Mining and Community in South Africa

Mining has played a key role in the growth of many towns in South Africa. This growth has been accompanied by a proliferation of informal settlements, by pressure to provide basic services and by institutional pressures in local government to support mining. Fragile municipal finance, changing social attributes, the pressures of shift work on mineworkers, the impact on the physical environment and perceived new inequalities between mineworkers, contract workers and original inhabitants have further complicated matters. Mining growth has, however, also led to substantial local economic benefits to existing business and it has contributed to a mushrooming of new enterprises.

While the relationship between mining and economic development at the country level has received adequate attention in existing literature, less is known about the consequences of mining at the local level. This book investigates the local impacts of mining in South Africa, focusing on employment, inequality, housing, business development, worker well-being, governance, municipal finance, planning and the environment.

Taking an interdisciplinary approach, *Mining and Community in South Africa* will be of interest to scholars of South Africa, economic development, labour and industry, politics and planning.

Lochner Marais is Professor in Development Studies at the Centre for Development Support, University of the Free State, Bloemfontein, South Africa.

Philippe Burger is Professor and Head of the Department of Economics at the University of the Free State, Bloemfontein, South Africa.

Deidré van Rooyen is currently the Programme Director for Development Studies and a researcher in the Centre for Development Support at the University of the Free State, Bloemfontein, South Africa.

Routledge Contemporary South Africa

Mining and Community in South Africa

From Small Town to Iron Town

**Edited by Lochner Marais,
Philippe Burger and
Deidré van Rooyen**

Routledge
Taylor & Francis Group

LONDON AND NEW YORK

First published 2018
by Routledge

2 Park Square, Milton Park, Abingdon, Oxfordshire OX14 4RN
52 Vanderbilt Avenue, New York, NY 10017

Routledge is an imprint of the Taylor & Francis Group, an informa business

First issued in paperback 2019

British Library Cataloguing-in-Publication Data
A catalogue record for this book is available from the British Library

Library of Congress Cataloging-in-Publication Data
A catalog record for this book has been requested

ISBN: 978-1-138-06113-2 (hbk)
ISBN: 978-0-367-88893-0 (pbk)

Typeset in Times New Roman
by Apex CoVantage, LLC

Contents

Figures

viii *Figures*

Tables

Contributors

Diane Abrahams, School of Tourism and Hospitality Management, University of Johannesburg, Johannesburg, South Africa.

Philippe Burger, Department of Economics, University of the Free State, Bloemfontein, South Africa.

Falko T. Buschke, Centre for Environmental Management, University of the Free State, Bloemfontein, South Africa.

Malène Campbell, Department of Urban and Regional Planning, University of the Free State, Bloemfontein, South Africa.

Jan Cloete, Centre for Development Support, University of the Free State, Bloemfontein, South Africa.

Stuart Denoon-Stevens, Department of Urban and Regional Planning, University of the Free State, Bloemfontein, South Africa.

Ernst Drewes, Department of Urban and Regional Planning, University of the North West, Potchefstroom, South Africa.

Lyndon Du Plessis, Department of Public Management, University of the Free State, Bloemfontein, South Africa.

Jean-Pierre Geldenhuys, Department of Economics, University of the Free State, Bloemfontein, South Africa.

Fiona Haslam McKenzie, Centre for Regional Development, University of Western Australia, Australia.

Chris Hendriks, Department of Public Management, University of the Free State, Bloemfontein, South Africa.

Mischka Jacobs, Department of Urban and Regional Planning, University of the Free State, Bloemfontein, South Africa.

Martina Kotzé, Business School, University of the Free State, Bloemfontein, South Africa.

Molefi Lenka, Centre for Development Support, University of the Free State, Bloemfontein, South Africa.

Lochner Marais, Centre for Development Support, University of the Free State, Bloemfontein, South Africa.

Kgosi Mocwagae, Department of Urban and Regional Planning, University of the Free State, Bloemfontein, South Africa.

Thulisile Mphambukeli, Department of Urban and Regional Planning, University of the Free State, Bloemfontein, South Africa.

Etienne Nel, Department of Geography, University of Otago, Dunedin, New Zealand and Visiting Professor at the Centre for Development Support, University of the Free State, Bloemfontein, South Africa.

Petrus Nel, Department of Industrial Psychology, University of the Free State, Bloemfontein, South Africa.

Verna Nel, Department of Urban and Regional Planning, University of the Free State, Bloemfontein, South Africa.

John Ntema, Department of Development Studies, University of South Africa, Pretoria, South Africa.

Rory Pilossof, Department of Economics and International Studies Group, University of the Free State, Bloemfontein, South Africa.

Johnica Riet, Centre for Development Support, University of the Free State, Bloemfontein, South Africa.

Maitland T. Seaman, Centre for Environmental Management, University of the Free State, Bloemfontein, South Africa.

Joost Sommen, Independent Consultant, Bloemfontein, South Africa.

Thomas Stewart, Department of Urban and Regional Planning, University of the Free State, Bloemfontein, South Africa.

Deidré van Rooyen, Centre for Development Support, University of the Free State, Bloemfontein, South Africa.

Johan van Zyl, Centre for Development Support, University of the Free State, Bloemfontein, South Africa.

Richard D. Williamson, Centre for Environmental Management, University of the Free State, Bloemfontein, South Africa.

Preface

Though South Africa's economy is no longer dependent on mining, this industry still plays an important role in the country's economy and its social fabric. Over the past 20 years, mining has also geographically moved to the periphery of the country. This means that mining and societal concerns in peripheral locations do not always receive appropriate academic responses from the universities that are situated in the large metropolitan areas of South Africa. Postmasburg represents one such peripheral location in which mining increasingly plays an economic and societal role. This small town has undergone a metamorphosis from a regional service centre to a relatively large mining town – a transformation directly linked to the global demand for iron ore (mainly from China). Over the past 10 years, the global demand for iron ore has affected Postmasburg in positive and negative ways. This book is an attempt to document some of these global implications on the local environment of a small town in South Africa. While we essentially employ a planning and policy lens in our scrutiny of mining towns, we also ask important questions about mining and society that have a wider sphere of influence. Among others, we ask about the consequences of increased numbers of contract workers; whether new inequalities are being created; how government and mines respond to local development concerns; whether anybody is planning for decline and what planning for decline actually means; how economic diversification is viewed; how trends in international mining production influence South Africa and Postmasburg; and how global power play influences a small town in a peripheral location in South Africa. It is hoped that this book will provide a point of departure for similar studies in other remote mining communities and that it will spark off many other comparative analyses, contradictory findings and debates.

Lochner Marais
Philippe Burger
Deidré van Rooyen

Acknowledgements

We would like to acknowledge the following people:

- The University of the Free State for funding a substantial part of the research.
- Di Kilpert for her excellent copy editing of the work.
- Mr Marius Pretorius for assisting technical editing.
- Two anonymous reviewers from Routledge.
- Prof Doreen Atkinson and Dr Anton De Wit from the Nelson Mandela Metropolitan University and Dr Manfred Spoctor from the University of Stellenbosch for reviewing earlier versions of the book.

Abbreviations

AMCU	Association of Mineworkers and Construction Union
ANC	African National Congress
BEE	Black economic empowerment
BIBO	Bus-in-bus-out
CE	Common era
CER	Centre for Environmental Rights
CSR	Corporate social responsibility
DIDO	Drive-in-drive-out
EIA	Environmental impact assessment
FIFO	Fly-in-fly-out
FGT	Foster-Greer-Thorbecke
GDP	Gross domestic product
GHS	General Household Study
GTZ	Gesellschaft für Technische Zusammenarbeit
GOS	Gross operating surplus
GVA	Gross value added
GWC	Griqualand West Centre
HIV	Human Immunodeficiency Virus
IDP	Integrated development plan
JSE	Johannesburg Stock Exchange
KHDC	Khumani Housing Development Company
LED	Local economic development
LUMS	Land Use Management System
LQ	Location quotient
MIG	Municipal Infrastructure Grant
NIDS	National Income Dynamic Study
NSDP	National Spatial Development Perspective
NUM	National Union of Mineworkers
PCA	Principal components analysis
PESTLE	Political, economic, social, technological, legal and environmental
PGM	Platinum group of metals
RDP	Reconstruction and Development Programme
SALDRU	South African Labour and Demographic Research Unit

SDF	Spatial Development Plan
SES	Socio-economic and ecological system
SISO	Ship-in-ship-out
SLP	Social and labour plan
SPLUMA	Spatial Planning and Land Use Management Act
UNEP	United Nations Environmental Programme
USA	United States of America
WNLA	Witwatersrand Native Labour Organisation

Section A

Setting the scene

South Africa has an extensive mining economy. A wide range of minerals is being mined, multinational corporations are involved and the history of the industry stretches well over a century. Mining directly contributes approximately 6 to 7% of GDP. Indirectly, its contribution is estimated at about 20% and approximately one-third of market capitalisation on the Johannesburg Stock Exchange (JSE) originates from mining. In fact, the establishment of the JSE was a direct consequence of gold mining on the Witwatersrand at the end of the 19th century. South Africa's development is thus closely associated with the mines. But mining must also take the blame for many of the country's inequalities.

It is difficult to get a clear picture of the positive or negative consequences of mining from the perspective of a single discipline. In conducting a case study of a single town from a variety of disciplinary perspectives, we aimed to provide an in-depth description of the local consequences of mining and explain the conflicts the mines can cause in such a town. We can claim to have achieved these aims, while at the same time acknowledging the inevitable shortcomings of a single case study, in particular its limited generalisability. Our findings relate largely to the highly mechanised open-cast iron-ore mines of the Northern Cape. We expect to find similarities with other open-cast mining regions, but there will be considerable differences between these and the regions that practise underground mining, such the North West Province's Platinum Belt or the Free State Goldfields.

We chose Postmasburg for a number of reasons. Research on small towns has been one of the anchors of research at the Centre for Development Support at the University of the Free State. Our study of how the mines have transformed Postmasburg fits into this research niche. Small town research is not necessarily restricted to a narrow focus; it allows for wide angle views as well. For example, our study investigates how the demand for iron and steel in China has had repercussions for this small town in a remote part of South Africa. It investigates the town's vulnerability to changes in global markets. It looks at how mining and multinational corporations have influenced government, planning, the environment and not only people but the movement of people. The open-cast mining and mainly mechanised mining operations also gave us an opportunity to investigate how mining as an industry has changed over time and how the changes have affected not only the people working for the mines but also the town's original residents.

Our main focus in this book is on mining *settlements*. Mining towns have been shaped by the settlement methods used by the mining companies, and by the neoliberal production processes of the past three decades. Though the consequences of these processes are less pronounced in South Africa than internationally (but not absent), the power of the mining companies still makes itself felt in many mining settlements and communities. With this in mind, we have given much thought to how public policy could or should be shaped. How policies either succeed or fail is a central concern in this book. Irrespective of the influence of neoliberalism, mining towns are inevitably at risk from mine downscaling and closure. Concern about this vulnerability was a major reason for undertaking this research. It prompted questions about how a town can plan for its future if the main driver of its economy is unsustainable in the long term.

Mining legislation has changed considerably since the introduction of the Mineral and Petroleum Development Act (2002). Many of these changes followed principles associated with the 'new natural resource policy agenda' and emphasised the importance of mining in local development efforts. Besides making changes in the ownership regime of mines, the Act also provided for a social licence, in the form of social and labour plans. Guidelines that have been developed to support social and labour plans require applicants to apply for mining and production rights. Key terms in such guidelines are *regeneration of mining economies* and *provision of adequate living conditions and housing*. A number of other strategies have followed. One is the Mining Charter (2002 and 2010), which is largely based on the premise that the economic inequalities associated with colonialism and apartheid need to be redressed. The increased participation of historically disadvantaged South Africans is therefore central to the Charter. The Charter's vision is to ensure transformation in the mining sector. One of its aims is to improve mineworkers' housing and living conditions and develop mining communities. It recommends that the mines should be involved in practical development and that their plans should work in harmony with the municipalities' integrated development plans, i.e. their strategic plans. As regards living conditions, the emphasis is on upgrading hostel units, reducing densities in existing hostels and enabling homeownership for mineworkers. In 2012 the South African government introduced the Strategy on the Revitalisation of Distressed Mining Towns. This strategy has five objectives: to ensure the rule of law, peace and stability; to strengthen labour relations; to improve mineworkers' living and working conditions; to provide short-to-medium-term measures to support growth and stability; and to identify long-term measures to support growth and stability. The emphasis on stability should be noted. No mention is made of either mine downscaling or managing economic decline.

The revitalisation strategy was a consequence of the Marikana tragedy of August 2012 in which the South African Police Services killed 34 mineworkers following local protests near the mining settlement of Marikana in the North West Province's Platinum Belt. The mineworkers' poor socio-economic and living conditions were identified as an underlying cause of the unrest. A living-out allowance (a means of getting rid of the compound system historically associated with the accommodation of mineworkers on mine property in South Africa) had not necessarily resulted in better living conditions. Furthermore, the allowances contributed to informal settlement development and served to shift the burden of infrastructural provision from the mining companies onto local government. Although mineworkers in the platinum industry had, by mid-2014, managed to negotiate relatively large salary increases, there is not much proof either that their living conditions have improved or that they are set to improve in the near future. The events of 2012 focused government attention on the challenges that mining areas face as a result of poor living conditions and mine closure. Given the emphasis on living conditions, many of the chapters in this book concentrate on issues of housing and inequalities.

This book investigates the effects of mining on the people who live and work in the small town of Postmasburg, situated in a remote and arid region of South Africa. The following intersecting themes run through the book and we return to them in the final chapter.

- *Increased numbers of contract workers.* The situations of contract mineworkers and mine-employed mineworkers are compared in several chapters. Though contract work is less evident in South Africa than in Australia, estimates are that nearly 30% of mineworkers in South Africa are contract workers, the result of outsourcing by the mining companies. They are paid lower salaries than the workers employed directly by the mines and to some extent they perpetuate the migrant labour system that was common in the apartheid period.
- *New inequalities.* According to the international literature, the mining booms of the 2000s have created new inequalities, including inequality between mineworkers and the original population. The Australian literature reveals inequality between mineworkers and local, particularly indigenous, communities. We consider inequalities in income, working hours, union protection, housing and well-being. Some of these kinds of inequality are related to the differences between contract mineworkers and mine-employed mineworkers. And new inequalities may spring from the environmental degradation caused by mining.
- *Government responses and hybrid governance models.* Worldwide, the histories of mining towns show that mining has had many negative effects on local governments. New mining developments have been known to place huge pressure on mining towns to develop and expand infrastructure. However, those who manage these towns seldom know how long such infrastructure will be used, which makes it difficult to manage the municipal budget. Municipalities have adopted three methods of dealing with these uncertainties: cooperative governance, collaborative planning and hybrid governance. We have found Postmasburg to represent an example of the hybrid governance model and we have examined it in detail.
- *Planning for growth and decline.* Having seen both substantial growth and the initial signs of decline in Postmasburg, we consider the problems involved in planning for both.

- *Economic diversification.* This issue is central to staples theory, the resource curse theory and the Dutch disease theory. We attempt to gauge how mining booms affect the economic development of a small town like Postmasburg and to determine how far business has devised plans to diversify the economy with a view to countering the effects of mine downscaling.
- *The relationship between mining town development and changes in production methods and labour regimes.* In Table 1.1 we set out the implications that changing patterns of production and labour regimes have had for mining towns. Central to all the chapters in the book is our conviction that to understand a town like Postmasburg we must understand its labour regimes and how they are implemented.
- *The role of economic power.* Power is a theme running through all the chapters. The reality is that many local residents, their local government, the local businesses and civil society operate in the same space in which large companies and multinational corporations operate.

The book has five sections. Section A sets the scene with three chapters covering our research design, mining-town research theories, international literature on local consequences of mining growth and decline, the history of mining in South Africa, and South African government policy. Chapter 1 (*The background to the Postmasburg study*) discusses theoretical frameworks that have been used to study mining towns and explains the research design of this book. Chapter 2 (*The literature on mining communities and mining growth and decline*) reviews the international literature on the effects of mining on mining towns. It covers the topics of social changes that mining brings to a town; pressures on planning, infrastructure provision and housing; and local economic development and diversification. Chapter 3 (*Migration and mine labour in South Africa*) lays the theoretical foundation for the book. It discusses the conceptual perspectives that inform much of the literature on migrant labour systems. It traces the evolution of scholarship on labour migration and the way that perspectives have shifted over time and describes the present state of the field. It provides historical background on labour migration and mining in South Africa. It scrutinises the present situation of mineworkers in South Africa, focusing on their financial situation and the implications of migrant lifestyles – particularly the issues of managing multiple households, job precariousness and dependency.

Section B of the book investigates governance, planning, environmental issues and power relationships, Section C considers whether mineworkers should own or rent in a town near a mine and Section D investigates the living conditions, well-being and business environment of Postmasburg. In the conclusion (Section E), the concluding chapter (Chapter 14, *The way forward for Postmasburg*), written after a workshop with experts Haslam McKenzie from Australia and Nel from New Zealand, we document the implications of our case study for theory and policy in South Africa.

1 The background to the Postmasburg study

Lochner Marais, Deidré van Rooyen,
Philippe Burger, Molefi Lenka, Jan Cloete,
Stuart Denoon-Stevens, Kgosi Mocwagae,
Mischka Jacobs and Johnica Riet

Introduction

Mining towns are a common feature of the international urban landscape. Many of them sprang up between 1950 and 1980. Typically they were established expressly for the business activities of a specific mining company and in most cases they were built, maintained and governed by the company itself (Littlewood, 2014). Indeed, mining leases often stipulated that the town had to be developed by the mining company (Carrington and Hogg, 2011). Many mining towns were created despite the existence of other towns in the vicinity of the new mine. The growth of these towns and the associated social dynamics have aroused much research interest (Lawrie et al., 2011).

Although mining towns vary greatly according to their location, the resources they mine and the companies that run them, they do have some things in common. Typical features are a planning and management approach that prioritises physical infrastructure and recreational services, ownership of all or most of the housing by the mining company, and basic services provided and often subsidised by the company (Petkova et al., 2009; Littlewood, 2014). The flip side of these positive features is underinvestment in social services (Lockie, 2011). Health and educational services are commonly provided but social support and community building are often neglected. Another typical downside is that mining towns struggle to sustain high growth over a long period, as they suffer from the volatility and vulnerability associated with global resource prices (Lawrie et al., 2011; Smith, 2015; Chapman et al., 2015). People who live in these towns thus have to learn to adapt not only to rapid growth but often also to rapid decline. Another problem is that small non-mining businesses struggle to get a hold, because the mining company is reluctant to sublet land to them or simply because the non-mining population tends to get displaced (Petkova et al., 2009). And the fact that mining towns are commonly situated in remote locations has negative implications for people's well-being, for economic diversification and for sustainable planning.

By the mid-1980s the mining-town model had come under scrutiny for a number of reasons. Inability to diversify the economies of these places was the main concern (Petkova et al., 2009). In addition, questions were asked about the adequacy of their social infrastructure, housing and sewerage. These questions were important because the lifespan of mining operations had a direct bearing on how to provide these services. A further question was who had to pay for the services. By the mid-1980s, falling mineral prices were dampening mining companies' enthusiasm for continuing to finance physical and social infrastructure. In many parts of the world, the falling prices and the mining towns' problems led to the handing-over of town administrations to government (Littlewood, 2014). The withdrawal of mining companies as managers of mining towns caused further concerns, such as the effect the withdrawal would have on taxpayers, the possible reduction in employment opportunities and uncertainty about the long-term maintenance of infrastructure. In South Africa, municipal dependence on the rates and taxes paid by mining companies has had long-term negative implications for municipal finance after the process of housing privatisation (Marais, 2013).

By the end of the 1980s mining companies and governments had become reluctant to establish new mining towns (Haslam McKenzie, 2013). In Australia, mining companies and state governments were curbing the development of new mining towns, with the limited lifespan of mining operations being the main reason. Changing labour processes were also instrumental in changing the mining-town landscape: larger numbers of contract workers and the increase in shift work (such as four days on, four days off, or two weeks on, one week off) meant increased mobility and consequently fewer permanent settlements. The overall logic was that if they lived in a central town or city and commuted to the mine site, mine employees and their families would be less likely to suffer when the mine closed. In 2005, it was estimated that only 53% of mineworkers in Australia were permanently located in mining towns (Carrington and Hogg, 2011).

Fly-in-fly-out (FIFO) arrangements in mining towns have been criticised for their negative effects on community building, social cohesion and health, and have been blamed for increasing family stress, substance abuse, social exclusion, vehicle accidents and crime (Torkington et al., 2011). Other negative findings have been a decline in local spending, and complaints from permanent residents that temporary mineworkers from outside contribute to antisocial behaviour and criminal activities. However, despite these drawbacks, it does seem that the fly-in-fly-out system has in many ways softened the consequences of the mining downturn for mining towns.

A mining town is obviously vulnerable to mine downscaling or closure; as Laurence (2005, p. 285) says, 'The excitement and fanfare that surrounds the opening of a new mine is never present when it finally closes'. The environmental and technical issues have received attention, but the socio-economic effects of downscaling or closure have been decidedly under-researched. The early work dealing with the socio-economic consequences originated from the Global North (Bradbury and St-Martin, 1983; Neil et al., 1992). Since the 2000s, the literature has begun to include case studies from, and of relevance to, the developing world (Acquah and Boateng, 2000; Jackson, 2002; World Bank and IFC, 2002; Haney and Shkaratan, 2003; McGuire, 2003). The most common local demographic implications of downscaling or closure reported in the international literature are ageing and depopulation (Petrov, 2010), substantial increases in artisanal and (in many cases) illegal mining (Hilson, 2010), and an overall loss of production and capital in the area (Bradbury and St-Martin, 1983). Declining living standards among former mineworkers (Haney and Shkaratan, 2003) and community instability (Jackson, 2002) are commonly reported. Negative health implications for mineworkers and the communities that are left behind have also been noted (Holton et al., 2002).

Having a diverse economy helps to mitigate the effects of mining decline. Mine closure can have particularly negative implications for companies if skilled people leave the region (Petrov, 2010). In general, mining communities are inappropriately trained for work outside the mining environment, and mitigation programmes designed to assist with economic development have generally been absent in areas of mine downscaling. Where mine closure regulations were in place, they were generally aimed at rehabilitating the area around the mine rather than dealing with the social and economic problems. Researchers increasingly argue that planning for downscaling and closure should start as early as possible, but at least during the main phase of profitable operations. Stated differently, mine closure should be part of the mine-planning cycle.

The creation of appropriate skills and business partnership programmes outside mining is also commonly proposed as a way to address the inevitable reality of mine downscaling. Collaborative planning and partnerships have become synonymous with the rhetoric on mining communities. However, Hamann (2004) notes that partnerships in areas of weak local government are commonly dominated by mining companies and that many of these companies have shifted their collaborative planning responsibilities onto corporate social responsibility. The result is a focus on short-term efforts that ignores long-term planning responsibilities. Some useful recent studies of the effects of mine downscaling and closure are Warhurst and Naronha (2000); Veiga et al. (2001); Hamann (2004); Upton et al. (2004); Andrews-Speed et al. (2005); Bowes-Lyon et al. (2009); Petrov (2010) and Stacey et al. (2010).

Theories for studying mining towns

The first papers in the body of research on mining towns originated in Canada. In the 1970s and 1980s a large number of studies were published in such journals as *Rural Sociology*, *Journal of Rural Studies* and *Journal of the Community Development Society*. One of the first books on the topic was Lucas (1971), and others have recently been published in the Global North (Crawford, 1995; Amundson, 2004) and Global South (Obeng-Odoom, 2014). Five research traditions have dominated the research on mining towns (although various other theoretical frameworks have been used to assess community interaction with mining companies). The five relevant theories are summarised below: staple theory, social disruption theory, the 'resource curse', the 'Dutch disease' and neoliberalism.

Staple theory

Staple theory was one of the first theoretical frameworks for analysing the role of mining in development. The theory originated in Canada with Watkins's seminal paper (Watkins, 1963). It was also later applied in the United States and it saw some limited application in the Global South. Gunton (2003) described this theory as integrating 'the physical geography of natural features with the theory of economic linkages to explain the spatial pattern and institutional structure of the development process in regions'. Stated in simple terms, staple theory sees economic development and growth as being based on the export of staple products. Staples are natural products which need little beneficiation, i.e. processing, before they are exported. From this viewpoint, economic growth is the result of direct investment in the mining industry and the spatial distribution of development associated with resource extraction.

According to Watkins (1963), the spatial distribution of development is influenced by four factors: forward linkages (those associated with the processing of minerals), backward linkages (those associated with inputs into the mining system), final demand linkages (the production of consumer goods to meet regional needs) and fiscal linkages (expenditure of rents and profits generated by the production process). The overall argument is that accessible regional resources create large-scale competitive advantages for regions. The global demand for these resources ensures that a country has access to global companies and capital rather than being dependent on local investments. More than 50 years ago, Robinson (1962, p. 118) noted that isolated mining communities in Canada 'make no contribution to the development of, nor do they receive any flows from, their surrounding environments'. Staple theory, as applied in Canada, laid the foundation for the 'resource curse' and 'Dutch disease' theories.

Social disruption theory

Social disruption theory was the basis of many studies of mining towns in the 1970s and 1980s. The theory emphasises the social and economic ills associated with fast-growing mining areas. It states that resource booms have negative implications for local people as they erode local culture and structures (Smith et al., 2001; Ennis et al., 2014). The body of work based on this theory deals with unaffordable housing, homelessness, increased local poverty, crime, high levels of drug and alcohol abuse, marital breakdown, mental problems, community disharmony and low levels of local employment (Bowes-Lyon et al., 2009; Argent, 2014; Ennis et al., 2014).

Social disruption theory dominated early work in mining towns but it did not escape criticism (Wilkinson et al., 1982). Some of the early studies were already showing mixed results, and by the mid-1980s a substantial body of work had started to challenge this theory. The original studies were criticised for being undiscerning, having weak empirical bases, favouring cross-sectional over longitudinal work, overgeneralising on the basis of single case studies, and idealising mining towns (Wilkinson et al., 1982; Lawrie et al., 2011; Ennis et al., 2014). Researchers have cautioned against viewing development around mining towns as a negative phenomenon per se (Amundson, 2004; Lawrie et al., 2011). High levels of growth should not automatically be seen as negative: if we take into account the differences between mining towns, and the different resources they mine, we get a more nuanced understanding of boom mining cycles. Wilson (2004, p. 266) notes that 'the rides of all communities will not be identical' and that 'some may experience a wild ride while others may feel only a little dip or bump from time to time'. The need for long-term research has been stressed. Smith et al. (2001) found that the mining-related social problems they first recorded were far less noticeable in the same towns two decades later, and that the mining companies had made substantial commitments to deal with them. The mixed results in the literature show that disruption occurs only in a particular place during a particular period of growth, and then only in particular sections of the mining town community. The theory that mine downscaling causes social disruption has not yet been sufficiently researched. Longitudinal studies are still needed on boom and bust cycles and how local communities adapt.

The 'resource curse'

The resource curse theory, which has its origins in staple theory, says that natural resources have negative implications for a country's development and economic growth and seldom help to reduce poverty. It states that the short-term dividends associated with resource extraction inhibit economic diversification in countries whose economy is dominated by resources, and that the availability of resources might directly displace non-mining enterprises. Furthermore, resource exports could overheat the economies of mining-dependent regions or countries, impeding their potential to diversify their economies and react to global changes. For example, overheating of the economy might create inappropriate exchange rates for the local currency, which might, in turn, negatively affect exports of manufacturing goods (Stedman et al., 2004). Besides these economic factors, political factors are often mentioned in the resource curse literature. Corruption, mismanagement and weak political institutions in mining-dependent countries contribute to the resource curse (Langton and Mazel, 2008; Hammond, 2011). However, some scholars have argued that a reverse causality exists (Brunnsch-weiler and Bulte, 2008). Corruption, mismanagement and weak political institutions in mining-dependent countries contribute to the resource curse (Langton and Mazel, 2008; Hammond, 2011), but the resource curse appears to have less effect in higher-income countries because they have well-designed public policies and strong institutions (Mehlum et al., 2006). The implications of the resource curse have been taken beyond political and economic manifestations to include the argument that mining has negative implications for education, health and the development of women.

Most of the work in this theory has been done at the level of countries, with only limited attention being devoted to cities in the Global South. There is empirical evidence that non-resource-dependent countries outperform resource-dependent countries (Langton and Mazel, 2008). However, the evidence in support of the resource curse theory is mixed and Larsen (2005) shows that rich countries may be exceptions to the rule. Haslam McKenzie (2013, p. 345) notes that the curse of resource dependence has local effects because mining-dependent areas 'are often under considerable housing, infrastructure and services pressure with a sudden influx of population and businesses supporting the resources industries', and the long-term local implications could be damaging to the community as it could struggle to 'retain non-resources businesses, key workers associated with health, education, policing and childcare, casual labour and the essential services that make a community liveable'. Haslam McKenzie (2013) further maintains that remote mining areas in particular have been on the receiving end of the negative consequences of mining growth. Some useful recent studies that examine the 'resource curse' are Randall and Ironside (1996); Gylfason (2001); Larsen (2005); Hajkowicz et al. (2011); James and Aadland (2011); Bryceson and MacKinnon (2013) and Eduful and Hooper (2015).

The 'Dutch disease'

Related to the 'resource curse' discussed above is the 'Dutch disease'. The name was coined by *The Economist* (1977) to describe the negative effects of the oil boom in the North Sea on manufacturing in the Netherlands. It is applied to situations where mining causes the exchange rate to rise and labour and capital to flow into a country. Generally, the Dutch disease also results in increased government involvement in the economy (which might have consequences for state budgets) and lower levels of tax collection (Chaudhry and Karl, 2001). The long-term consequences of these effects are higher production costs, a reduction in the global competitiveness of locally produced goods and services and a rise in wages.

Rolfe et al. (2007) suggest two ways to cure the Dutch disease: to hold some of the resource revenues elsewhere to reduce local spending surges, or to intervene in those factors that caused specific industries to lose competitiveness. They also note that negative social consequences are associated with the Dutch disease (even if positive social consequences are equally possible). Rising local prices, especially for housing, could lead to social exclusion or relocation. The Dutch disease could also cause job losses because of the lack of competitiveness of specific industries (other than mining). Prominent studies of the Dutch disease are Chaudhry and Karl (2001), Karl (2004), Rolfe et al. (2007), Langton and Mazel (2008) and James and Aadland (2011).

Neoliberalism

Neoliberalism in the mining environment involved the rise of multinational corporations, increased emphasis on value for shareholders, outsourcing of mine activities, outsourcing or out-phasing of peripheral activities, substantial increases in salaries and more use of shift work (see Table 1.1). The neoliberal view has influenced both the mining production process and government responses, which means that mining towns have had to deal with these changing trends. Neoliberal governments emphasise property rights, free markets and free trade. Bryceson and MacKinnon (2013) argue that neoliberalism in government reduces the role of national and local governments in mining and their ability to manage mining investments. What is more, neoliberalism in government causes the state to adopt 'a narrow sectoral approach to mining as a source of export revenue and a magnet for investment' (Bryceson and MacKinnon, 2013, p. 515). Haslam McKenzie (2013) speaks of the retreat of government, and argues that it results in smaller funding allocations to some of the remote mining settlements (Haslam McKenzie, 2013). Pick et al. (2008) observe that governments commonly shift the risks associated with mining onto local communities, often blaming low levels of development on inappropriate local responses and in the process playing down structural problems.

Neoliberalism in a mining company means a greater emphasis on shareholders, productivity and local infrastructure, which could make the company reluctant to focus on development goals. Some consequences of this approach have been larger numbers of contract workers (outsourcing), the introduction of block-roster shifts, and an emphasis on global networks and outsourcing.

The role of neoliberalism in mining has not escaped criticism. The literature shows that an overemphasis on global competitiveness leads mining companies to disregard social cohesion, ignore long-term planning, dispossess indigenous populations, underplay sustainability, inhibit local participation, encourage cheating in respect of local taxes or leases and possibly damage the local economy.

There have been a number of responses to increased neoliberalism in the mining environment. International funding institutions, for instance, and even governments in the Global South, have started to emphasise local decision making, citizen participation in how mining revenues should be spent, and particularly partnerships. Arellano-Yanguas (2008) refers to this change as a 'new natural resource agenda'.

Politico-economic trends in mining town development

Table 1.1 summarises the changing trends in mining-town development from a politico-economic perspective. Although the table shows changes in the labour regime and changes in mining towns separately, it must be remembered that the interrelationship between these issues remains crucial. These changing trends and their local implications have also influenced South African mining. They are important in the chapters of this book. In our assessment of the literature on social and economic consequences that follows, we specifically distinguish between the two distinct periods identified in Table 1.2 – the initial period up to the mid-1980s and the second period since the mid-1980s.

Table 1.1 Changing patterns of labour and mining-town development

	Criteria	Modern/industrial period, 1950–mid-1980s	Post-industrial/neoliberal period, since mid-1980s
Nature of mining companies and global mining trends	How far multinational corporations dominate mining	Largely dominated by local mining companies	Largely dominated by multinational corporations
	Major trend in the mining economy	Boom period ended in the mid-1980s	Boom since early 2000s ended in 2014/15
Changes in the labour regime	Working hours	40-hour working week Daytime work only Full-time mine employment	Block-roster shifts (e.g. 4 days on, 4 days off, or 2 weeks on, 2 weeks off) Shifts (usually 12-hour periods day or night) 24-hour production cycles Contract work Production 7 days a week Extended periods off
	Nature of employment	Employed full-time by the mining company	Increasingly employed as contract workers
	Duration of work	Lifelong or for as long as the mine is in operation	Short-term contracts
	Salary package	Large-scale non-salary benefits Moderate salaries	Only salary benefits Large salaries
	Mining production methods	Labour intensive	Capital intensive Mechanisation Production oriented Outsourcing – for non-direct as well as direct services
	Labour legislation	Strict labour legislation Labour is unionised	Smaller role for unions
Changes in mining towns	Settlement permanency	Mostly permanent (as long as mine production continues) Company towns	Mostly non-permanent workforces Worker camps/'fly-in-fly-out' workers
	Housing types	Houses provided by the mining company	Privatisation Worker camps 'Hotbedding'* Informal settlement development Re-emergence of compounds
	Town management	Many towns initially managed by mines	Transferred to local government
	Community cohesion	Seen as permanent	Increasingly seen as temporary

Criteria		Modern/industrial period, 1950–mid-1980s	Post-industrial/neoliberal period, since mid-1980s
	Implications for host communities	Positive local implications but long-term negative consequences depending on mine's lifespan	Economic exclusion Less local spending
	Local financial risks	National government	Local communities
	Social infrastructure	Some underinvestment	Continued underinvestment
	Governance models	Mining towns managed by mines, or by local municipalities (where they existed) that depended heavily on mine housing	Mining companies had withdrawn by late 1980s Recently, corporate social responsibility (CSR) used as means of providing social infrastructure Increasing emphasis on partnerships for development Hybrid governance models
Impacts of mine closure	Local impacts	Extreme	Local consequences of mine closure reduced by 'fly-in-fly-out' mining

* 'Hotbedding' refers to shift work in which two people use the same bed one after the other in a 24-hour cycle.

Gaps in the research on mining towns

The original work on mining towns usually took the form of one-off case studies and, where household surveys were used, favoured cross-sectional methods. Most of these studies focused on boom cycles and seldom considered the long-term implications of mining for local communities (Wilson, 2004). A number of researchers have noted that the specific time in the mining cycle at which case studies or individual or household surveys are done is a crucial factor in influencing the results (Nord and Luloff, 1992; Freudenburg and Wilson, 2002). The importance of longitudinal work is also often emphasised in the literature (for example Hajkowicz et al., 2011; Chapman et al., 2015). Smith et al. (2001) observed 15 years ago that there was a dearth of studies following longitudinal research designs, and they noted that the few studies that could account for long-term change had found that most of the original negative social consequences of rapid growth had been negated over time and, what is more, that the notion of 'mining dependence' as the main variable in research was questionable. Twenty-five years ago, Machlis et al. (1990) found that impacts usually lag behind specific events in mining production.

A substantial body of work is available on resource towns and the research generally makes meaningful contributions towards understanding mining towns. Often, these studies emphasise regional variations, but they are nevertheless generally 'unable to account for variability between locations on the basis of factors such as commodity, company structure, remoteness and demographic structure' (Chapman et al., 2015, p. 630). Consequently, they either neglect the relationship between a town's performance and its business cycles or fail to make comparisons between towns. This in turn underplays the diversity of mining towns. There is a gap in the research for comparisons of mining towns across different commodities and different companies.

Very few studies have focused on periods of economic decline. Although long-term evaluations should include bust as well as boom periods, the overall focus has been on mining growth. Finally, not enough local case studies have been done in Africa. Littlewood (2014) and Eduful and Hooper (2015) note that there is an urgent need to increase the number of case studies from the Global South.

History of Postmasburg

The region has been associated with mining for many centuries. From as early as CE 800 the Khoi and the Tswana peoples mined specularite (a variety of haematite) in the region, using it primarily as a cosmetic to stain the skin red. The miners stayed at the site only for short periods of time and did not settle in the area permanently (Beaumont and Boshier, 1974; Thackeray et al., 1983).

Postmasburg started life in the 1800s, after the migration of the Griqua into the area in the 1820s. It began as Sibling, a mission station of the London Missionary Society. In 1882 its name was changed to Blinkklip. The establishment of the town occurred shortly after the area, then known as Griqua West, was annexed into the Cape Colony, a move prompted primarily by the discovery of diamonds in the wider region. Prospecting in the region began shortly after the town's establishment, and manganese was discovered in the region in 1886. Around this time, the first farms in the area were surveyed, and in 1892 the town was formally proclaimed and renamed Postmasburg after the Reverend Dirk Postma, one of the founding ministers of the Dutch Reformed Church. The next significant event in Postmasburg's history occurred between October 1899 and June 1900, when the town fell into Boer hands during the Anglo-Boer War. This occupation was short-lived, lasting only eight months. See Snyman (1985), Van Vollenhoven and Pelser (2010) and Küsel (2011) for further details of this history.

Although manganese had been discovered in the region in as early as 1886, the mining history of the town really begins between 1923 and 1926, with the discovery of the first economically viable deposits of manganese on the farm Gloucester, 26 km west of present-day Postmasburg. In 1929 the Union Manganese and South African Manganese Company was formed. It was later to become Assmang, the mining company that owns the Beeshoek mine today. In the following year an extension of the railway from Kimberley to Postmasburg was completed, allowing freight transport of the manganese ore. Assmang mined manganese at Beeshoek for five years, until 1935, and then turned to mining iron ore at the same Beeshoek mine a few years later. This mine closed down during World War II.

The Beeshoek Iron Ore Mine was re-opened just outside Postmasburg in 1960 (Sabatini and Middleton, 2014). In 1962, electricity was supplied to Beeshoek and Gloucester, enabling a transition from traditional to modern mining techniques. Assmang began exporting ore in 1964. After a relatively uneventful 40 years, the next big change was in 1999, with the opening of a new open-cast mine, Beeshoek South. A second expansion of this mine is still in progress and a new eastern pit is expected to be opened in 2016, which will extend the mine's life by between two and 10 years. Parallel to this, Kumba Iron Ore, a subsidiary of Anglo American, opened the Kolomela Mine just outside Postmasburg in 2011. This mine is expected to have a lifespan of around 29 years. More detailed reference to the history of Postmasburg and mining in the area can be found in Assore (2010), Van Vollenhoven and Pelser (2010), Küsel (2011), Sabatini and Middleton (2014) and Mining Technology (2016).

Figure 1.1 and Figure 1.2 provide a overview of Postmasburg in national and regional context while Figure 1.3 provides a town layout of Postmasburg. Today, Postmasburg is part of the Tsantsabane Local Municipality.

Table 1.2 shows the changes in population numbers in Postmasburg since 1996 and Figure 1.4 shows the annual growth rates of GVA and the mining workforce in the broader Tsantsabane Local Municipality. The high levels of volatility in production and employment, evident in Figure 1.4, make it extremely difficult to plan

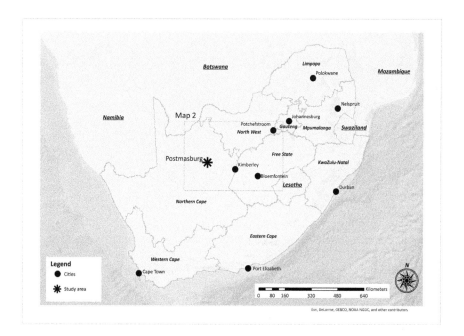

Figure 1.1 Location of Postmasburg in South Africa

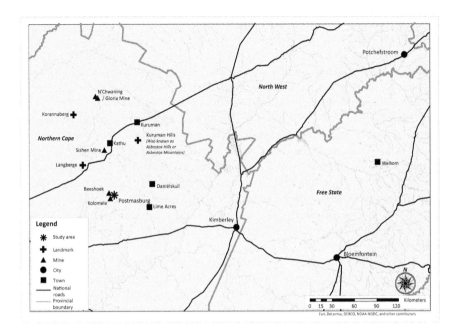

Figure 1.2 The location of Postmasburg in its regional context

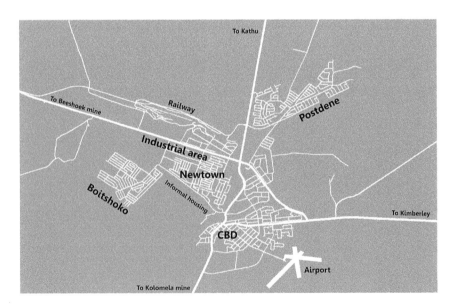

Figure 1.3 Layout plan of Postmasburg

Table 1.2 Population changes in Postmasburg, 1996–2011

Year	Postmasburg	
	Population	*% increase since previous period*
1996	19,005	
2001	21,191	11%
2011	30,089	42%
2015 (estimate)	35,000	14%

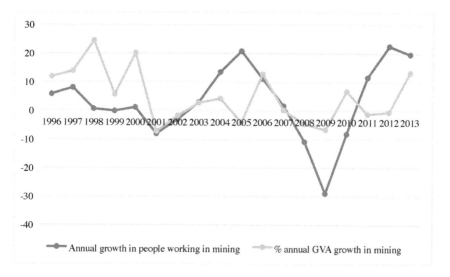

Figure 1.4 Annual growth rate of GVA and mining employment in Tsantsabane, 1996–2013
Source: Quantec, 2016

in the long term as regards settlement and social infrastructure. Basic services provided today could turn out to be inappropriate tomorrow, but not providing them could result in large-scale informal settlements and poor living conditions. Several chapters of this book discuss the implications of these fluctuations in population, workforce numbers and GVA.

How the study was done

The research was both qualitative and quantitative. We assessed the current situation in the town by means of a case study approach that provided a holistic view of Postmasburg. We started from the position of knowing little about Postmasburg and wanting to answer some 'how' and 'why' questions, but guided by some general ideas or expectations about mining towns in South Africa. We wanted to find out what people thought, what they valued and expected, how they related to each other, how they behaved, what resources they had and what social institutions were important in their town. In this way, we could explore attitudes to the mining development in this small town and the surrounding region. We collected data by conducting semi-structured interviews with three key informants from mining companies, five from the municipality and 12 from the business sector and civic organisations. To select these participants we used snowballing purposive sampling.

We also conducted three quantitative surveys: a household survey, a well-being survey and a business survey. In the household survey we collected completed 1029 questionnaires from households in all areas of Postmasburg: 529 from households with members employed in mining, 273 from non-mining households and 227 from informal settlements surrounding the town. To obtain the samples we used systematic random sampling based on cadastral information (site numbers based on information obtained from the Surveyor General). As our interest was in mining in the area, we deliberately over-sampled mining households in order to allow for comparison between sub-groups (such as directly employed and contractor-employed employees and the employees of the different mining companies). For the informal settlements sample we used random cluster sampling. We divided these settlements into eight sub-areas and obtained 25 completed questionnaires from each. In each household a fieldworker administered the questionnaire to the person who self-identified as best able to act as respondent for the household and who thus answered on behalf of all members of the household. The questionnaire elicited information such as number of household members, income, assets, migration patterns, employment and municipal services in the house. It consisted of closed-ended multi-choice questions. More specifically we were interested in comparing mining households and non-mining households.

From the household survey we compiled a population of individual mineworkers and then conducted our second survey, this time inquiring about the well-being of 253 of these mineworkers, randomly selected from the compiled list. The questionnaire elicited information about matters to do with trust, challenges, satisfaction, safety, burnout, self-awareness and psychological capital. It required the respondents to rate statements on a Likert scale. We conducted these as either face-to-face or telephonic interviews, depending on the preference and availability of the respondent.

Our third survey was of 55 businesses (32 formal and 23 informal) in Postmasburg, using a questionnaire completed by the proprietors themselves. We obtained a random sample of formal businesses from the telephone directory and, as with the informal settlements survey, we obtained a sample of informal businesses by means of clustered random sampling. The questionnaire elicited information about the owner's background, the business's turnover, profits and assets, the services the business received and any problems it was experiencing.

The fieldworkers who conducted the surveys were local unemployed youths who received intensive training in fieldwork and the instruments. The household and well-being questionnaires were completed electronically on tablets using CSPro software for Computer Assisted Personal Interview applications. The data were then emailed to a team member for processing. The business survey was completed on hard copies.

In addition to the surveys and interviews we also analysed documents from both the mining companies and the local government. We assessed a variety of municipal documents such as the local economic development strategy, integrated development plan and spatial development framework and a range of reports from the mining companies. Unfortunately, the mining companies' social and labour plans are not public documents and were not available for analysis.

References

Acquah, P. and Boateng, A., 2000. Planning for mine closure: Some case studies in Ghana. *Minerals and Energy*, 15, pp. 23–30.

Amundson, M., 2004. *Yellowcake Towns: Uranium Mining Communities in the American West*. Houston, TX: University of Texas Press.

Andrews-Speed, P., Ma, G., Shao, B. and Liao, C., 2005. Economic responses to the closure of small-scale coal mines in Chongqing, China. *Resource Policy*, 30, pp. 39–54.

Arellano-Yanguas, J., 2008. *A Thoroughly Modern Resource Curse? The New Natural Resource Policy Agenda and the Mining Revival in Peru*. IDS Working Paper No. 300. Institute of Development Studies, Brighton, UK.

Argent, N., 2014. Reinterpreting core and periphery in Australia's mineral and energy resources boom: An Innisian perspective on the Pilbara. *Australian Geographer*, 44(3), pp. 323–340.

Assore, 2010. *Assore Annual Report 2010*. www.assore.com/financials/annual_2010/history_ of_the_group.html (accessed 17 May 2016).

Beaumont, P. and Boshier, A., 1974. Report on test excavations in a prehistoric pigment mine near Postmasburg, Northern Cape. *South African Archaeological Bulletin*, 29, pp. 41–59.

Bowes-Lyon, L., Richards, J. and McGee, T., 2009. Socio-economic impacts of the Nanisivik and Polaris Mines, Nunavut, Canada. In: J. Richards, ed. *Mining, Society, and a Sustainable World*. Heidelberg: Springer, pp. 371–396.

Bradbury, J. and St-Martin, I., 1983. Winding down in a Quebec mining town: A case study of Schefferville. *Canadian Geographer*, 27(2), pp. 128–144.

Brunnschweiler, C. and Bulte, E., 2008. The resource curse revisited and revised: A tale of paradoxes and red herrings. *Journal of Environmental Economics and Management*, 55, pp. 248–262.

Bryceson, D. and MacKinnon, D., 2013. Eureka and beyond: Mining's impact on African urbanisation. *Journal of Contemporary African Studies*, 30(4), pp. 513–537.

Carrington, K. and Hogg, R., 2011. The resource boom's underbelly: Criminological impacts of mining development. *Australian and New Zealand Journal of Criminology*, 44(3), pp. 445–453.

Chapman, R., Plummer, P. and Tonts, M., 2015. The resource boom and socio-economic well-being in Australian resource towns: A temporal and spatial analysis. *Urban Geography*, 36(5), pp. 629–653.

Chaudhry, K. and Karl, T., 2001. Booms and busts: Theorising institutional formation and change in the oil states. *Review of International Political Economy*, 8(1), pp. 163–180.

Crawford, M., 1995. *Building the Workingman's Paradise: The Design of American Company Towns*. London: Verso.

The Economist, 1977. The Dutch disease. 26 November, pp. 82–83.

Eduful, A. and Hooper, M., 2015. Urban impacts of resource booms: The emergence of oil-led gentrification in Sekondi-Takoradi, Ghana. *Urban Forum*, 26, pp. 283–302.

Ennis, G., Tofa, M. and Finlayson, M., 2014. Open for business but at what cost? Housing issues in boomtown Darwin. *Australian Geographer*, 45(4), pp. 447–464.

Freudenburg, W. and Wilson, L., 2002. Mining the data: Analyzing the economic implications of mining for nonmetropolitan regions. *Sociological Inquiry*, 72, pp. 549–575.

Gunton, T., 2003. Natural resources and regional development: An assessment of dependency and comparative advantage. *Economic Geography*, 79(1), pp. 67–94.

Gylfason, T., 2001. Natural resources, education, and economic development. *European Economic Review*, 45(4–6), pp. 847–859.

Hajkowicz, S., Heyenga, S. and Moffat, K., 2011. The relationship between mining and socio-economic wellbeing. *Resources Policy*, 36(1), pp. 30–38.

Hamann, R., 2004. Corporate social responsibility, partnerships, and institutional change: The case for mining companies in South Africa. *Natural Resources Forum*, 28, pp. 278–290.

Hammond, J., 2011. The resource curse and oil revenues in Angola and Venezuela. *Science and Society*, 75(3), pp. 348–378.

Haney, M. and Shkaratan, M., 2003. *Mine Closure and Its Impact on the Community: Five Years after Mine Closure in Romania, Russia and Ukraine*. Washington, DC: World Bank.

Haslam McKenzie, F., 2013. Delivering enduring benefits from a gas development: Governance and planning challenges in remote Western Australia. *Australian Geographer*, 44(3), pp. 341–358.

Hilson, G., 2010. 'Once a miner, always a miner': Poverty and livelihood diversification in Akwatia, Ghana. *Journal of Rural Studies*, 26(3), pp. 296–307.

Holton, D., Kelly, M. and Baker, A., 2002. Paradise lost? Assessment of liabilities at a uranium mine in the Slovak Republic: Novoveska Huta. *Geological Society Special Publication*, 198, pp. 355–377.

Jackson, R., 2002. *Capacity Building in Papua New Guinea for Community Maintenance during and after Mine Closure*. London: International Institute for Environment and Development.

James, A. and Aadland, D., 2011. The curse of natural resources: An empirical investigation of US counties. *Resource and Energy Economics*, 33, pp. 440–453.

Karl, T., 2004. Oil-led development: Social, political and economic consequences. *Encyclopedia of Energy*, 4, pp. 61–672.

Küsel, U., 2011. *Heritage Management Plan for Kolomela Mine in the Postmasburg District Municipality of the Northern Cape Province*. Unpublished Report for Kumba Iron Ore, Kolomela Mine, Postmasburg.

Langton, M. and Mazel, O., 2008. Poverty in the midst of plenty: Aboriginal people, the 'resource curse' and Australia's mining boom. *Journal of Energy and Natural Resources Law*, 26(1), pp. 31–65.

Larsen, E., 2005. Are rich countries immune to the resource curse? *Resources Policy*, 30, pp. 75–86.

Laurence, D.C., 2005. Optimisation of the mine closure process. *Journal of Cleaner Production*, 14, pp. 285–298.

Lawrie, M., Tonts, M. and Plummer, P., 2011. Boomtowns, resource dependence and socio-economic well-being. *Australian Geographer*, 42(2), pp. 139–164.

Littlewood, D., 2014. 'Cursed' communities? Corporate Social Responsibility (CSR), company towns and the mining industry in Namibia. *Journal of Business Ethics*, 120, pp. 39–63.

Lockie, S., 2011. Intimate partner abuse and women's health in rural and mining communities. *Rural Society*, 20, pp. 198–215.

Lucas, R., 1971. *Minetown, Milltown, Railtown: Life in Canadian Communities of Single Enterprise*. Toronto: University of Toronto Press.

Machlis, G., Force, J. and Balice, R., 1990. Timber, minerals, and social change: An exploratory test of two resource-dependent communities. *Rural Sociology*, 55, pp. 411–424.

Marais, L., 2013. Mine downscaling in the Free State Goldfields. *Urban Forum*, 24, pp. 503–521.

McGuire, G., 2003. *Managing Mine Closure Risks in Developing Communities: A Case Study*. Indonesia: Kelian Equatorial Mining.

Mehlum, H., Moene, K. and Torvik, R., 2006. Institutions and the resource curse. *Economic Journal*, 116, pp. 1–20.

Mining Technology, 2016. *Kolomela Iron Ore Mine, Northern Cape, South Africa*. www.mining-technology.com/projects/kolomela-iron-ore-mine-northern-cape/ (accessed 17 May 2016).

Neil, C., Tykkylainen, M. and Bradbury, J., 1992. *Coping with Closure: An International Comparison of Mine Town Experiences*. London: Routledge.

Nord, M. and Luloff, A., 1992. Socioeconomic heterogeneity of mining-dependent counties. *Rural Sociology*, 58(3), pp. 492–500.

Obeng-Odoom, F., 2014. *Oiling the Urban Economy: Land, Labour, Capital and the State in Sekondi-Takoradi, Ghana*. London: Routledge.

Petkova, V., Lockie, S., Rolfe, J. and Ivanova, G., 2009. Mining development and social impacts on communities: Bowen basin case studies. *Rural Society*, 19(3), pp. 211–228.

Petrov, A., 2010. Post-staple bust: Modeling economic effects of mine closures and post-mine demographic shifts in an Arctic economy (Yukon). *Polar Geography*, 33(1–2), pp. 39–61.

Pick, D., Dayaram, K. and Butler, B., 2008. Neo-liberalism, risk and regional development in Western Australia: The case of the Pilbara. *International Journal of Sociology and Social Policy*, 28(11–12), pp. 516–527.

Quantec, 2016. *EasyData Regional Database*. Pretoria: Quantec Research.

Randall, J. and Ironside, G., 1996. Communities on the edge: An economic geography of resource-dependent communities in Canada. *Canadian Geographer*, 40(1), pp. 17–35.

Robinson, I., 1962. *New Industrial Towns on Canada's Resource Frontier*. Chicago: University of Chicago.

Rolfe, J., Miles, B., Lockie, S. and Ivanova, G., 2007. Lessons from the social and economic impacts of the mining boom in the Bowen Basin, 2004–2006. *Australasian Journal of Regional Studies*, 13(2), pp. 134–153.

Sabatini, R. and Middleton, J., 2014. Early manganese mining in the Northern Cape. *Railway History Group of Southern Africa*, 21.

Smith, B., 2015. The resource curse exorcised: Evidence from a panel of countries. *Journal of Development Economics*, 116, pp. 57–73.

Smith, D., Krannich, R. and Hunter, L., 2001. Growth, decline, stability, and disruption: A longitudinal analysis of social well-being in four western Australian communities. *Rural Sociology*, 66(3), pp. 425–450.

Snyman, P., 1985. Postmasburg en die Tweede Vryheidsoorlog. *South African Military Society*, 6(6). http://samilitaryhistory.org/vol066ps.html (accessed 17 May 2016).

Stacey, P., Naude, A., Hermanus, M. and Frankel, P., 2010. The socio-economic aspects of mine closure and sustainable development: Guideline for the socio-economic aspects of closure: Report 2. *Journal of the Southern African Institute of Mining and Metallurgy*, 110(7), pp. 395–413.

Stedman, R., Parkins, J. and Beckley, T., 2004. Resource dependence and community well-being in rural Canada. *Rural Sociology*, 69(2), pp. 213–234.

Thackeray, A., Thackeray, J. and Beaumont, P., 1983. Excavations at the Blinkklipkop specularite mine near Postmasburg, Northern Cape. *The South African Archaeological Bulletin*, 38(137), pp. 17–25.

Torkington, A., Larkins, S. and Gupta, T., 2011. The psychosocial impacts of fly-in fly-out and drive-in drive-out mining on mining employees: A qualitative study. *Australian Journal of Rural Health*, 19, pp. 135–141.

Upton, B., Harrington, T. and Mendenhall, S., 2004. Sustainable development and mine closure planning: A case study, Golden Sunlight mine, Jefferson County Montana. *2004 SME Annual Reprints*, pp. 1061–1066.

Van Vollenhoven, A. and Pelser, A., 2010. *A Report on the Heritage Relating to the Closure EMP of the Assmang Glosum Mine close to Postmasburg: 2010*. Wonderboompoort: Archaetnos.

Veiga, M., Scoble, M. and McAllister, M., 2001. Mining with communities. *Natural Resources Forum*, 25(3), pp. 191–202.

Warhurst, A. and Naronha, L., 2000. Corporate strategy and viable future land use: Planning for closure from the outset of mining. *Natural Resources Forum*, 24, pp. 153–164.

Watkins, M., 1963. A staple theory of economic growth. *Canadian Journal of Economics and Political Science*, 29(2), pp. 141–158.

Wilkinson, K., Reynolds, R., Thompson, J. and Ostresh, J., 1982. Local social disruption and western energy development: A critical review. *Pacific Sociological Review*, 25(3), pp. 275–296.

Wilson, L., 2004. Riding the resource roller coaster: Understanding socioeconomic differences between mining communities. *Rural Sociology*, 69(2), pp. 261–281.

World Bank and IFC, 2002. *It's Not Over When It's Over: Mine Closure around the World*. Washington, DC: World Bank and International Finance Corporation.

2 The literature on mining communities and mining growth and decline

Lochner Marais and John Ntema

Introduction

In this chapter, to provide background to our case study of Postmasburg, we review the various bodies of international and South African literature dealing with the effects of mining growth and decline on mining communities. Initially the international research came mostly from North America, but more recently it has been dominated by Australian case studies. The bulk of the international research, commonly framed within the social disruption theory, considers the consequences of mining growth for such matters as health and well-being, security, planning and local economic development in mining towns. More recently there has been a focus on the effects of mine decline and closure, emphasising the long-term socio-economic consequences. Disappointingly, there have been very few South African mining town case studies of the effects of mining growth, but a small body of work has emerged on the socio-economic consequences of mine closure in South Africa. The Postmasburg case study helps to fill a gap in the South African literature.

Mining towns, mining booms and the well-being of communities

Social implications

The original work on the effects of mining on mining communities was heavily influenced by the social disruption theory (Gillmore and Duff, 1975; Freudenberg, 1984). This theory was questioned in the mid-1980s and it was shown that the effects of mining on communities are seldom permanent (Smith et al., 2001). It is nevertheless important to consider some of the social problems that mining towns experience in their early days.

Social dislocation and community dissatisfaction in mining towns are often associated with rapid population growth, high levels of mobility, male domination and local government's inability to provide the growing population with basic social infrastructure (Chapman et al., 2015). Lack of community trust has, in some cases, been associated with rapid population growth (Smith et al., 2001). Conflict between existing residents and newcomers and increased crime have also been noted as causes of dissatisfaction in mining towns (Petkova et al., 2009). Income disparities between long-time residents and the mineworkers can also contribute to social and political conflict (Chapman et al., 2014). High levels of population turnover, too, are not conducive to community building (Haslam McKenzie, 2013).

Lack of social infrastructure planning is often pointed out as one reason why mining towns have difficulty in creating close-knit communities (Petkova et al., 2009; Chindo, 2011). Many mining communities have expressed the view that their quality of life is poor (Christopherson and Rightor, 2011).

Health and well-being

The health implications of mining for mineworkers and mining communities have been noted in the literature (Castranova and Vallyathan, 2000; Stephens and Ahern, 2001; Graber et al., 2014; Mactaggart et al., 2016). Noise and dust are common causes of environmental health problems associated with mining (Petkova et al., 2009). The dust particles originating from mine dumps commonly contain traces of metals such as manganese, lead, cadmium and arsenic (Meza-Figueroa et al., 2009; Moreno et al., 2010). The negative health consequences for communities surrounding mine dumps have received some attention (Alonso et al., 2001; Paoliello et al., 2002; Mapani et al., 2010; Nkosi et al., 2015). Low-income households and children are at higher risk (Nkosi et al., 2015). Nkosi et al. (2015) noted that residents in towns adjacent to mine dumps have an increased likelihood of presenting symptoms associated with asthma, such as wheezing and rhinoconjunctivitis. A case study in Portugal associated proximity to mine dumps with higher incidences of respiratory disease and cancer (Mayan et al., 2006), while in Brazil higher levels of cadmium (associated with mine dumps) were found to lead to higher levels of loss of the sense of smell (Paoliello et al., 2002). Persons who live in close proximity to active surface coal mining present with higher levels of blood inflammation (Hendryx and Entwhistle, 2015), while poorer self-reported health outcomes have also been documented in these locations (Nkosi et al., 2015).). In the Niger Delta, research has shown increases in the incidence of cough, fever, abdominal pain and diarrhoea, and cancer (Chindo, 2011).

Shandro et al. (2011) find that the lack of employment opportunities for women is related to negative health outcomes for women, and that mining towns have increases in pregnancies, sexually transmitted diseases and injuries. Our focus in the book is not on labour-sending areas, but it is worth noting that the health implications of mining activities extend to these areas (Trapido et al., 1998).

Mental health issues in mining towns have received substantial research attention. As far back as the mid-1970s, research had already found that mining was associated with a higher incidence of neural disorders (Burvill, 1975). More recent research has supported this (Sharma, 2009; Hajkowicz et al., 2011; Lockie, 2011). These disorders are commonly associated with long working hours, remote locations (separation from relatives and friends), a patriarchal culture, a lack of social integration among women and, more recently, with changing labour regimes (Sharma, 2009). Women who have lived in mining towns up to the age of 18 have been found to be more at risk of psychological abuse (Lockie, 2011). In general, women in mining towns have small social networks (Sharma, 2010) and divorce levels are also reported to be higher in mining towns (Lockie, 2011). Sharma (2010, p. 201) suggests that the psychological well-being of women in a remote mining community 'might be improved through better local medical services, increased efforts at social inclusion and community connectedness, greater access to child care and better community infrastructure and pleasant surrounds'.

Crime

Mining booms have been associated with increases in crime, and in alcohol and drug abuse (Kramnich, 1985; Doukas et al., 2008; Hajkowicz et al., 2011; Lockie, 2011; Shandro et al., 2011). Some of the consequences of crime and drug abuse are directly related to the higher household incomes that accompany mining booms (Doukas et al., 2008). The issue of increased crime against people and property has been recorded in early work on social disruption (Smith et al., 2001) and also in more recent research conducted in Australia, for example by Haslam McKenzie (2013), who found the increased crime to be associated with high population growth, the transient nature of the population, rising inequality, rising living costs and workplace pressures. Increased numbers of cases of violence against women, including domestic violence, have also been reported (Sharma and Rees, 2007; Sharma, 2010; Shandro et al., 2011).

A longitudinal study of mining towns in Australia found that 'none continued to show reductions in social integration, neighbouring ties, trust in other community residents, or community satisfaction; when residents were surveyed in 1995, none continued to show increases in fear of crime', which led the researchers to conclude that where social disruption does occur, it does not seem to be permanent (Smith et al., 2001, p. 446).

Indigenous communities

In Australia, mining towns and mining development have had negative effects on indigenous communities (Langton and Mazel, 2008; Ennis et al., 2014; Carrington et al., 2011). As mines tend to favour prospective workers with a history in mining, this has tended to exclude indigenous populations from employment in mining (Petkova et al., 2009). Haslam McKenzie (2013, p. 355) describes the situation of excluded indigenous populations as 'the paradox of plenty'. Several authors have documented negative effects of mining on local communities in Africa, such as lack of access to markets, increases in transport costs, declining agricultural production, exclusion from employment in the mining sector, an influx of strangers to the mining areas and in some cases even resettlement (Christopherson and Rightor, 2011; Negi, 2014; Büscher, 2015). Chindo (2011) mentions the exclusion of women from the mining sector in Africa, and Eduful and Hooper (2015) note the outright displacement of local residents, sometimes because residents sell their houses in upmarket neighbourhoods and move to low-income neighbourhoods.

Carrington et al. (2011, p. 340) note that many mining towns 'are unaffordable for those who do not work in the resources industry or benefit directly from it'.

Implications of the new labour regime

The new production and labour regimes of the past 20 years have had the effect of creating new social problems in mining towns. Carrington et al. (2011) say that although these post-industrial production systems have raised incomes they have also eroded worker rights, increased short-term employment (contract work) and reduced work security. They say that the 'longer-term, more holistic view of the role of work in relation to well-being, personal identity, family and community is giving way to a narrower, shorter-term focus on immediate economic benefits' (2011, p. 338). Smith et al. (2001) found much variation in social engagement and proposed that the assumptions made by the social disruption theory should not be accepted unquestioningly. Haslam McKenzie (2013) argues for a more nuanced understanding of place and context.

The switch from permanent employment to shift work, which some researchers call 'atypical' work, has reduced workers' participation in family life (Grosswald, 2003; Sharma, 2009). Shift work has been blamed for the increase in the divorce rate (Presser, 2000). Sharma and Rees (2007) have shown that shift work, often imposed by company policy, can cause sleep disorders, gastrointestinal problems, increased irritability and impaired mental health, and can lead to reduced participation in family activities, changes in gender roles and unfair burdening of female partners – women in mining towns spend more time at home performing duties as housewives and mothers than women do elsewhere.

Planning, housing and infrastructure in mining towns

New mining operations increase the pressure on land, planning systems, the provision of housing and the accompanying infrastructure. Mining towns' local planning problems have been noted in Europe (Feagin, 1990), North America (Halseth, 1999) and more recently in Australia (Haslam McKenzie, 2013). Mining development is usually accompanied by rapid population growth, resulting in enormous pressure to release land for new housing developments (and thus to provide infrastructure) (Haslam McKenzie, 2013) and rapid increases in house prices and rental fees (Rolfe et al., 2007; Carrington et al., 2011; Grieve and Haslam McKenzie, 2011; Lawrie et al., 2011; Akbar et al., 2013; Chapman et al., 2015). Referring to Pilbara in Australia, Haslam McKenzie (2013, p. 349) notes that housing (whether owned or rented) becomes too expensive for potential residents and for most retirees, thereby preventing the community from 'functioning in a traditional manner'.

Exorbitant prices of housing (whether owned or rented), accompanied by government inability to provide infrastructure, have contributed to widespread informality in African countries (Littlewood, 2014; Negi, 2014). Large-scale informal settlements or unsafe compound housing are common in Africa. Informality manifests somewhat differently in Australia and may include tents, makeshift housing, caravans or garages, overcrowding, 'hotbedding' (two shift workers using the same bed one after the other in a 24-hour cycle), and the illegal subdivision of land on the urban periphery (Haslam McKenzie, 2013). Spending more than 30% of income on housing is not uncommon in many mining towns (Akbar et al., 2013). The 'fly-in-fly-out' system in Australia has led to the development of worker camps (a new form of informal or temporary housing), encouraged housing speculation and block-booking of motels (Lawrie et al., 2011; Ennis et al., 2014), and made it more difficult to forecast housing and settlement patterns (Akbar, et al., 2013). High prices have also negatively affected the housing conditions of existing communities, low-income households and indigenous communities (Haslam McKenzie et al., 2009; Lawrie et al., 2011; Ennis et al., 2014). Ennis et al. (2014, p. 338) note that for 'residents living in the economic shadow of major projects, the resultant housing shortages and high living costs generate economic insecurity, especially among already vulnerable populations and those on low or fixed incomes'.

Local economic development

In Chapter 1 we discussed the negative effects of mining at the country level and we noted that the empirical results of 'Dutch disease' or 'resource curse' studies are mixed. Here we shift our focus from the national perspective to the local economy of mining towns. Economic diversification is one of the crucial concerns about these towns. Their economy is constrained by their dependence on mining, the remote locations of many of them and their limited economic activity beyond resource extraction (Robertson and Blackwell, 2015).

Christopherson and Rightor (2011) note poor local economic results from mining. Mining contributes to economic development and employment in general, but the distribution of positive and negative effects varies in scale and across space and time (Franks et al., 2011). Some mining towns may indeed be worse off as a result of resource extraction. For example, it is not uncommon for mining areas to have smaller populations and poorer economies after the initial boom period is over – an outcome that is well documented in the case of shale gas extraction (Christopherson and Rightor, 2011; Weber, 2012). Wilson (2004) likens the boom-bust cycle to a roller coaster ride.

Escalating house prices (for ownership or rental) in many mining towns have discouraged the local entrepreneurs who are essential for economic diversification. Often, many non-mining residents have been pushed out by the increase in living costs. The dominant role of mining companies in establishing and managing mining towns has further meant that many mining companies have been reluctant to make land available for non-mining enterprises (Petkova et al., 2009). The environmental damage caused by mining has also served to inhibit economic diversification (Kemp, 2010). Specific problems caused by mining include negative effects on wildlife, disruption of water supplies to households, power outages and earth tremors (Petkova et al., 2009).

The changing labour regimes of the past two decades, which have meant reduced investment in new mining towns, have also had negative local economic implications for existing mines. The increasing use of contract workers (for construction and maintenance), and block-shift and fly-in-fly-out systems, have reduced local spending and investment in mining towns (Tonts, 2010). Local economies have also often been affected by skills shortages in mining areas (Rolfe et al., 2007). A limited pool of people with specialist skills, limited training opportunities and the remote locations of many mining towns have all contributed in this regard. A general lack of skills beyond those used in mining makes it difficult for non-mining business enterprises to find suitable employees. Lawrie et al. (2011) point out that in many cases local employees are being locked into mining towns because the skills they have do not allow them to find employment outside the industry.

Outsourcing work to local companies has not always been easy. In many small mining towns, 'there are few opportunities to spend locally without compromising service delivery to the community' (Haslam McKenzie, 2013, p. 351). The strict health, safety and environmental requirements of these services do not permit the generation of larger local procurement systems.

The proponents of mining generally emphasise the local employment opportunities, the associated economic opportunities and the social benefits that mining brings (Littlewood, 2014). They further hold that population growth around mines and the spending patterns of mine employees, who generally receive high salaries, commonly bring positive local economic effects (Petkova et al., 2009; Rolfe et al., 2007). Boom periods commonly generate increased employment. Yet in reality the projected employment figures seldom materialise (Christopherson and Rightor, 2011). Lawrence (2005, p. 555) observes that the 'excitement and fanfare that surrounds the opening of a new mine is never present when it finally closes'. In the next section we review the literature on mining decline.

Mining towns and decline

Singh (2011, p. 259) predicts that mine closure is 'destined to be the big mining issue of this millennium'. Mine closure usually results in unemployment and loss of income, with the inevitable negative social consequences (Chindo, 2011). Warhurst and Naronha (2000, p. 154) ask whether mining can be done in a manner that 'does not result in impoverishment at the close of mining operations, and that avoids long-term or permanent damage to ecosystems that have a positive value to local communities and business activities'. The literature on the socio-economic consequences of mine closure was originally dominated by work on the Global North (Bradbury and St-Martin, 1983; Neil et al., 1992). Since the 2000s, there has been an increase in case studies on developing countries (Acquah and Boateng, 2000; Jackson, 2002; World Bank and IFC, 2002; Haney and Shkaratan, 2003; Littlewood, 2014).

Mining towns are generally ill-prepared for mine closure. It is usually associated with economic decline, a loss of production and a loss of capital (Bradbury and St-Martin, 1983). The peripheral location of many mining towns renders this decline even more problematic, particularly as it makes economic diversification difficult (Neil et al., 1992). Using old infrastructure that accompanied the development of the mine, and maintaining it, can be a long-term burden for post-mining communities (Jackson, 2002; World Bank and IFC, 2002). Mine closure further serves to increase the pressure on existing jobs and can lead to community conflict (Haney and Shkaratan, 2003). For those who cannot leave the town after the mine closes, insecure and informal employment becomes the norm. The reality that mineworkers seldom have a wider set of skills adds to their inability to find work in a diversified economy. Mineworkers with a set of skills earmarked for mining moreover find it hard to contribute to economic diversification by means of self-employment (Jackson, 2002). Increasingly, the importance of diversifying economies while mining is in operation is being promoted as a means of avoiding the negative implications of decline (Bowes-Lyon et al., 2009). So far, success has been limited (Littlewood, 2014).

Ageing populations and decreasing populations are among the most commonly reported negative consequences of mine downscaling in the international literature (Upton et al., 2004; Petrov, 2010; Stacey et al., 2010; Christopherson and Rightor, 2011). Research points to community instability (Jackson, 2002) and negative health implications for both mineworkers and the communities left behind (Holton et al., 2002). The stress of unemployment is further exacerbated by the loss of social networks that results from the out-migration of mining populations (Neil et al., 1992). The level of resistance to moving seems to be higher in areas where mining companies have raised living standards artificially by means of subsidies (Bradbury and St-Martin, 1983). Mine closure is also commonly associated with the weakening of community ties and the closure of sports and recreation facilities (Neil et al., 1992). The maintenance of social infrastructure – such as school and health facilities – also comes under pressure (Jackson, 2002). Direct physical opposition to mine closure can also develop (Bradbury and St-Martin, 1983; Nygren and Karlsson, 1992) and community upheaval in areas of mining decline is not uncommon (Jackson, 2002). Increased levels of alcohol and drug abuse and crime have also been associated with mine downscaling (Rao and Pathak, 2009). Mine closure also leads to increased poverty and declining living standards (Haney and Shkaratan, 2003). In the USA, mining busts have caused poverty to return to levels that were prevalent before the boom (Black et al., 2005).

The communities that remain have to deal with the environmental degradation caused by mining. They may have to live with poor water quality, river and underground water problems and dust (Smith and Underwood, 2000; McGuire, 2003). While the large parcels of land used during mining operations are abandoned after the mining cycle, not all mining land can be rehabilitated (Smith and Underwood, 2000).

Mine closure has implications for health. It can bring an increase in mental health problems such as stress, anxiety and alcoholism, affecting not only mineworkers but also their families (Shandro et al., 2011). The main concern in the literature is not mine closure itself but rather how the mining companies deal with it, and how they deal with people who feel betrayed, resentful, exasperated and anxious (Pini et al., 2015).

   Mining bust cycles have serious effects on housing and how housing is planned (Graves et al., 2009). In some cases, the dominant role of homeownership and policies promoting homeownership has been questioned. Graves et al. (2009, p. 138) warn that in mining towns, policies promoting homeownership 'make homeownership attractive even in the face of variable employment prospects, [thereby] increasing adjustment costs in stagnating regions'. Homeownership can also effectively lock households into specific locations as it makes it difficult to trade houses and thereby compromises mobility (Graves et al., 2009). Those who live in mining towns are only too familiar with lock-ins (Lawrie et al., 2011). Because many mineworkers have difficulty finding employment in other sectors of the economy, residents of such towns are vulnerable to industry change (Lawrie et al., 2011). Planning for mining decline is further complicated by the fact that, depending on their age and education, substantial numbers of former mineworkers might want to continue living in the town (Eikeland, 1992). In addition, municipal finance is generally adversely affected by mine downscaling, and subsequent declines in property values have also been recorded (Acquah and Boateng, 2000). In some of the older mining towns, mining companies owned the houses and paid the rates and taxes (Bradbury and St-Martin, 1983). Mine closure therefore meant that these became the responsibility of the individuals living in those towns. Transfer of municipal function to local authorities is a common result of mine closure (Jackson, 2002; Littlewood, 2014). Some scholars see the transfer of assets to municipalities as a mechanism used by mining companies to avoid long-term implications (Littlewood, 2014). It is difficult to maintain the infrastructure when mining decline has reduced the municipal income (Acquah and Boateng, 2000).

   All of the above problems point to the importance of intergovernmental support. Conflict between national and local governments over who should carry the cost of mine downscaling has been recorded in the literature (Nygren and Karlsson, 1992). A big concern is that many mining companies have started to address the problem of decline through their corporate social responsibility programmes (see for example Kapelus, 2002). The unintended outcome is a focus on short-term benefits and a danger that the longer-term considerations (what happens beyond mining) will be ignored (Kapelus, 2002). Collaborative planning by means of partnerships and starting to plan while the mine is still fully operational have been suggested as possible ways of dealing with the problem (Hamann, 2004).

South African mining towns

Despite the existence of a considerable body of research on mining towns internationally, little research has been done on mining towns in South Africa, and few of the studies that have been done take into account the theories used in mining town research. Given the volume of work available on migrant labour, labour issues and mining development in general, the dearth of research – particularly on mining towns – strikes us as rather odd.

The work that is available tends to take a local economic development point of view, with some emphasis on diversifying the economy through partnerships (Rogerson, 2011, 2012) and the local economic development consequences of mine closure and decline (Binns and Nel, 2001, 2002; Nel and Binns, 2002; Marais et al., 2005; Marais, 2013a, 2013b; Marais and Cloete, 2013; Marais and Nel, 2016). Since the demise of apartheid, some attention has also been devoted to mining housing (Demissie, 1998; Marais and Venter, 2006; Cloete and Marais, 2009; Cloete et al., 2009; Cronje, 2014). A recent edited book on secondary cities in South Africa (Marais et al., 2016a) highlights the problems associated with the growth in coal-mining in Emalahleni (Campbell et al., 2016), mining decline in the gold industry of the City of Matlosana (Van Rooyen and Lenka, 2016) and a long-term dependence on coal mining in Emfuleni and uMhlathuze (Marais et al., 2016b; Wessels and Rani, 2016). Furthermore, Marais and Cloete (2016) have noted that growing mining towns struggle to provide their inhabitants with adequate infrastructure.

Four main points need to be noted as regards mining towns in South Africa. Firstly, increased pressure on mining companies to focus on core mining issues has affected the kind of settlement that springs up around the mine. This focus on core mining issues in South Africa is accompanied by pressure from government to minimise the number of mineworkers living in compound housing. In practice, this has led mining companies to provide living-out allowances to mineworkers. The result has been that mineworkers' living conditions have not necessarily changed for the better. In fact, the literature shows that housing outcomes are worse for mineworkers in gold and platinum mining (Marais and Venter, 2006; Cronje, 2014). It further seems that these policy shifts by government and mining companies have resulted in more pressure being placed on local municipalities to provide appropriate housing (Cronje, 2014; Marais and Cloete, 2016).

Secondly, as elsewhere in the world, mining towns in South Africa differ considerably from one another. To mention but a few differences, these towns differ in respect of the commodities being mined, the mining companies that operate in their areas and the mines' location in relation to other economic activities (Marais et al., 2015). Research has also shown that, because of the complex reasons mentioned above, mining decline in the gold-mining industry also differs between any two prominent mining areas (Marais et al., 2015). The Free State Goldfields and Matjhabeng have experienced slight population decline. However, in the City of Matlosana the population has continued to grow despite a decline in the mining economy.

Thirdly, despite increased mining activity, mining decline is a reality in gold-mining areas and in some coal-mining areas. Although mining decline has had disastrous consequences for many gold-mining towns, local economic development efforts to address the consequences of decline have been limited (Marais, 2013b). Mining decline in itself has placed increased pressure on municipal planning and finance (Marais, 2013a). Mining decline usually also goes hand in hand with a loss of people's sense of place. In the Free State Goldfields, mining decline has led to the closure of the local airport and sports clubs, and a resultant decline in sporting excellence.

Mine downscaling also has negative implications for municipal finance. The historical dependence of municipal finance on mining has been noted in the South African literature (Marais et al., 2005; Marais, 2013a). In both the Free State Goldfields and Koffiefontein, the mine owned in excess of 50% of the existing housing stock. Mine downscaling and closure meant that these houses were privatised. Obviously, dumping large numbers of houses onto the market leads to a price slump. However, it also entails risks for the municipality in that, under the mining dispensation, the mines had paid the rates and taxes for these houses. In many cases, the mines had paid these fees well in advance of the payment dates stipulated by the various municipalities. Pre-payment had a positive influence on municipalities' cash flow. Privatising houses to individual households has also meant that the risks have likewise been transferred to individual households (Marais et al., 2005; Marais, 2013a).

Finally, it should be noted that mine growth and mine decline occur at times when nobody expects them (Marais and Nel, 2016), this being partly due to the vulnerabilities associated with global mining practice. Yet it cannot be ruled out that the Free State Goldfields failed to plan for mining decline or to obtain provincial and national support for its plans (Marais, 2013b).

Conclusion: major differences between the experiences of mining towns in South Africa and internationally

This chapter has reviewed a wide range of literature on growth and decline in mining towns, looking particularly at the socio-economic implications of mine downscaling, and ending with a focus on research on mining towns in South Africa. The chapter lays the foundation for the rest of the chapters which concern the mining town of Postmasburg. We conclude by pointing out six ways in which the international situation might differ from the situation currently encountered in South Africa.

The first major difference lies in the historical mining landscape. The role of the compound for housing mineworkers is important and the compound system should be seen against the background of institutionalised migrant work. The migrant worker system was to some extent a fly-in-fly-out – or rather 'bus-in-bus-out' – system. Despite the inhumane nature of the system (and its negative implications for labour-sending areas), it nevertheless helped to reduce the long-term risks of mining for mining communities (Marais and Cloete, 2013). However, despite the existence of a migrant system not being regulated by government, migrant workers still constitute a large part of the mining workforce in South Africa. This, together with a larger emphasis on contract workers, has contributed to the development of large-scale informal settlements around many mining towns.

The second major difference is in the number of contract workers involved in the South African mines. Although there has been a substantial increase in contract work in mining in South Africa, the scale of this phenomenon is much smaller than in either Australia or Canada. Furthermore, contract work in South Africa is largely focused on peripheral and not core mining activities so there are likely to be inequalities between contract workers, who are part-timers, and the mineworkers, who are permanent employees.

A third difference is that, despite the continued labour migration to mining areas, substantial investments are still being made in mining towns in the form of housing for mineworkers. Although the format of these housing investments has changed from mine-provided to mine-enabled, they continue to drive local development.

A fourth difference is in the level of mechanisation. This is substantially higher in Australia and Canada than in South Africa, where most mining is still labour intensive. Even though open-pit mining has brought increased mechanisation, underground mining of platinum and gold still requires large numbers of unskilled labourers.

A fifth difference is that the South African government seems to be far more interventionist than governments elsewhere in the world. The Strategy on the Revitalisation of Distressed Mining Areas, the Mining Charter and various other pieces of legislation (referred to in Chapter 1) attempt to regulate and direct the behaviour of mining companies. This makes for interesting comparisons between South African mining towns and mining towns in Australia.

And finally, the extent to which mine work in South Africa is still unionised differs markedly from the situation in Australia and Canada. Higher levels of unionism in South Africa have resulted in slower swings to shift work or to less extensive shift work than elsewhere in the world.

References

Acquah, P. and Boateng, A., 2000. Planning for mine closure: Some case studies in Ghana. *Minerals and Energy*, 15, pp. 23–30.

Akbar, D., Rolfe, J. and Kabir, Z., 2013. Predicting impacts of major projects on housing prices in resource based towns with a case study application to Gladstone, Australia. *Resources Policy*, 38, pp. 481–489.

Alonso, E., Cambra, K. and Martinez, T., 2001. Lead and cadmium exposure from contaminated soil among residents of a farm area near an industrial site. *Archives of Environmental Health*, 56(3), pp. 278–282.

Binns, T. and Nel, E., 2001. Gold loses its shine: Decline and response in the South African goldfields. *Geography*, 86, pp. 255–260.

Binns, T. and Nel, E., 2002. The village in the game park: Community response to the demise of coal mining in KwaZulu-Natal, South Africa. *Economic Geography*, 79, pp. 41–66.

Black, D., McKinnish, T. and Sanders, S., 2005. The economic impact of the coal boom and bust. *Economic Journal*, 115, pp. 449–476.

Bowes-Lyon, L., Richards, J. and McGee, T., 2009. Socio-economic impacts of the Nanisivik and Polaris Mines, Nunavut, Canada. In: J. Richards, ed. *Mining, Society, and a Sustainable World*. Heidelberg: Springer, pp. 371–396.

Bradbury, J. and St-Martin, I., 1983. Winding down in a Quebec mining town: A case study of Schefferville. *Canadian Geographer*, 27(2), pp. 128–144.

Burvill, P., 1975. Mental health in isolated new mining towns in Australia. *Australian and New Zealand Journal of Psychiatry*, 9, pp. 77–83.

Büscher, B., 2015. Investing in irony? Development, improvement and dispossession in southern African coal spaces. *European Journal of Development Research*, 27(5), pp. 727–744.

Campbell, M., Nel, V. and Mphambukeli, T., 2016. eMalahleni. In: L. Marais, E. Nel and R. Donaldson, eds. *Secondary Cities and Development*. London: Routledge, pp. 63–82.

Carrington, K., Hogg, R. and McIntosh, A., 2011. The resource boom's underbelly: Criminological impacts of mining development. *Australian and New Zealand Journal of Criminology*, 44(3), pp. 335–354.

Castranova, V. and Vallyathan, V., 2000. Silicosis and coal workers' pneumoconiosis. *Environmental Health Perspectives*, 108(4), pp. 675–684.

Chapman, R., Plummer, P. and Tonts, M., 2015. The resource boom and socio-economic well-being in Australian resource towns: A temporal and spatial analysis. *Urban Geography*, 36(5), pp. 629–653.

Chapman, R., Tonts, M. and Plummer, P., 2014. Resource development, local adjustment, and regional policy: Resolving the problem of rapid growth in Pilbara, Western Australia. *Journal of Rural and Community Development*, 9(1), pp. 72–86.

Chindo, M.I., 2011. Understanding community characteristics in resource development: A case study of the Nigerian Oil Sands. *The Social Sciences*, 6(4), pp. 283–290.

Christopherson, S. and Rightor, N., 2011. How shale gas extraction affects drilling localities: Lessons for regional and city policy makers. *Journal of Town and City Management*, 2(4), pp. 350–368.

Cloete, J. and Marais, L., 2009. Mining, aridness and housing: The case of the village under the trees. *Town and Regional Planning*, 55, pp. 31–38.

Cloete, J., Venter, A. and Marais, L., 2009. Breaking new ground, social housing and mineworker housing: The missing link. *Town and Regional Planning*, 54, pp. 27–36.

Cronje, F., 2014. *Digging for Development: The Mining Industry in South Africa and Its Role in Socio-Economic Development*. Johannesburg: South African Institute for Race Relations.

Demissie, F., 1998. In the shadow of the gold mines: Migrancy and mine housing in South Africa. *Housing Studies*, 13(4), pp. 445–469.

Doukas, A., Cretney, A. and Vadgama, J., 2008. *Boom to Bust: Social and Cultural Impacts of the Mining Cycle*. Calgary: The Pembina Institute.

Eduful, A. and Hooper, M., 2015. Urban impacts of resource booms: The emergence of oil-led gentrification in Sekondi-Takoradi, Ghana. *Urban Forum*, 26, pp. 283–302.

Eikeland, S., 1992. National policy of economic redevelopment, and how the working class copes with uncertainty. In: C. Neil, M. Tykkylainen and J. Bradbury, eds. *Coping with Closure: An International Comparison of Mine Town Experiences*. London: Routledge, pp. 119–130.

Ennis, G., Tofa, M. and Finlayson, M., 2014. Open for business but at what cost? Housing issues in boomtown Darwin. *Australian Geographer*, 45(4), pp. 447–464.

Feagin, J., 1990. Extractive regions in developed countries: A comparative analysis of the oil capitals, Houston and Aberdeen. *Urban Affairs Quarterly*, 25, pp. 591–619.

Franks, D., Brereton, D. and Moran, C., 2011. Managing the cumulative impacts of coal mining on regional communities and environments in Australia. *Impact Assessment and Project Appraisal*, 28(4), pp. 299–310.

Freudenberg, W., 1984. Boomtown's youth: The differential impacts of rapid community growth upon adolescents and adults. *American Sociological Review*, 49, pp. 697–715.

Gillmore, J. and Duff, M., 1975. *Boomtown Growth Management: A Case Study of Rock Springs-Green River, Wyoming*. Boulder, CO: Westview.

Graber, J., Stayner, L., Cohen, R., Conroy, L. and Attfield, M., 2014. Respiratory disease mortality among US coal miners: Results after 37 years of follow-up. *Occupational and Environmental Medicine*, 70(1), pp. 30–39.

Graves, P., Weiler, S. and Tynon, E., 2009. The economics of ghost towns. *Journal of Regional Analysis and Policy*, 39(2), pp. 131–140.

Grieve, S. and Haslam McKenzie, F., 2011. Local housing strategies: Responding to the affordability crises. In: I. Alexander, S. Greive and D. Hedgcock, eds. *Planning Perspective in Western Australia: A Reader in Theory and Practice*. Freemantle: Freemantle Press, pp, 66–85.

Grosswald, B., 2003. Shift work and negative work-to-family spillover. *Journal of Sociology and Social Welfare*, 30(4), pp. 31–56.

Hajkowicz, S., Heyenga, S. and Moffat, K., 2011. The relationship between mining and socio-economic wellbeing. *Resources Policy*, 36, pp. 30–38.

Halseth, G., 1999. 'We came for the work': Situating employment migration in B.C.'s small, resource-based communities. *The Canadian Geographer*, 43(4), pp. 363–381.

Hamann, R., 2004. Corporate social responsibility, partnerships, and institutional change: The case for mining companies in South Africa. *Natural Resources Forum*, 28, pp. 278–290.

Haney, M. and Shkaratan, M., 2003. *Mine Closure and Its Impact on the Community: Five Years after Mine Closure in Romania, Russia and Ukraine*. Washington, DC: World Bank.

Haslam McKenzie, F., 2013. Delivering enduring benefits from a gas development: Governance and planning challenges in remote Western Australia. *Australian Geographer*, 44(3), pp. 341–358.

Haslam McKenzie, F., Phillips, R., Rowley, S., Brereton, D. and Birdsall-Jones, C., 2009. *Housing Market Dynamics in Resource Boom Towns*. Perth: Australian Housing and Urban Research Institute.

Hendryx, M. and Entwhistle, J., 2015. Association between residence near surface coal mining and blood inflammation. *The Extractive Industries and Society*, 2, pp. 246–251.

Holton, D., Kelly, M. and Baker, A., 2002. Paradise lost? Assessment of liabilities at a uranium mine in the Slovak Republic: Novoveska Huta. *Geological Society Special Publication*, 198, pp. 355–377.

Jackson, R., 2002. *Capacity Building in Papua New Guinea for Community Maintenance during and after Mine Closure*. London: International Institute for Environment and Development.

Kapelus, P., 2002. Mining, corporate social responsibility and the 'community': The case of Rio Tinto, Richards Bay minerals and the Mbonambi. *Journal of Business Ethics*, 39, pp. 275–296.

Kemp, D., 2010. Mining and community development: Problems and possibilities of local-level practice. *Community Development Journal*, 45(2), pp. 198–218.

Kramnich, R., 1985. A comparative analysis of factors influencing the socioeconomic impacts of electric generating facilities. *Socio-Economic Planning Sciences*, 13, pp. 41–46.

Langton, M. and Mazel, O., 2008. Poverty in the midst of plenty: Aboriginal people, the 'resource curse' and Australia's mining boom. *Journal of Energy and Natural Resources Law*, 26(1), pp. 31–65.

Lawrence, D., 2005. Optimisation of the mine closure process. *International Journal of Environmental Studies*, 62(5), pp. 555–570.

Lawrie, M., Tonts, M. and Plummer, P., 2011. Boomtowns, resource dependence and socio-economic well-being. *Australian Geographer*, 42(2), pp. 139–164.

Littlewood, D., 2014. 'Cursed' communities? Corporate Social Responsibility (CSR), company towns and the mining industry in Namibia. *Journal of Business Ethics*, 120, pp. 39–63.

Lockie, S., 2011. Intimate partner abuse and women's health in rural and mining communities. *Rural Society*, 20, pp. 198–215.

Mactaggart, F., McDermott, L., Tynan, A. and Gericke, C., 2016. Examining health and well-being outcomes associated with mining activity in rural communities of high-income countries: A systematic review. *Australian Journal of Rural Health*, 24(4), pp. 230–237.

Mapani, B., Ellmies, R., Kamona, F., Khibek, B., Majer, V., Knest, I., Pasava, J., Mufenda, M., Mbingoneeko, F. 2010. Potential human health risks associated with historic ore processing at Berg Aukus, Grootfontein area, Namibia. *Journal of African Earth Sciences*, 58, pp. 638–637.

Marais, L., 2013a. The impact of mine downscaling on the Free State Goldfields. *Urban Forum*, 24, pp. 503–521.

Marais, L., 2013b. Resources policy and mine closure in South Africa: The case of the Free State Goldfields. *Resources Policy*, 38, pp. 363–372.

Marais, L. and Cloete, J., 2013. Labour migration, settlement and mine closure in South Africa. *Geography*, 98(2), pp. 77–84.

Marais, L. and Cloete, J., 2016. The role of secondary cities in managing urbanisation in South Africa. *Development Southern Africa*, 34(2), pp. 182–195.

Marais, L., Lenka, M., Grobler, W. and Cloete, J., 2016b. Emfuleni. In: L. Marais, E. Nel and R. Donaldson, eds. *Secondary Cities and Development in South Africa*. London: Routledge, pp. 83–100.

Marais, L. and Nel, E., 2016. The dangers of growing on gold: Lessons from the history of the Free State Goldfields, South Africa. *Local Economy*, 31(1–2), pp. 282–298.

Marais, L., Nel, E. and Donaldson, R., 2016a. *Secondary Cities and Development*. London: Routledge.

Marais, L., Pelser, A., Botes, L., Redelinghuys, N. and Benseler, A., 2005. Public finances, service delivery and mine closure in Koffiefontein (Free State, South Africa): From stepping stone to stumbling block. *Town and Regional Planning*, 48, pp. 5–16.

Marais, L., Van Rooyen, D., Nel, E. and Lenka, M., 2015. Responses to mine downscaling: Evidence from secondary cities in the South African Goldfields. *The Extractive Industries and Society*, 4(1), pp. 163–171.

Marais, L. and Venter, A., 2006. Hating the compound, but . . . Mineworker housing needs in post-apartheid South Africa. *Africa Insight*, 36(1), pp. 53–62.

Mayan, O., Gomes, M., Henriques, A., Silva, S. and Begonha, A., 2006. Health survey among people living near an abandoned line: A case study: Jales Mine, Portugal. *Environmental Monitoring and Assessment*, 123, pp. 31–40.

McGuire, G., 2003. *Managing Mine Closure Risks in Developing Communities: A Case Study, Kelian Equatorial Mining, Indonesia*. Mining Risk Management Conference, 9–12 September 2003, Sydney, Australia.

Meza-Figueroa, D., Maier, R., de la O-Villanueva, M., Gomez-Alvarez, A., Moreno-Zazueta, A., Rivera, J., Campillo, A., Grandlic, C., Anaya, R. and Palafox-Reyes, J.,2009. The impact of unconfined mine tailings in residential areas from a mining town in a semi-arid environment: Nacozari, Sonora, Mexico. *Chemosphere*, 77, pp. 140–147.

Moreno, M., Acosta-Saavedra, L., Meza-Figueroa, D., Vera, E., Cebrian, M., Ostrosky-Wegman, P., Calderon-Aranda, E. 2010. Biomonitoring of metal in children living in a mine tailings zone in Southern Mexico: A pilot study. *International Journal of Hygiene and Environmental Health*, 213, pp. 252–258.

Negi, R., 2014. 'Solwezi mabanga': Ambivalent developments on Zambia's new mining frontier. *Journal of Southern African Studies*, 40(5), pp. 999–1013.

Neil, C., Tykkylainen, M. and Bradbury, J., 1992. *Coping with Closure: An International Comparison of Mine Town Experiences*. London: Routledge.

Nel, E. and Binns, T., 2002. Decline and response in South Africa's Free State Goldfields: Local economic development in Matjhabeng. *International Development Planning Review*, 24(3), pp. 249–269.

Nkosi, V., Wichmann, J. and Voyi, K., 2015. Mine dumps, wheeze, asthma, and rhinoconjunctivitis among adolescents in South Africa: Any association? *International Journal of Environmental Health Research*, 25(6), pp. 583–600.

Nygren, L. and Karlsson, U., 1992. Closure of the Stekenjokk mine in north-west Sweden. In: C. Neil, J. Tykkylainen and J. Bradbury, eds. *Coping with Closure: An International Comparison of Mine Town Experiences*. London: Routledge, pp. 99–118.

Paoliello, M., de Capitani, E., Goncalves da Cunha, F., Matsuo, T., Carvahlo, M., Sakuma, A., Figueiredo, B. 2002. Exposure of children to lead and cadmium from a mining area of Brazil. *Environmental Research*, 88(2), pp. 120–128.

Petkova, V., Lockie, S., Rolfe, J. and Ivanova, G., 2009. Mining development and social impacts on communities: Bowen basin case studies. *Rural Society*, 19(3), pp. 211–228.

Petrov, A., 2010. Post-staple bust: Modeling economic effects of mine closures and post-mine demographic shifts in an Arctic economy (Yukon). *Polar Geography*, 33(1–2), pp. 39–61.

Pini, B., Hayes, B. and McDonald, P., 2015. The emotional geography of a mine closure: A study of the Ravensthorpe nickel mine in Western Australia. *Social and Cultural Geography*, 11(6), pp. 559–574.

Presser, H., 2000. Nonstandard work schedules and marital instability. *Journal of Marriage and Family*, 62(1), pp. 93–110.

Rao, P. and Pathak, K., 2009. Impacts of mine closure on the quality of life of the neighbouring community. *Eastern Journal of Psychiatry*, 12, pp. 10–15.

Robertson, S. and Blackwell, B., 2015. Remote mining towns on the rangelands: Determining dependency within the hinterland. *The Rangeland Journal*, 27, pp. 583–596.

Rogerson, C., 2011. Mining enterprise and partnerships for socio-economic development. *African Journal of Business Management*, 5(14), pp. 5405–5417.

Rogerson, C., 2012. Mining-dependent localities in South Africa: The state of partnerships for small town local development. *Urban Forum*, 23, pp. 107–132.

Rolfe, J., Miles, B., Lockie, S. and Ivanova, G., 2007. Lessons from the social and economic impacts of the mining boom in the Bowen Basin, 2004–2006. *Australasian Journal of Regional Studies*, 13(2), pp. 134–153.

Shandro, J., Veiga, M., Shoveller, J., Scoble, M. and Koehoorn, M., 2011. Perspectives on community health issues and the mining boom-bust cycle. *Resources Policy*, 36(2), pp. 178–186.

Sharma, S., 2009. An exploration into the wellbeing of the families living in the 'suburbs in the bush'. *Australian and New Zealand Journal of Public Health*, 33(3), pp. 262–269.

Sharma, S., 2010. The impact of mining on women: Lessons from the coal mining Bowen Basin of Queensland, Australia. *Impact Assessment and Project Appraisal*, 28(3), pp. 201–215.

Sharma, S. and Rees, S., 2007. Consideration of the determinants of women's mental health in remote Australian mining towns. *Australian Journal of Rural Health*, 15, pp. 1–7.

Singh, G., 2011. Environmental and social impact assessment studies and operations requirements for mine closure. *Journal of Mines, Metals and Fuels*, 59(9), pp. 251–260.

Smith, D., Krannich, R. and Hunter, L., 2001. Growth, decline, stability, and disruption: A longitudinal analysis of social well-being in four western Australian communities. *Rural Sociology*, 66(3), pp. 425–450.

Smith, F. and Underwood, B., 2000. Mine closure: The environmental challenge. *Mining and Technology*, 109(3), pp. 202–209.

Stacey, P., Naude, A., Hermanus, M. and Frankel, P., 2010. The socio-economic aspects of mine closure and sustainable development-guideline for the socio-economic aspects of closure: Report 2. *Journal of the Southern African Institute of Mining and Metallurgy*, 110(7), pp. 395–413.

Stephens, C. and Ahern, M., 2001. *Worker and Community Health Impacts Related to Mining Operations Internationally: A Rapid Review of the Literature*. London: London School of Hygiene and Tropical Medicine.

Tonts, M., 2010. Labour market dynamics in resource dependent regions: An examination of the Western Australian Goldfields. *Geographical Research*, 48(2), pp. 148–165.

Trapido, A., Mqoqi, N., Williams, B., White, N., Solomon, A., Goode, R., Macheke, C., Davies, A. and Panter, C. 1998. Prevalence of occupational lung disease in a random sample of former mineworkers, Libode District, Eastern Cape Province, South Africa. *American Journal of Industrial Medicine*, 34, pp. 305–313.

Upton, B., Harrington, T. and Mendenhall, S., 2004. Sustainable development and mine closure planning: A case study, golden sunlight mine, Jefferson County Montana. *2004 SME Annual Reprints*, pp. 1061–1066.

Van Rooyen, D. and Lenka, M., 2016. City of Matlosana. In: L. Marais, E. Nel and R. Donaldson, eds. *Secondary Cities and Development in South Africa*. London: Routledge, pp. 49–62.

Warhurst, A. and Naronha, L., 2000. Corporate strategy and viable future land use: Planning for closure from the outset of mining. *Natural Resources Forum*, 24, pp. 153–164.

Weber, J., 2012. The effects of a natural gas boom on employment and income in Colorado, Texas, and Wyoming. *Energy Economics*, 34, pp. 1580–1588.

Wessels, J. and Rani, K., 2016. uMhlathuze. In: L. Marais, E. Nel and R. Donaldson, eds. *Secondary Cities and Development*. London: Routledge, pp. 141–158.

Wilson, L., 2004. Riding the resource roller coaster: Understanding socioeconomic differences between mining communities. *Rural Sociology*, 69(2), pp. 261–281.

World Bank and IFC, 2002. *It's Not Over When It's Over: Mine Closure around the World*. Washington, DC: World Bank and International Finance Corporation.

3   Migration and mine labour in South Africa

Rory Pilossof and Philippe Burger

A long history

Between 2005 and 2010, it is estimated, over three million people migrated across internal borders in Africa. Prominent among these were labour migrants. This level of internal migration, unequalled on any other continent, reflects a long history of labour migration in Africa. South Africa in particular has seen massive labour migration, both internal and external. The discovery of gold and diamonds in the late 19th century, combined with the march of colonialism across the region, drew vast numbers of migrants to Kimberley and the Witwatersrand. The ensuing system of migrant labour played a large part in shaping the country's economic, social and political systems throughout the 20th century, and continues to play a large part in the early 21st century.

Theories of labour migration

This section outlines some theories that have been used to explain labour migration. It looks at their strengths and shortcomings and describes how the field has evolved. This theoretical outline will help to explain trends in the history of South African labour migration in the section that follows.

The literature on labour migration is dauntingly extensive: this has become a major field of study, incorporating many disciplines and approaches. Over the course of the 20th century, the theories that were used to explain migration evolved, as scholars responded to each other and new ways of thinking emerged, producing some sharply opposed viewpoints.

Most early accounts of migration in this literature, such as Todaro (1969), were based on neoclassical economics. They described rural populations responding to opportunities and incentives in urban areas or on mines or farms. In neoclassical economic theory, differences in wages and job opportunities were seen as the main reason people migrated. The assumption was that migrants were 'rational self-interested, maximisers, responsive to market signals, who would *choose* to go where the commodity they sold (labour) was best remunerated' (Niño, forthcoming. Emphasis in the original).

Human capital theory evolved from neoclassical theory. The view was now that migrants' decisions to move were based on their assessment of possible future benefits. The theory showed that the benefits need not necessarily be monetary, or immediate. Its main drawback was its failure to examine critically the ways that information is received and digested by the prospective migrants. Information was treated as perfect, accurate and complete, which it could never be (Becker, 1964; Boyle et al., 2013, p. 62).

Behavioural theories were the next step. These theories gave more attention to individuals. Behavioural theorists looked at the mechanisms behind acts of migration, taking into account the process of decision making, the context of rural and urban experiences and people's aspirations to find work elsewhere. The information that migrants have is often imperfect, inaccurate and incomplete, but what they are doing is simply aiming for a better life, rather than making a perfect rational choice to maximise their capital earning. The main problem with behavioural theories, and neoclassical theories too, is that they tend to see migration as a benevolent system that will help the rural worker.

Neoclassical and behavioural theories were criticised as reductionist because they did not take into account the larger context in which decisions and choices are made. Structuralist theory attempted to correct this defect by looking behind everyday actions to find structuring forces that dictated people's actions (Frank, 1966; Wallerstein, 1974, 1980). Studies in 1970s began to look into migrants' backgrounds to see how they were coerced into a predatory system. In southern Africa, slavery, colonial occupation and the emergence of large-scale farming and mining changed the nature of labour needs and practices. Colonial and settler regimes created ways of extracting labour that, even if they were not outright slavery, were not entirely voluntary, in that they obliged migrants to sell their labour under unfavourable conditions (Arrighi, 1970; Wolpe, 1972; Amin, 1974)

Structuralism, however, provided little room for individual agency or action. Delius and Phillips (2014, p. 7) say that although the structuralist view 'provides important insights into the nature and impact of the [labour migration] system', it 'tends to diminish the lives, experience and agency of the men and women at its heart'. In response, many scholars sought to reintroduce individual experience and motivation. Humanist theory, arguing that migrants must first and foremost be seen as people who make their own decisions, foregrounded migrants' motives. Studies based on this theory often relied heavily on in-depth qualitative methodologies, usually using detailed life histories. Researchers began to look at migrants' cultural experiences and to consider how the social character of migrants' origin and destination locations affected their culture and practices. Ethnographic studies of migrants' life stories in home villages and work compounds have flourished (e.g. Moodie, 1983; Moodie and Ndatshe, 1994; Delius, 2014).

Paton (1995, p. 9) argues that the basic principles of structuralist theories of labour migration have proven correct. He says that labour migration is 'best understood as part of a global capitalist dynamic mobilising a series of types of "unfree" or less-than-equal labourers' and that

> from its most coercive to its most voluntary forms, [it] represents a part of the historical spectrum of "unfree" labour that became important in the 19th century

and continues to be a vital ingredient in the recipe for nodal capital accumulation today.

As we show in the historical section below, this is partly why structuralist approaches have dominated the South Africa literature. Labour migration in southern Africa conforms to the pattern described above, and the revisionist boom in literature, confronting the repressive apartheid state, used structuralist theory to show how the migrant labour system benefited the settler authorities over the course of the 20th century.

The theories outlined above have produced large quantities of literature, offering an array of insights into the workings and machinations of labour migration in southern Africa. Much of the current research takes important cues from this literature. New trends in migrant research tend to look at what might be loosely termed 'migrant livelihoods' (O'Laughlin, 2013) rather than labour dynamics more specifically (Nino, forthcoming). We must stress, furthermore, that the older theories have not disappeared. They are still used in much of the current literature on migration and issues such as development, poverty reduction and rural agency in Africa.

Overview of labour migration in South Africa

The discovery of diamonds and gold in the second half of the 19th century radically changed the political and economic scene in South Africa. Significant capital investment was poured into the mines and there was a huge demand for labour. The end of the 19th century and the beginning of the next saw a massive increase in the number of black mineworkers. By the 1920s, 100,000 migrants from the region were working on the Witwatersrand mines, 78,000 of them Mozambicans, and the number continued to rise, peaking at over 265,000 in the 1970s (Crush et al., 2005, p. 3). Southern Africa provides one of the oldest and largest examples of circular migration patterns in the world, due in large part to the mining industries in South Africa but also to those in Zimbabwe and Zambia. The rise in migration rates came at a time of state formation and border regularisation in the region – processes which created a great deal of friction that is still evident today, in the form of large numbers of illegal or undocumented workers in South Africa. As Paton (1995, p. 3) has noted, it is vital that we recognise the role of the state in processes of labour migration (and labour export).

Up to the 1960s, the conventional wisdom in South Africa, promoted by the government and the mining bosses, was that the migrant labour system was normal and natural. They argued, in characteristic neoclassical fashion, that the mining sector had to offer low wages because the ore was of a low grade and profit margins were small, which also meant that there was no excess to pay for workers' families and larger population relocations. Neoclassical scholars also believed that migrants (internal and external) benefited from the security of subsistence agricultural production in the rural areas (Delius, 2014, p. 314). This viewpoint was strongly criticised in the 1960s and 1970s by revisionists who questioned the neoclassical assumptions and the human capital theories that had been used up to that point. Underdevelop-ment scholars, such as Arrighi (1970) and Wolpe (1972), sought to disprove the notion that market forces alone drove migration patterns and questioned the notion of 'voluntary' participation. Arrighi in particular argued that African economies, local and regional, had been deliberately undermined by the colonial project. Colonists had introduced a variety of measures – taxes, alienation of land, creation of reserves and the introduction of labour laws and regimes – to ensure the creation and mobili-sation of the necessary labour forces. In South Africa, and other settler colonies such as Rhodesia, draconian laws were enacted to control the movement and activities of domestic black populations, along with the recruitment and settlement of migrant workers and communities (Arrighi, 1970; Wolpe, 1972; Amin, 1974; Niño, forth-coming). The main point is that rural areas subsidised wages.

In his seminal work on the gold mines, Wilson (1972a, 1972b) contradicts the common perception that profits were low: from 1910 to 1969, profit margins fluc-tuated between 17 and 23%. He also notes that the migrant labour system caused a dramatic decline in agricultural production in areas where people had left to work on the mines. This undercuts the notion that the system was a rural safety net for migrants. Following on from Wilson, Van Onselen (1976) and Bundy (1979) investigated the question of 'voluntary' labour participation in such systems in South Africa and southern Africa. Other authors have described coercive means of recruitment, by both local elites and specific organisations (such as the Witwa-tersrand Native Labour Organisation, WNLA), and other means of labour creation, such as the alienation of land, formation of reserves, introduction of taxes and undermining of rural subsistence agriculture (Palmer and Parsons, 1977; White-side, 1988; Crush et al., 1991). The negative effect on miners' lives attracted much attention. The physical demands of mining, combined with the generally poor working conditions and inadequate safety precautions, had long-lasting conse-quences for the health of black mineworkers. Studies have revealed a high preva-lence of scoliosis (McCulloch, 2013), tuberculosis and HIV (ARASA, 2008) in mining and ex-mining populations, and also the attempts by the mining industry to cover up these issues and deny responsibility (McCulloch, 2013). McCulloch (2013, p. 13) argues that 'the industry's failure to create safe workplaces and to compensate migrant workers for occupational disease underpinned its commercial success and allowed the costs of production to be shifted to rural communities'.

The important research on migrant labour in the 1960s, 1970s and 1980s was largely structuralist. It focused on the systems in place and the way migrants were coerced into exploitative labour practices. The colonial state, the power it wielded and its intentions in creating and maintaining a migrant labour system were central to this research. Much of it illustrated the connection between 'the development of labour-importing areas and the underdevelopment of labour-exporting areas', whether internal or external (Paton, 1995, p. 3). The revisionist school emerged from academic frustrations with Afrikaner political hegemony and the absence of the decolonisation or African advancement that could be seen elsewhere on the continent. Histories of African achievements and experiences began to emerge. This was a time of critical investigation into the formation of the settler state and migrant labour, and European control of assets and land became a key area of study. Issues of labour and labour migration became central themes for scholars with leanings towards Marxist historical materialism in the struggle against the apartheid system.

From the 1980s onwards, however, research turned to understanding how forces in both the rural and urban areas had affected migrants' lives and choices. The focus was now on the agency of migrants and how they sought to contest the boundaries of their working and rural lives. Moodie has written a great deal on the lives of migrant workers (e.g. Moodie, 1980, 1983). He notes the connection between waged work and rural agriculture:

> Tenacious attachment to the land and to agrarian production along with the necessity for infusions of capital into rural agriculture . . . gave rise to cultural patterns in which migrant men (and the women, children, and elders they left at home) forged continuities between wage work and subsistence agriculture.
> (Moodie and Ndatshe, 1994, p. 22)

Many people resisted the processes of proletarianisation (incorporation into wage labour structures) – this can be seen in the way they defined themselves by the choices they made. Moodie and Ndatshe (1994, p. 32) note 'the tenacity with which rural pro-prietors resisted proletarianisation and sustained rural production' (see also Moodie, 1980, 1983). They note that South African-born men could and did exercise choice about where and how to work. They chose gold mines over coal, copper, salt or asbestos mines and over farm labour. Some chose to work in secondary industries in urban settings, or on the railways, or as domestic servants. Though still hampered by a repressive government, many black South Africans were able to exercise some agency and had at least some leeway to choose where to work. Research in the 1980s mapped out the vast area that migrants came from – not only from nearby Lesotho, Swaziland, Mozambique and Zimbabwe, but also from as far afield as Angola, Tanzania, Malawi and Zambia. Entire coal mines in the Highveld were manned almost exclusively by Mozambicans (Crush et al., 1991, 2005). With these new insights and information, more research was devoted to the various cultures on the mines and the boosting of worker consciousness (Beinart, 1987; Miles and Crush, 1993; Harries, 1994).

During the 1970s, following the independence of Mozambique, the South African Chamber of Mines introduced a mandate to reduce the foreign component of the mining labour force. As a result, this component fell from 37% in 1974 to 16% in 1979 (Harington et al., 2004; Nite and Stewart, 2012). As well as the internal directives, political changes in southern Africa also affected labour accumulation from the region. From the late 1960s, President Kaunda of Zambia tried to stop Zambian miners leaving to work in apartheid South Africa. After the crash of an airplane in a flight from Malawi in 1974 that killed 74 Malawian miners, President Banda also banned Malawians from heading to South African gold mines. By the mid-1980s, mines in South Africa were beginning to expand, due to the rise in the gold price and the favourable exchange rates offered by a weakening rand. Over 700,000 people were now employed in the industry.

With the passing of the Industrial Conciliation Amendment Act of 1979, black mineworkers obtained the right to unionise. The National Union of Mineworkers (NUM) was formed in 1982 and in 1983 it secured bargaining recognition from the

Chamber of Mines. The NUM campaigned against the system of job reservation, whereby the best jobs were allocated to white miners. It became the largest single trade union in South Africa's history and, despite hostile conditions, managed to win a great many concessions for black mineworkers, even before majority rule in 1994.[1] However, the NUM's success came at a cost.

In 1987 a study supported by the International Labour Organization predicted that there would be no foreign miners working on the mines by 1995 (De Vletter, 1987). This forecast turned out to be spectacularly wrong. By 1990, foreigners still accounted for 47% of the mining labour force, and this percentage grew to 57% in 2000 (Crush et al., 2005, p. 8). This 'externalisation' of the workforce was in direct response to the growing power of the NUM, as mines sought to lay off local workers at faster rates than foreigners. From 1987 the mines increased their recruitment of non-South African labour, 'to attenuate the presence of the new generation of highly politicized local labour' (Nite and Stewart, 2012, p. 42). While migrant numbers rose, the total number of people employed in the mining industry fell. In 1985 the gold mines employed over 477,000 workers. This number fell to just over 300,000 in 1994. By 2000, it was barely 200,000. Between 1985 and 2000, 'the value of mine output had increased 250%, whereas employment had fallen by 50%' (Harington et al., 2004, p. 68).

Majority rule and mineworkers today

Majority rule in 1994 brought widespread hope for a brighter future for all South Africans. Expectations were high that the African National Congress (ANC), led by Nelson Mandela, would reform the economy, help labourers in industries such as mining and improve the quality of life for lower income families. A host of new research confirmed how unevenly the country's wealth had been distributed. However, as the hardships many workers faced in the new South Africa began to fall away, so too did the academic focus on labour. This change in focus was also partly due to a general move away from labour histories globally in the 1990s.

The negotiated end to apartheid and the triumphant elections brought the new government a great deal of goodwill. Many commentators were therefore willing to give it time to address the country's problems of wealth disparity and massive inequality. However, as the new millennium progressed, questions began to be asked about whether the introduction of democracy had improved workers' lives and long-term futures. The promises of 1994 went unfulfilled for many ordinary South Africans. The failure of the ANC to provide employment and better future possibilities for many, and the concomitant high levels of corruption, self-enrichment and individual largesse within the ANC, have led to widespread public dissatisfaction. As is shown below, nothing has typified this shift more than the Marikana strikes of 2012. As a result, more and more studies have been devoted to the failings of the ANC and the struggles of post-apartheid South Africa. And labour has emerged as a vital area of this new research agenda.

Black mineworkers had achieved a great deal during the 1980s, especially with the formation of the NUM and the right to unionise. But they were constrained by the negotiated settlement that ended apartheid, which recognised the strategic economic importance of mining. As a result, the industry saw little change throughout the 1990s.

In the late 1990s the new democratic government introduced a number of labour Acts that dealt with bargaining and conditions of employment. The Labour Relations Act of 1995 updated the bargaining structure of labour, and allowed for central bargaining, and bargaining councils. But central bargaining has been a long-standing feature in the mining industry, with the Chamber of Mines for decades representing in particular the gold and coal mines. In Postmasburg both the Beeshoek iron ore mine, part of Assmang, and the Kolomela iron ore mine, part of Kumba, negotiate directly with the labour unions. The Basic Conditions of Employment Act of 1998 sets out, among other things, arrangements for leave, termination of service and fringe benefits. The introduction of new labour legislation led to changes in mining companies' labour recruitment practices and a much more elaborate use of subcontracting and outsourcing (Bezuidenhout and Buhlungu, 2007, pp. 253–256). From the mid-1990s, mining operations increased their subcontracting of core mining operations. By 2003, over 90,000 mineworkers were outsourced, up from 46,000 in 2000. This was roughly 20% of the total workforce. These workers were lower paid, had fewer benefits and, most importantly, were not eligible to join organised unions such as the NUM. This has gradually undermined the success and importance of the NUM. The NUM had secured some wage increases for its members during the 2000s, but employment in the sector stagnated.

Figure 3.1 shows the real percentage changes in the mining sector's gross value added (GVA), i.e. the contribution of mining to the country's gross domestic

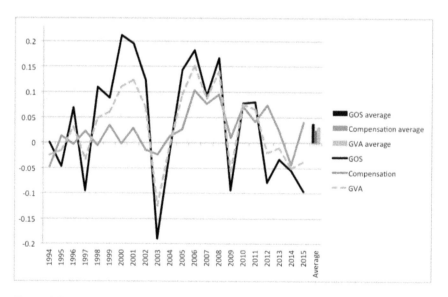

Figure 3.1 Percentage changes in gross value added, gross operating surplus and labour compensation in mining in South Africa, 1994–2015

Source: Stats SA (2016)

product (GDP). The GVA of mining is therefore the total income generated by the mining sector. GVA has two components: labour compensation and the gross operating surplus (GOS) allocated to the owners of the mines. Figure 3.1 also presents the real percentage change in GOS and labour compensation. Note that with the exception of 2003, when the rand appreciated significantly, and 2009, when the global financial crisis hit, the GVA of mining increased by more than 5% a year between 1998 and 2011. Indeed, in some years the increase even exceeded 10%. The increase in GOS from 1999 to 2002 was largely the result of the rand depreciating, thereby increasing the rand price that minerals received and contributing significantly to the GOS of mines. It can be seen that the increase in GVA was allocated quite differently between the owners of mines and labour. With the exception of 1997 (when the emerging market crisis occurred), 2003 (when the rand appreciated) and 2009 (when the global financial crisis occurred), and until 2011 the increase in GOS exceeded the increase in labour compensation by some significant margin. It therefore seems that, at least until 2011, mine owners benefited more than workers and that the benefits that workers expected from the new South Africa did not all materialise. Unhappiness about this fed into the Marikana strike of 2012 and the more general mine sector strikes of 2014. However, by 2012 the mining industry was beginning to face more difficult times as the commodity boom came to an end.

How the world economy affected mining in South Africa

In the mid-2000s the world experienced a commodity boom. Figure 3.2 shows the real prices of some commodities for the period 1980–2015. From about 2003 to 2008 prices rose steeply. The All Commodity Index in real terms increased from roughly 100 in 2003 to 261 in June 2008. The second half of 2008 saw a drop in real commodity prices but they resumed their high levels after that, with the All Commodity Index reaching 234 in March 2011. This resurgence was largely because emerging market countries were less affected by the fallout from the global financial crisis in the period between 2008 and 2011. As a result, the commodity demand from these countries sustained the high commodity prices during this period. Commodity prices were also buoyed up by the US Federal Reserve's quantitative easing strategy that pumped high levels of liquidity into markets, with large amounts of this liquidity spilling over into international commodity markets.

However, after 2011 the commodity bubble burst, as growth in China and other emerging markets fell, placing a damper on global commodity demand. The Chinese economic growth rate fell from over 12% in the late 2000s to approximately 6% by 2015. With the fall in commodity demand, the All Commodity Index fell to 101 at the end of 2015. The price of iron, the commodity mined at Postmasburg, displayed similar bubble behaviour, with the nominal price increasing from $15 per metric tonne in 2003 to $167 in 2011 and the real price from $15 in 2003 to $118 in 2011. However, after 2011 the price imploded, bringing the nominal price down to $55 and the real price to $40 in 2015 (see Figure 3.3). (In January 2016

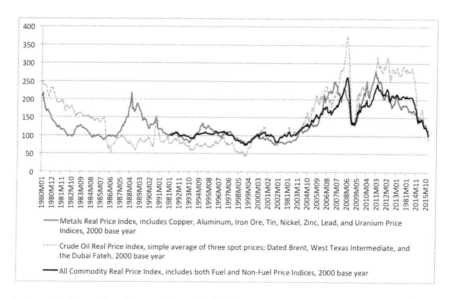

Figure 3.2 International commodity price indices, 1980–2015

Source: IMF (2016); OECD (2016)

Note: Commodity price series and indices were obtained from the IMF. The nominal series and indices were deflated using the US producer price index for manufacturing obtained from the OECD database. All data are monthly (year and month indicated on the x-axis).

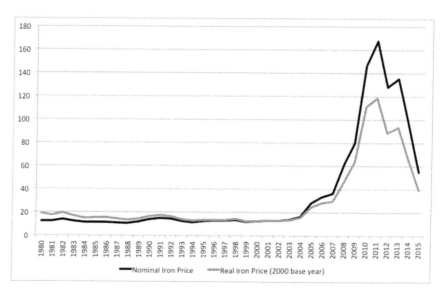

Figure 3.3 International nominal and real iron price indices, 1980–2015

Source: IMF (2016); OECD (2016)

the nominal iron price plummeted to below $40, but rebounded after that to about $50 in mid-March 2016.)

With the fall in commodity prices after 2011, the South African mining sector's GVA and GOS shrank in all four years of the period 2012–2015. The fall in the GOS meant that in general the mining sector was running at a loss and profits vanished. Labour compensation continued to increase during the period, except in 2014, a year marked by a five-month strike in the platinum sector. The increases in the GOS in excess of the increases in labour compensation between 1998 and 2011 meant that labour's share in the mining sector's total income shrank. As Figure 3.1 shows, the increase in GOS considerably exceeded the increase in labour compensation in the period 1998–2002 and as a result, as Figure 3.4 shows, this resulted in a fairly steep fall in labour's share, from 53% in the early 1990s to 37% in 2002 and to 35% in 2008. However, from 2009 the share increased and stood at 45% in 2015. The increase is largely the result of the sector running at a loss (i.e. the GOS decreased – see Figure 3.1), while labour compensation kept on increasing in most years.

The increase in mining's GVA and GOS, and thus its profits between 1998 and 2011, originated largely from the commodity price bubble. Compare Figure 3.5, which shows the nominal rand value of mining production during the period 1980m1 to 2016m1, to Figures 3.6 and 3.7, which show the volume of gold and iron produced during the same period. The first point to note is that in nominal rand terms total commodity production displays a continuous steady increase (see Figure 3.5), despite an acceleration in the mid-2000s and a deceleration since then. However, when we look at the total volume of commodities, we see no sustainable increase

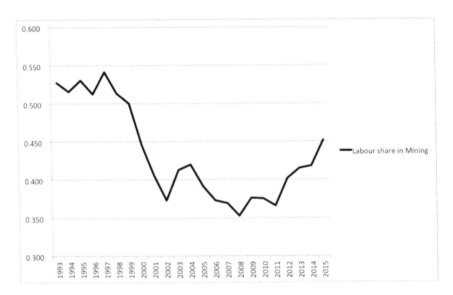

Figure 3.4 Labour's percentage share in GVA of the mining sector in South Africa, 1993–2015

Source: Stats SA (2016)

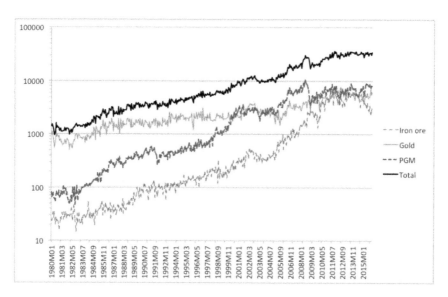

Figure 3.5 Total rand value of mining production in South Africa, 1980–2015

Source: Stats SA (2016)

Note: Figures 3.6, 3.7 and 3.8 are presented in logarithmic scale. The benefit of using logarithmic scale is that if the slope of the line in two places on the graph is the same, it also means that the percentage rate change in those two places is the same. Thus, whereas in a normal graph an increase from 1000 to 1100 will look steeper than an increase from 100 to 110, on a logarithmic graph the slope of these two increases will look the same. All data are monthly (year and month indicated on the x-axis).

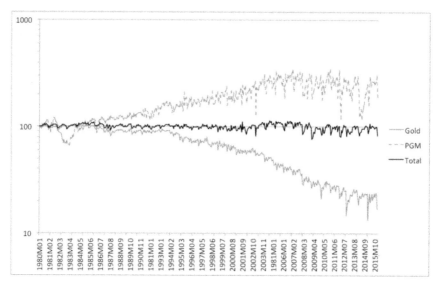

Figure 3.6 Volume index of gold production in South Africa, 1980–2015 (1980 = 100)

Source: Stats SA (2016)

Note: All four indices presented in Figures 3.6 and 3.7 were drawn with 2010 set equal to 100. So although we could compare the levels at two different dates for any one of the commodities, we cannot compare the levels of two commodities. Thus, the indices are not drawn to show sizes relative to each other. All data are monthly (year and month indicated on the x-axis).

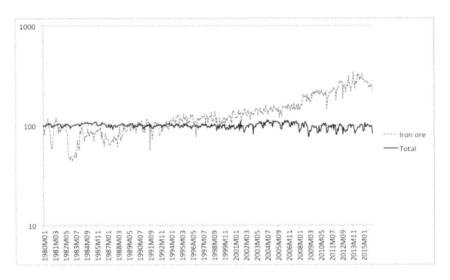

Figure 3.7 Volume index of iron production in South Africa, 1980–2015 (1980 = 100)
Source: Stats SA (2016)

since 1980 (see Figures 3.6 and 3.7). Not even during the commodity boom of the mid- and late-2000s did production react by increasing the volume.

The overall movement hides movements in some of the more important commodities. For instance, even though the nominal rand value of gold produced continues to increase, albeit at a slow rate, the volume of gold produced has fallen sharply since 1980. Figure 3.6 shows that, with the index set to 100 in January 1980, it decreased to approximately 20 in the last months of 2015 – i.e. the volume of gold produced in South Africa in 2015 was approximately one fifth of what it was in 1980.

The production of iron ore and the platinum group of metals (PGM) increased in both nominal rand and real volume terms. The PGM index, set at 100 in 1980, averaged 164 in the 1990s (Figure 3.6). Though very volatile, it averaged 254 during the 2000s, ending the decade at 343. However, from 2011 to 2015 the average fell to 234, largely because of the fall in production, to a low point of 119 during the first half of 2014 that coincides with the five-month platinum mine strike, the longest strike in South African history. (It is also interesting to note that although the level of output during 2012 was lower than in 2011, the Marikana incident in August 2012 was not accompanied by a slowdown in platinum production – indeed, in August 2012 the index stood at 278.)

The index for iron ore, the commodity mined at Postmasburg, increased from an average of 110 in the 1990s, to 158 during the 2000s. During the period 2011–2015 the index increased further to 254 (Figure 3.6). However, there was a marked slowdown after 2013, largely because of the slowdown in international demand for iron, with the index standing at 249 at the end of 2015.

Considering the mining industry in the aggregate, however, it was the rise in commodity prices, and not an increase in the volume of minerals produced, that fed the higher real GVA of the period 1998 to 2011. The fact that during this period, on average, the GOS increased at a faster rate than labour compensation, explains to some extent the discontent on the part of mineworkers and labour unions in the period 2012–2014 and their demand for a wage increase. It also explains why some mineworkers felt that the NUM had not represented their interests fully in the preceding years, and why they shifted their membership to the Association of Mineworkers and Construction Union (AMCU). However, by 2012 the commodity boom was largely over and mine profitability came under heavy pressure.

Drama on the mines

The trouble and violence at Marikana and the continued labour unrest in many of South Africa's mining areas remind us that social and labour plans since 1994 have had little effect (Cronje, 2014). Labour relations in the South African mining industry are strained and salary scales are contested by the mineworkers.

August 2012 saw the Marikana incident during which the police killed 34 protesting mineworkers (Dlangamandla et al., 2014). At the time, they received salaries of between R5,000 and R6,000 a month and were now demanding a basic monthly salary of R12,500.[2] Following this incident, the first half of 2014 saw a five-month-long strike by platinum workers – the most protracted strike in South African history – again with demands for a basic salary of R12,500 (Seekings, 2014). The mines followed a two-pronged defence strategy: on the one hand, they argued that they could not afford such a wage; on the other, they argued that when overtime and benefits were taken into consideration, remuneration was not very far short of the R12,500 that was demanded. Workers rebutted this second claim, arguing that it might be true for permanently employed workers, but not for workers employed by labour brokers, who receive no benefits.

The bursting of the commodity price bubble affected both employment and earnings from 2012 onwards. Table 3.1 shows that employment by the total mining sector increased from 495,150 workers in 2007 to 524,873 by 2012, a 6% increase in five years. This is not a large increase for a five-year period, but from 2012 to

Table 3.1 Average number of employees, 2007–2014

Year	Total		Males		Females	
	All mines	Iron ore	All mines	Iron ore	All mines	Iron ore
2007	495,150	13,858	470,491	12,821	24,659	1,037
2008	518,729	13,256	487,700	12,080	31,029	1,176
2009	491,794	13,727	457,362	12,312	34,432	1,415
2010	498,906	18,216	459,032	16,316	39,874	1,900
2011	512,878	22,361	468,592	19,890	44,286	2,471
2012	524,873	23,380	476,471	20,611	48,402	2,769
2013	509,914	21,126	459,750	18,573	50,164	2,553
2014	495,592	21,794	443,066	19,041	52,526	2,753

Source: DMR (2016)

2014 employment fell back to 495,592 workers. Iron ore mining saw a much more significant increase of 69% over the same five-year period, from 13,858 workers to 23,380, before falling to 21,794. However, early in 2016 Anglo American announced that it planned to retrench 4,000 workers in its Kumba mines, the biggest of which is the mine at Kathu, followed by the Kolomela mine in Postmasburg and the Thabazimbi mine.

The fall in commodity prices – including the price of steel – and the fall in commodity demand from emerging market economies, such as China, have limited the extent to which South African mines can address labour demands.[3] Figure 3.8 shows the average real and nominal earnings in mining in South Africa. It shows that in 2012, the year in which platinum mineworkers were protesting to get a R12,500 monthly salary (culminating in the Marikana incident), the average annual earning per mineworker was R178,387, or R14,865 a month (DMR, 2016 and authors' own calculations – see Table 3.2).[4] In 2012 real earnings stagnated, increasing again the year after, but then decreasing in 2014 (see Figure 3.8 and Table 3.2). Thus, the trouble in mining, associated with the fall in commodity prices since 2012, did register in real earnings (Figure 3.9).

In the unfolding of the labour drama it became clear that remuneration was not the only issue causing the strained relationship. Firstly, it was clear that there was widespread dissatisfaction with the NUM among mineworkers, who saw the union

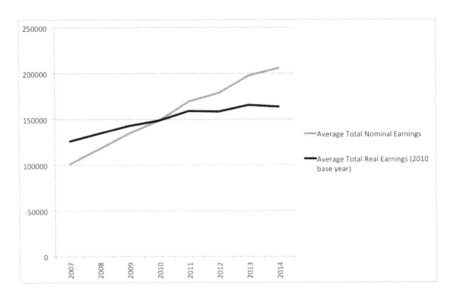

Figure 3.8 Real and nominal earnings in the mining sector in South Africa (rand), 2007–2014

Source: DMR (2016) and authors' own calculations

Note: Real earnings strips out the effect of inflation so that one rand in 2014 is the same as one rand in the base year (2010 in this case).

Table 3.2 Average earnings in the mining sector, 2007–2014 (rand per annum)

Year	Nominal earnings			Real earnings (2010 base year)		
	Total	Males	Females	Total	Males	Females
2007	101,127	100,665	109,936	125,831	125,257	136,793
2008	117,376	116,922	124,513	134,199	133,679	142,359
2009	134,389	133,674	143,887	142,924	142,163	153,026
2010	148,963	148,330	156,249	148,963	148,330	156,249
2011	169,577	168,714	178,706	159,000	158,191	167,560
2012	178,387	177,468	187,431	158,523	157,707	166,560
2013	197,588	196,826	204,567	165,669	165,031	171,521
2014	206,187	205,231	214,252	163,409	162,651	169,800

Source: DMR (2016), and authors' own calculations

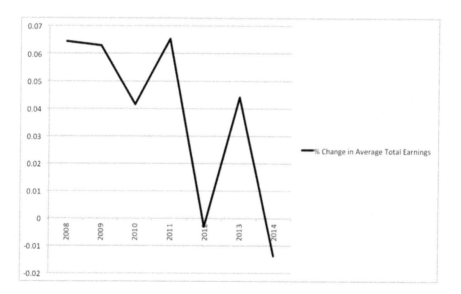

Figure 3.9 Percentage change in real earnings in the mining sector in South Africa, 2008–2014

Source: DMR (2016) and authors' own calculations

as too closely aligned with the ruling ANC and no longer having their interests at heart. This led to the establishment of the AMCU in 1998, which in 2016 represented over 70% of miners at Lonmin platinum mines and was the majority union at Amplats and Impala Platinum.

Secondly, the socio-economic conditions and local planning problems have apparently proven to be equally important. Migrant workers often prefer to receive a living-out allowance from the mine instead of accommodation in the mine compound. Evidence suggests that workers opting for a living-out allowance are worse off than those who stay in the mining compound (Cronje, 2014). Most of the mineworkers are migrants, and anecdotal evidence suggests that many maintain two households – one in the labour-sending area and another in the mining town where they work. Pressure to maintain two households also means that many workers end up with significant debt and garnishee orders against their salaries.

Conclusion

With the start of industrial-scale mining in South Africa during the 19th century, migratory labour became a fundamental part of the process. This holds true even today, with internal and external migrants being essential to mining operations across the country. A neoclassical approach to labour migration would view migrants as possessing individual agency in deciding to work on the mines and choosing which mine to work on. But when we look at the way the mining companies and the government over decades have fashioned and moulded labour movement, the structuralist view that labour migration is driven by power relations in society seems more plausible. Individual agency should therefore be understood as *a constrained agency*, the limits of which are set by the broad structural forces shaping migration. For instance, to earn money to pay a poll tax on land, a subsistence farmer might have weighed up his options and decided he could earn more at a gold mine than at a coal mine. However, it was nevertheless the power relations behind migration that were ultimately responsible for the farmer's decision to migrate to the mines in the first place.

Recognising human agency within a broader structure allows for the study of people's decisions *within a framework of structurally constrained human agency.* Even today many of the mineworkers in places like Postmasburg are migrants from rural labour-sending areas who come to the mines to support their families at home. However, once on the mines, their aspirations and hopes are constrained by the realities of the mine, and indeed by the performance of the mine itself. The situation they face reflects not only current power relations in the mining sector but also global economic changes. The commodity boom in the mid- to late-2000s and the fall in commodity prices since 2013 are two of the most important global economic changes that have affected workers' lives in far-flung mining towns like Postmasburg. Falling iron ore prices since 2013 are threatening the mines' profitability and hence the employment of workers in a town that is predominantly dependent on iron ore mining.

Falling commodity prices and sales, and labour retrenchments by mines and by businesses directly or indirectly dependent on the mines, may in time bring social and political pressures to Postmasburg, although this is not yet evident. As the Marikana incident and the five-month long platinum strike demonstrated, such pressures are not beyond the realm of possibility, and once they occur, can do severe damage to the lives of migrant mineworkers. The study on which this book is based came at an opportune time: it enabled us to investigate the economic and social realities of mineworkers and their families at a very troubled time in the history of South African mining.

Notes

1 For the success and early history of the NUM, see Bezuidenhout and Buhlungu (2007, p. 254–265).
2 In 2012 $1=R7.50, while at the time of writing it was $1=R15.00.
3 This boom-bust cycle of mining also places heavy planning pressures on mining areas. The long-term environmental and socio-economic implications of mining are high on the agenda (Warhurst and Naronha, 2000). Postmasburg happens to be one such example in which a mushrooming of informal settlements has placed pressure on water and sanitation services and on urban infrastructure.
4 Note that this is the average earning of *all* mineworkers, which unfortunately does not tell us much about the distribution of earnings or the median earnings. The protesting mineworkers therefore found themselves at the bottom end of the mine sector's income distribution. This explains why they demanded a R12,500 monthly salary, while the average monthly salary was R14,865.

References

Amin, S., 1974. *Modern Migrations in West Africa*. London: Oxford University Press.
ARASA (AIDS and Rights Alliance for Southern Africa), 2008. *The Mining Sector, Tuberculosis and Migrant Labour in Southern Africa*. Johannesburg: ARASA.
Arrighi, G., 1970. Labour supplies in historical perspective: A study of the proletarianization of the African peasantry in Rhodesia. *Journal of Development Studies*, 6(3), pp. 197–234.
Becker, G., 1964. *Human Capital*. New York: Columbia University Press.
Beinart, W., 1987. Worker consciousness, ethnic participation and nationalism: The experiences of a South African migrant. In: S. Marks and S. Trapido, eds. *The Politics of Race, Class and Nationalism in Twentieth-Century South Africa*. London: Longman, pp. 286–309.
Bezuidenhout, A. and Buhlungu, S., 2007. Old victories, new struggles: The state of the National Union of Mineworkers. In: S. Buhlungu, J. Dabiel, R. Southall and J. Lutchman, eds. *State of the Nation: South Africa 2007*. Cape Town: HSRC, pp. 245–265.
Boyle, P., Halfacree, K. and Robinson, V., 2013. *Exploring Contemporary Migration*. New York: Routledge.
Bundy, C., 1979. *The Rise and Fall of a South African Peasantry*. London: Heinemann.
Cronje, F., 2014. *Digging for Development: The Mining Industry in South Africa and Its Role in Socio-Economic Development*. Johannesburg: South African Institute for Race Relations.
Crush, J., Jeeves, A. and Yudelman, D., 1991. *South Africa's Labor Empire: A History of Black Migrancy to the Gold Mines*. Boulder, CO: Westview.
Crush, J., Williams, V. and Peberdy, S., 2005. *Migration in Southern Africa*. Johannesburg: Global Commission on International Migration.
Delius, P., 2014. The making and changing of migrant workers, *Worlds* (1800–2014). *African Studies*, 73(3), pp. 313–322.
Delius, P. and Phillips, L., 2014. Introduction. In: P. Delius, L. Phillips and F. Rankin-Smith, eds. *A Long Way Home: Migrant Worker Worlds, 1800–2014*. Johannesburg: Wits University Press, pp. 118–137.
De Vletter, F., 1987. Foreign labour on the South African gold mines: New insights on an old problem. *International Labour Review*, 126(2), pp. 199–218.
Dlangamandla, F., Jika, T., Ledwaba, L., Mosamo, S., Saba, A. and Sadiki, L., 2014. *We Are Going to Kill Each Other: The Marikana Story*. Cape Town: Tafelberg.

DMR (Department of Mineral Resources), 2016. *Mineral Volume Data*. www.dmr.gov.za/publications/viewcategory/149-statistics.html (accessed 10 April 2016).

Frank, A.G., 1966. The development of underdevelopment. *Monthtly Review*, 18(4), pp. 17–31.

Harington, J.S., McGlashan, N.D. and Chelkowska, E.Z., 2004. A century of migrant labour in the gold mines of South Africa. *Journal of the South African Institute of Mining and Metallurgy*, 104(2), pp. 65–71.

Harries, P., 1994. *Work, Culture and Identity: Migrant Labourers in Mozambique and South Africa, c.1860–1910*. London: James Currey.

IMF (International Monetary Fund), 2016. *Commodity Prices*. www.imf.org/external/np/res/commod/index.aspx (accessed 14 March 2016).

McCulloch, J., 2013. *South Africa's Gold Mines and the Politics of Silicosis*. Johannesburg: Jacana.

Miles, M. and Crush, J., 1993. Personal narratives as interactive texts: Collecting and interpreting migrant life-histories. *Professional Geographer*, 45(1), pp. 95–129.

Moodie, D., 1980. The formal and informal structure of a South African gold mine. *Human Relations*, 33(8), pp. 555–574.

Moodie, D., 1983. Mine culture and miner's identity on the South African gold mines. In: B. Bozzoli, ed. *Town and Countryside in the Transvaal*. Johannesburg: Ravan, pp. 88–102.

Moodie, D. and Ndatshe, V., 1994. *Going For Gold: Men, Mines and Migration*. Johannesburg: Wits University Press.

Niño, H.P., (forthcoming 2017), A survey of labour migration in Africa since 1900. In: *General Labour History of South Africa*. Geneva: ILO (International Labour Organisation) (*Editors, publisher and place of publication not yet finalised at time of writing*).

Nite, D. and Stewart, P., 2012. *Mining Faces: An Oral History of Work in Gold and Coal Mines in South Africa: 1951–2011*. Sunnyside: Fanele.

OECD (Organisation for Economic Cooperation and Development), 2016. *US Producer Price Index for Manufacturing*. https://data.oecd.org/price/producer-price-indices-ppi.htm#indicator-chart (accessed 14 March 2016).

O'Laughlin, B., 2013. Land, labour and the production of affliction in rural southern Africa. *Journal of Agrarian Change*, 13(1), pp. 175–196.

Palmer, R. and Parsons, N., 1977. *The Roots of Rural Poverty in Central and Southern Africa*. London: Heinemann.

Paton, B., 1995. *Labour Export Policy in the Development of Southern Africa*. Harare: University of Zimbabwe.

Seekings, J., 2014. *How to Reduce Inequality in South Africa*. PoliticsWeb. www.politicsweb.co.za/news-and-analysis/how-to-reduce-inequality-in-south-africa?sn=Marketingweb+detail (accessed 31 May 2016).

Stats SA (Statistics South Africa), 2016. *GDP Tables: 4th Quarter 2015*. P0441. www.statssa.gov.za/?page_id=1847 (accessed 14 March 2016).

Todaro, M.P., 1969. A model of labor migration and urban unemployment in less developed countries. *American Economic Review*, 59(1), pp. 138–148.

Van Onselen, C., 1976. *Chibaro: African Mine Labour in Southern Rhodesia 1900–1933*. London: Pluto Press.

Wallerstein, I., 1974. *The Modern World System I, Capitalist Agriculture and the Origins of the European World Economy in the Sixteenth Century*. New York: Academic Press.

Wallerstein, I., 1980. *The Modern World System II, Mercantilism and the Consolidation of the European World-Economy, 1600–1750*. New York: Academic Press.

Warhurst, A. and Naronha, L., 2000. Corporate strategy and viable future landuse: Planning for closure from the outset of mining. *Natural Resources Forum*, 2\, pp. 153–164.

Whiteside, A., 1988. *Labour Migration in Southern Africa*. Braamfontein: South African Institute of International Affairs.

Wilson, F., 1972a. *Migrant Labour in South Africa: Report to the South African Council of Churches*. Johannesburg: South African Council of Churches and SPRO-CAS.

Wilson, F., 1972b. *Labour in the South African Gold Mines 1911–1969*. Cambridge: Cambridge University Press.

Wolpe, H., 1972. Capitalism and cheap labour-power in South Africa: From segregation to apartheid. *Economy and Society*, 1(4), pp. 425–456.

Section B

Governance, planning, the environment and power

Many of the initial mining settlements were company towns, developed, planned and managed by mining companies. This practice drew criticism because it did not allow for much private initiative. In some cases, mining companies even started to perform local government functions. Company towns still exist today. However, many mines have now handed over management and control to the municipality. This means the municipality has to start levying rates and taxes and providing infrastructure and amenities, and mining households have to start budgeting and paying for services.

However, since the early 1990s new policies have been developed for mining towns. In Australia the fly-in-fly-out arrangements introduced in the 1990s have effectively halted the development of mining towns. South Africa has taken a different course: its policy guidelines say mining companies have a responsibility to create integrated mining communities. This has promoted the development of formal and permanent mining towns close to the mines. The emphasis on integrated communities is a reaction against the apartheid system. A further development, in line with international trends under the 'new natural resource agenda', the post-apartheid government has introduced the principle of collaborative planning. Mines have had to develop social and labour plans and extensive environmental management plans. The granting of the company's mining licence depends directly on these plans. The local strategic plans, called integrated development plans, have to be dovetailed with the social and labour plans – the ideal outcome being collaborative plans. In the real world, however, the local strategic plans are of questionable quality, and the social and labour plans are linked to the licencing agreements for mining that are managed by a national government department and not by the local government. In a situation complicated by the power of multinational organisations and the fact that local government happens to be the weakest sphere of government in South Africa, the prospects are less than promising.

Two further principles are entrenched in the 'new natural resources agenda': partnerships, and planning for mine closure before mining commences. Just as the principle of collaborative planning has not really gained general acceptance, so the notion of partnerships has not always received sufficient attention. And as some scholars have pointed out, partnerships do not work when the power relationships are unbalanced. Multinational corporations have much inherent power and capacity but the local municipalities do not. Planning for mine closure is entrenched in environmental legislation and largely pertains to how the mined land will be rehabilitated. Though South African policy guidelines are mostly silent on the social and economic issues of mine downscaling, they do advise that ideally mining should not create ghost towns. How then is a municipality to plan infrastructure for areas whose reason for existing may eventually disappear?

This section comprises five chapters that ask crucial questions about governance, planning, the environment and power.

- Should all mines develop settlements in their vicinity? Government policy promotes these settlements, but are there not more appropriate alternatives that will minimise the consequences of mine downscaling? Could mineworkers not be bussed in over longer distances – for example from Kathu to Postmasburg or vice versa?
- Our case study offers an example of a fairly good partnership approach to developing housing and settlement structures for the mine workforces. Two mining companies, Kumba and Assmang, have successfully collaborated with the municipality in developing land and infrastructure in Postmasburg. As a consequence, the long-term maintenance has been transferred to the municipality. Is this an appropriate response or should the mining companies take responsibility for the longer-term implications of mining? Already there are indications that the municipality is struggling to provide adequate funding for maintenance.
- What hampers collaborative planning? Does the failure to plan collaboratively stem from unequal power relations?
- Is the Tsantsabane Local Municipality able to perform its role of collecting rates and taxes from the newly established settlements? How much support does the municipal fiscus receive from the national and provincial governments and how well do these levels of government respond to the needs of a mining town?
- How does one simultaneously plan for growth and decline? To what extent is planning based on best-case scenarios? Can a case not be made for planning for more than one scenario? How can one plan engineering services for mining towns that will first grow and then shrink over time?
- To what extent does new-order mining legislation make mining environmentally more sustainable?

These five chapters attempt to answer the above questions. Chapter 4 (*The Tsassamba Committee*) assesses the role of a private-public partnership in Postmasburg. The Tsantsabane Local Municipality and the two mining companies came together in a novel kind of partnership, the Tsassamba Committee, with official representation from all three entities. The committee functioned on both management and technical levels. It opened a bank account for the companies and the municipality to deposit their contributions to the town's bulk services needs and land needs. Master plans and projects to address these needs were developed and were to be rolled out and managed by the committee. However, as the authors show, this partnership had its share of problems. Chapter 5 (*Spatial planning for Postmasburg*) looks at how mining and government relations affect spatial and land-use planning in Postmasburg. It investigates the consequences of mining booms for spatial planning and asks whether it is possible to plan for such rapid changes. The authors express concerns about the single growth scenario that underlies planning in Postmasburg. Chapter 6 (*Government, mining and community relations*) considers the dynamics of power relationships in Postmasburg. It looks at the ways in which collaborative planning is either inhibited or promoted. The authors emphasise that a lack of trust between the parties remains a major obstacle. Chapter 7 (*Mining and municipal finance*) explains how mining development affects municipal finance in Postmasburg. The authors analyse, among other documents, the audited financial statements of the Tsantsabane Local Municipality. Trends discernible in the financial statements are discussed in detail and compared with those specifically associated with mining development. The chapter also considers the consequent pressures on planning, infrastructure and housing. Chapter 8 (*Environmental legislation, mining and ecosystems*) describes the ecological consequences of mining near Postmasburg over the past century. The authors examine the efficacy of environmental legislation by contrasting the ecological impacts of the early mines established before the advent of modern environmental legislation with those of modern mines.

4   The Tsassamba Committee

Ernst Drewes and Malène Campbell

A hybrid model of governance for Postmasburg

The presence of a mine places extraordinary pressure on a town, obliging it to invest in large-scale infrastructure and land development to serve the influx of people, particularly during periods of mining growth. Planning and providing services in a mining town is a challenge, complicated by factors such as volatility in resource prices (Chapman et al., 2015) and uncertainty about how long a boom will last.

To alleviate the negative effects of the extraction of natural resources, the 'natural resource policy agenda' calls for public participation when mining revenue is allocated, decentralisation of the government and cooperation, such as public-private-partnerships (Arellano-Yanguas, 2008). The natural resource policy agenda says that planning should go beyond mining operations and consider the planning implications of mine closure, such as the maintenance of infrastructure (ICMM, 2008; Ayelazuno, 2014). Although much of the emphasis on planning beyond the life of a mine is on the mining operations, it should also be applied to the mining settlements created as a result of those operations. The natural resource agenda policy also emphasises the concepts of social partnerships, such as partnerships between a local government and a mining company, and hybrid models of governance. This shift to partnerships and hybrid governance models came after the period, mainly the 1980s and early 1990s, during which mining companies commonly performed local government functions (IIED, 2002). The formation of partnerships is intended to prevent mining companies taking over local government functions and those towns becoming company towns. The partnerships are collaborations between government, the private sector and civil society and are typically formed in mining towns so that joint responsibility will be taken for the pressures on local governments (Rogerson, 2012). Such partnerships can be formed within or outside the ambit of social and labour plans or local strategic plans although the social and labour plans in principle make provision for such collaborative planning projects (Rogerson, 2011).[1]

The Tsassamba Committee, the topic of this chapter, is a coordinating committee formed in Postmasburg to assist in the development of bulk and internal infrastructure[2] and to provide land for housing for the employees of the two largest mines, Kolomela (owned by Kumba) and Beeshoek (owned by Assmang). The provision of bulk infrastructure posed a major challenge to the Tsantsabane Local Municipality. The mines were concerned that the municipality did not have the human resource capacity to deal with the pressure caused by mining in the area, so in 2008 the Tsassamba Committee was established between the Tsantsabane Local Municipality, Kolomela mine and Beeshoek mine. This is largely a technical committee. It includes a civil engineer, an urban and regional planner, munici-pal officials and mining employees. Members of the business chamber and civil society organisations are not involved. The funds come mainly from the mining companies, with some contributions from government. The Tsassamba Committee conducted a thorough needs assessment, focusing on the immediate need for bulk infrastructure and serviced stands for housing.

In this chapter we critically assess the Tsassamba Committee against the back-ground of the need for partnership and a hybrid model of governance in Post-masburg. We based our study on interviews, our assessment of the Committee's minutes, and the background knowledge and direct involvement in the Tsassamba Committee of an author of this chapter, Ernst Drewes who is the Technical Advisor of Beeshoek Mine. The interviewees were a spatial planner employed by the North-ern Cape Provincial Administration, spatial planners consulting in Tsantsabane, the general manager of Beeshoek mine, the principal engineer at Kolomela mine, other mining employees, the head of technical services at the Tsantsabane Municipality, other municipal officials, a municipal councillor and local business people.

The literature on governance, planning and collaboration

The need for partnership and collaboration in planning is discussed in a body of literature beyond the ambit of relations between mining companies and the local government in mining towns. Planning theory increasingly emphasises partner-ships and collaboration (for example, the well-known Healy, 1998, 2006). The UK has seen the spread of collaborative governance, and various forms of partnerships in community development are becoming common in other parts of the world, including North America. Healy (2006) recommends that planning and policy-making be based on interactive social processes. Hillier and Gunder (2003) empha-sise that urban planning is, after all, about the city of the future and its impact on people. But Watson (2009) argues that neither communities nor the market will solve urban problems. The implementation of plans should ideally be a process of negotiation and compromise (Healy, 2006). Planners must understand the local dynamics and context and assess the impact of interventions on people.

Healy (1998) asks whether governments have the capacity to make the improve-ments necessary to create places of quality. She argues that an essential part of such capacity is the character of municipal policy, which should be integrated and con-nected. She notes that collaborative methods result in cooperation between stake-holders in policy development and delivery. Whereas urban governance in Europe was top-down after the World War II and policies were developed at national level, local governments have now come under pressure to become entrepreneurial, in addition to improving the social and environmental qualities of cities. Healy (1998) argues that this is impossible to achieve without private sector partners. She therefore suggests that collaborative relationships with stakeholders should be encouraged, to generate a culture of urban governance that will ensure that all citizens can flourish. She says that potential stakeholders should be identified and asked how their voices could be heard during the development process, which would help to build capacity by mobilising social capital and knowledge of resources.

Van Horen (2002) describes a participatory project aimed at social empowerment that was successfully implemented by GTZ (Gesellschaft für Technische Zusammenarbeit) in a war-torn area of Sri Lanka. He argues that long-term improvement depends on the extent to which institutional capacity is built. The project's dependence on financial support was a problem, because it meant that the development process might not be sustainable once the funding was exhausted. This problem was addressed by building relationships on an understanding of local relationships and institutions. Relationships between the project and the central government were also positive and participatory on a local as well as central government level.

In 2005, after a period of council amalgamations,[3] Australian policy makers agreed there was a need to increase the efficiency of local governments. For effective service delivery and an efficient local government, several cooperative models were possible, such as joint boards, virtual local governments, agency models and municipal corporations. Dollery and Johnson (2005) considered that the emphasis on council amalgamation was inappropriate. Bel et al. (2007) found that efficiency, financial constraints and the management of political and citizen interest groups were the driving forces behind the reform process. Their research showed that municipalities are aware of the importance of managing markets, political interests and public participation in the service delivery process. Several authors note that committed leadership, an ethical approach, community involvement and public support are the prerequisites for successful partnerships, while acting responsibly is always good for business (Hamann, 2003; Bel et al., 2007; Osei-Kyei and Chan, 2015). Social responsibility is on the rise in South Africa partly as a result of policy adjustments – this is especially relevant to the mining sector in South Africa (Hamann, 2003).

Turner (1994) notes that in the United States social partnerships came to be considered an ideal way to reform industrial relations. He observes that negotiation and collaboration are the foundation stones of participatory social partnerships and that four elements are present in successful partnerships: mutual recognition and acceptance, direct participation and cooperation, training to raise the level of skills and institutional infrastructure. Some have criticised social partnerships, saying they are not democratically formed and are thus unrepresentative, but they can work to reduce conflict and bring economic benefits (Boyd, 2002).

Spatial planning policy in South Africa

In line with international trends, South Africa is moving away from company towns where the mining companies perform local government functions. The White Paper on Mining and Minerals states that 'the whole structure of mining towns and settlements must be altered to integrate mineworkers into the local economy and to end the racially discriminatory provisions that apply to housing' (DME, 1998, p. 27). It also proposes that a tripartite structure be established between the state, the mining industry and selected representatives of employees to seek ways to improve the lot of mineworkers. The Mineral and Petroleum Resources Development Act of 2002 requires the mining industry to intensify its social corporate initiatives and commitment to local development because mining in the past did not always benefit rural economies (Rogerson, 2011).

South African mining towns are of two types: those controlled and managed by the company, where all the housing belongs to the company and is only for mineworkers, and those where some housing is owned by the mine and the rest is privately owned. Lime Acres near Danielskuil in the Northern Cape Province is an example of the first kind where formal township establishment did not occur. Welkom in the Free State province is an example of the second kind, a hybrid. The resource slump of the mid-1980s caused many mining companies to privatise their housing, thus reducing their expenditure on non-mining activities and shifting the financial obligations to households and the responsibility for long-term infrastructure maintenance to local government. Besides the slump, the move was also prompted by the government's call for a move away from company towns. The National Spatial Development Perspective (NSDP), for example, required mining companies to 'ensure empowerment of employees through home ownership; and move away from providing housing at unsustainable locations on mine land' (RSA, 2006, p. 18). The NSDP further encouraged mining companies to promote housing development in sustainable towns near the mining operations and not as isolated villages on mine-owned land. This was the first direct guidance from the government, asking mining companies to house their employees in integrated settlements rather than in on-site housing in company towns. The government's Strategy for the Revitalisation of Distressed Mining Towns also emphasises homeownership and the development of settlements around mines (Tshangana, 2015). The government's policy stresses the importance of social stability and large-scale industry investment in mining towns.

Assmang originally developed a mining settlement or company town at its operations at Beeshoek, but by the late 2000s it had decided to disband the town and settle its employees in Postmasburg. In 2011 Kumba's new mine, Kolomela, started production. Given the above policy guidelines, Assmang and Kumba decided to settle their workforce in Postmasburg. Initial plans required the development of land, bulk infrastructure and 2000 houses in a small town which already had approximately 6500 houses. The main challenge was therefore to supply increased institutional capacity and support to provide for the new houses. The lack of institutional capacity at local government level (Rogerson, 2011, 2012) and the speed with which the infrastructure had to be provided required an alternative governance model. Some kind of partnership arrangement or hybrid governance model had to be secured. The Tsassamba Committee was established to address these concerns.

The operations of the Tsassamba Committee

The Tsassamba Committee's main function was to plan and develop the 2000 stands for housing for mining company employees and their families. In this section we look at its role against a background of the development responsibilities and functions of municipalities in South Africa, and the South African Constitution (RSA, 1996). Sections 80 and 81 of the Municipal Systems Act (RSA, 2000) make provision for service delivery agreements with social partners, thus promoting a hybrid model of governance. The municipalities are obliged to create formal integrated development plans (IDPs) and a Spatial Development Framework (SDF). In its IDP a municipality must develop a plan that links, integrates and coordinates sector plans and takes into account proposals for the development of the municipality; aligns the resources and capacity of the municipality with the implementation of the IDP; forms the policy framework and general basis on which annual budgets must be based; and is compatible with national and provincial development plans and planning requirements binding on the municipality in terms of legislation (RSA, 2000). The SDF is a plan for achieving the objectives of local government set out in section 152 of the Constitution; giving effect to its developmental duties as required by section 153 of the Constitution; and, together with other organs of state, contributing to the progressive realisation of the fundamental rights contained in Sections 24, 25, 26, 27 and 29 of the Constitution (RSA, 1996). The infrastructure which the Committee developed was in line with the Tsantsabane Municipality's IDP and SDF.

To ensure collaboration, the Tsassamba Committee first had to find common ground between the partners, so that there could be agreement on the Committee's tasks (Tsassamba Committee, 2008). The common ground and tasks were a long and cumbersome process which started out in 2008. The final "service level agreement" was only signed in 2010 after numerous meetings and informal discussions. The main issues reflected on the size of the contribution of the mines, as well as each mine's share in the forthcoming development process. The Municipality didn't have any funds available, only land.

These tasks were to:

- specify the role of each partner in the envisaged development efforts;
- determine the status of the land where development was envisaged;
- decide which bulk services were in need of upgrading;
- set out the responsibilities of Assmang and Kumba for town planning applications, the design of bulk services, a tender procedure for contractors, bulk service contributions per partner, the process for transfer of land and the construction of houses;
- specify the role of the municipality in supporting these endeavours while maintaining its primary role as service provider to the community;
- develop a budget for each of the three partners' contributions to the bulk services that needed to be constructed or expanded; and
- schedule formal monthly meetings of the three partners.

The first step was to open a bank account in the municipality's name, earmarked to finance the various projects. The private partners (the two mining companies) and the government would pay their contributions into this account and statements would be available for scrutiny and audit every month. Legislation doesn't allow for private bank accounts for such purposes, so an additional bank account in the municipality's name was opened and "ringfenced" for the Committee's purposes. Control of the account was at the Municipality's discretion, but they reported on cash flow monthly and provided statements. As mentioned, some of the money was used to pay salaries when there was financial problems in the Municipality.

Considering the overall need for human settlement, it is not surprising that the focus was mainly on bulk infrastructure projects. The main projects, the total value of which stood at R145 million in 2009 (Tsassamba Committee, 2014), were new main water facilities throughout the town, three new sewage pump stations, two new pressure towers and a water reservoir, four new tarred roads, new electrical and mechanical equipment for the water and sewerage facilities, two 11 kV electrical networks, and the upgrading of two substations. Sufficient land was available for the project because the municipality owned most of the vacant and available land in the town and surrounds. But no spatial planning, bulk infrastructure planning or statutory processes to formalise agricultural land had been initiated. "Formalise" in this context reflected on the SLA which defined formalised land as residential stands with internal engineering services, a General Plan and a Title Deed.

Importantly, we noted that the Committee's minutes make no reference to mine downscaling, though this is an important issue raised in the natural resource policy agenda. This issue was not part of the Committee's planning framework. Mine downscaling was never raised or discussed as the focus was on the projects.

The day-to-day management of the process was dealt with by the head of the municipal technical department and a representative from each of the mining companies. Detailed feedback on each infrastructure project and the relevant cash flows was prepared for each monthly meeting. Contractors were appointed by agreement between the partners, and all contractors and consultants had to provide verbal and written feedback at the monthly meetings. The legal requirements for a municipality in terms of the municipal financial act, i.e. procurement, and feedback to the Municipal Council, also formed part of management and collaboration process. Where relevant, departments such as Water Affairs also attended the monthly meetings. Except for the physical development of bulk services, the Committee members recognised that policy guidance, as required by legislation, was lacking: the municipality did not have an updated SDF and Land Use Management System (LUMS). None of the envisaged developments had been foreseen by the 2009 SDF. This required a speedy process to help the municipality create a new SDF and Master Plans for the various bulk services components, i.e. roads, water, sewerage and electricity. To some extent the Committee functioned as a committee of technical officials outside the ambit of local government.

The bulk infrastructure design and construction were carried out at the same time as the planning by the Committee, including the rezoning and development of stands for houses for mineworkers throughout various neighbourhoods in the town. This approach is quite new in South Africa, where the stands and housing are constructed at the same time as the bulk services. In short, the strategic planning components (the SDF and the Master Plans) were compiled ahead of physical development of infrastructure and stands, but were closely linked in terms of timeframes and budgets. The advantage was that there was no time lag between these policy documents as is usually the case.

The details were spelled out in the service level agreement, designed by all parties, which stipulated the role of each party in the envisaged development efforts, the status of the land where development was envisaged, and the bulk services in need of upgrading. It stipulated the role of the two developers with regard to town planning applications, design of bulk services, tender procedure for contractors, bulk service contributions per party, procedures for transfer of land and construction of houses. It also set out the detailed role of the Municipality in supporting these endeavours while maintaining its primary role as service provider to the community, a detailed budget for each of the three parties' contributions to the construction or expansion of bulk services, and the structure and representation for the three parties' formal monthly meetings.

How successful was the Tsassamba Committee?

On the face of it the positive contribution of the Tsassamba Committee seems obvious: stands were developed and bulk and internal infrastructure were created for a settlement that had not seen much expansion previously. Eight years after the Committee was formed in 2008, we reflected on its collaborative approach. We could see that enormous growth had been dealt with successfully, in terms of spatial planning and infrastructure development, but we felt it was time for a balanced assessment. In the following we look first at the positive achievements and then at some shortcomings.

Given the town's arid environment, providing water was the most crucial of the bulk infrastructure projects. Many people, including a municipal councillor who is also a local businessman, told us in interviews that the Committee had done a good job. Bulk water was ensured through Sedibeng's Gamagara Water Line.[4] Underground water is available because the mining companies pump water into the underground water system. According to our household survey (see Chapter 1 of this volume for our survey methods), 78% of Postmasburg's households have access to municipal water inside their dwellings and 99% have water-borne sanitation and electricity. As Table 4.1 shows, formal housing increased from 71.8% in 2011 to 77.9% in 2015, and flush and chemical toilets increased by 8.4%. These achievements are laudable considering that this was a period when informal settlements mushroomed in Postmasburg.

Interviews with the mining companies showed they were in general extremely positive about the Committee. Funding the various projects was a way for them to be seen as actively participating in local development. It helped them fulfil their responsibilities in terms of the Mining Charter (DMR, 2010) and retain their

Table 4.1 Housing types and toilet facilities in Tsantsabane Municipality, 2011 and 2015 (%)

Main dwelling								Toilet facility					
2011 – total 9838				2015 – total 11,821				2011 – total 9838			2015 – total 11,821		
Formal	*Traditional*	*Informal*	*Other*	*Formal*	*Traditional*	*Informal*	*Other*	*Flush/chemical*	*Other*	*None*	*Flush/chemical*	*Other*	*None*
71.8	0.9	25.8	1.5	77.9	0.3	19.7	2.2	70.0	11.6	18.3	78.4	9.7	11.9

Source: Stats SA (2012, 2016)

mining licence (RSA, 2002). Our interviewees emphasised the importance of the Committee as a forum that enables the municipality to cooperate with the mines to build and develop infrastructure together. A business interviewee said the Committee facilitated the free flow of information and regular meetings. The municipal councillor mentioned above praised those who were involved in maintaining the infrastructure, despite some shortcomings. He also commended the Committee's commitment to problem solving and working towards solutions.

But it should be noted that the collaboration is a direct consequence of a gap created by incapacity at the local municipality. And in contrast to the positive remarks, our interviewees also voiced some criticisms. Spatial planners that we interviewed expressed concern about the sustainability of the projects. The transfer of the operation and maintenance of the new housing developments to the municipality created a new challenge for the municipality, which was a serious concern given the lack of human capacity at the municipality to deal with the additional tasks. The root cause of the problem may be the fact that the mines used to dominate the process and did not help the municipality to create the capacity to deal with the long-term implications of development. The mining companies did not focus on the operation and maintenance of services after construction of the infrastructure was completed, and the municipality did not appoint additional capacity to cope with the much larger scope of operating and maintaining the infrastructure, such as the water pumps. Interviewees from both the public and private sector expressed concerns about the maintenance of the infrastructure, particularly water provision and the maintenance of water pumps. An employee from the Beeshoek mine said some houses currently have no water, but when the mine handed over the houses the pumps were working and water was available. This casts doubt on the ability of the municipality to operate the existing water system. Some municipal employees said the municipality only manages to deliver a low level of services.

Further concerns were expressed about the municipality's inability to deal with pressing issues. Several private sector interviewees said the municipality lacked a sound financial system, mainly because the post of Chief Financial Officer was unfilled most of the time, and was unable to send out accounts efficiently. Municipal income from property tax has increased rapidly because of the housing development (see Chapter 7 of this volume), but service delivery has not improved accordingly. Interviewees attributed this to poor capacity in the municipal finance department and a poor working relationship with the provincial treasury. A national survey on partnerships in rural mining towns showed that local municipalities like Postmasburg are indeed poorly capacitated (Rogerson, 2012).

We ourselves noted that the focus of the Committee was on providing bulk infrastructure and the creation of housing (mainly for mineworkers). There was no reference in the minutes to long-term viability or the risks associated with future mine downscaling. Responsibility for the long-term maintenance of the infrastructure was handed over to the municipality after the construction phase, as per legislation with regard to public utilities in South Africa.

One of the Committee's main objectives was to coordinate action between the 'social partners' (the mines and the municipality) to ensure that housing was delivered to the people employed at the town's two largest mines, Kolomela and Beeshoek, and in so doing prevent the development of informal settlements. The Committee indeed successfully coordinated housing opportunities for the mineworkers, but it did not curb the growth of informal settlements (see Chapter 9 of this volume). The important point is that collaboration should also consider the unintended consequences of mining and the living conditions of those not directly employed as mineworkers.

We heard other critical comments about spatial planning in Postmasburg. A retired spatial planner who had been an employee of the Northern Cape Provincial Administration said the Tsantsabane municipal council made most of its decisions in an uncoordinated manner and planning was not synchronised. This was probably because of the mining companies' immediate and pressing need to provide housing for their employees. He added that public participation is also a challenge and he doubts whether residents are fully informed of what is happening in Postmasburg. However, the fact that the municipality owned most of the well-located land made some of the planning easier for the Committee.

In 2014, after the general elections, a new municipal council was formed and some officials were replaced. With this change, the municipality's support for and collaboration with the Committee diminished and it became harder for the Committee to function. Our qualitative surveys made it clear that operating and maintaining the infrastructure is challenging, and it is clear from the minutes of the Committee meetings that the mining companies were pressurised into financing the operation and maintenance of the installed engineering services. In terms of the Mineral and Petroleum Resources Development Act (RSA, 2002), a mining company gets no points towards retaining their mining licence for community development initiatives that involve the operation and maintenance components of bulk infrastructure. The mining companies were thus not keen to finance the upkeep of services and as a result the Committee began to break down and meetings were no longer held regularly after that. The question of maintenance also became a stumbling block.

As we have said, the Committee represents an encouraging example of collaborative work. But its long-term viability seems doubtful. The council re-shuffle after the elections of 2014 meant that several management and political positions changed at the municipality. The Municipal Manager and the Head of Technical Services (who was the Chair of the Committee) were replaced and transferred to other municipalities in the Northern Cape. The motivation behind this restructuring was apparently political, and it seriously affected the functioning of the Committee. Municipal support was no longer guaranteed. It became increasingly difficult to get the representatives from the municipality to attend the monthly meetings and thus virtually impossible to make formal decisions (Tsassamba Committee, 2015). Fortunately, the bulk of the infrastructure projects had been completed and handed over to the municipality. Service provision was functional for the existing town as well as all the new developments. Therefore, the main problem with the continuance of the Committee was lack of municipal support, or rather direct attempts from them, under new leadership, to see the end of the Committee. Previous support from the Municipality was outstanding, and relationships between the mining companies are well established and continue until today.

Lessons can be learned from the Tsassamba Committee's experience, should other municipalities consider using a coordination committee of social partners to deliver infrastructure. Firstly, a collaborative approach between government departments, the private sector and other local stakeholders, including the traditional leadership, can be beneficial for South African towns. Most rural and small municipalities in South Africa struggle to survive financially and new developments of even basic services suffer as a result. Collaboration provides the country with a viable alternative management and development model, supported by success stories and best practices of developed countries (Minnaar, 2005; Ndoni and Elhag, 2012; Straussman, 2007). Planning should be done in such a manner as to ensure the attainment of social, economic and physical goals in small towns like Postmasburg. The collaborative approach is supported by the natural resource policy agenda (Arellano-Yanguas, 2008), which advocates social partnerships like the Tsassamba Committee.

Some interviewees described the Committee as a technical committee, yet critical remarks were made about the governance and oversight associated with this committee. During our survey we heard allegations of mismanagement and corruption. It is seems that on some occasions the municipality borrowed money from the Tsassamba account to pay salaries. Of importance though, is that the Committee was made aware of this, as an officer in the financial department had to present account statements every month.

Conclusion

The Tsassamba Committee was an attempt to create a social partnership between two mining companies and the local municipality in Postmasburg, mainly to provide housing and infrastructure for the employees of the two mines. Its successes lie squarely with the personalities that made this initiative work over an extended and extremely stressful period during a mining boom. Four shortcomings of the process must be mentioned. Firstly, it happened largely during the boom phase. No consideration was given to mine downscaling and its consequences. Secondly, the Committee did not stand the test of time. Collaboration did occur, but the Committee did not establish long-term collaborative planning and partnerships. Thirdly, the intention of the partnership can also be questioned when one considers that the long-term risks associated with the development were shifted onto the municipality. The partnership did not include generating capacity for operations and maintenance. Although this could well be attributed to the inefficiency of the local municipality, it was equally a result of the power relationships between powerful mining companies and weak local government structures. Finally, there also seems to have been a policy issue. According to the Department of Mineral Resources (RSA, 2002), if the mines pay for the operations and maintenance of settlements created by mining companies it does not count towards their social licence. We would argue that if mining companies contribute financially to operations and maintenance (and not only via the property rates from their employees' houses), they should be given credit for this in the licencing agreements.

Our final assessment is that the Committee's achievements can be measured against the characteristics of successful social partnerships: mutual recognition and acceptance, direct participation and cooperation, vocational training to raise the level of skills, institutional infrastructure and community involvement. Our survey found that the Committee was mutually recognised and accepted by the Tsantsabane Local Municipality, Kolomela mine (Kumba) and Beeshoek mine (Assmang). The Committee participated and cooperated in the development of bulk infrastructure and land to provide housing for the employees of these two mines, which had posed a major challenge to the municipality. The municipal officials on the Committee were trained and mentored to raise their vocational level of skills, but although institutional infrastructure was built through participation and coordination, members of the business chamber and civil society organisations were unfortunately not involved.

For over a decade the emphasis in planning theory has been on collaborations and partnerships. Although we learned from the literature that neither communities nor the market will solve urban challenges, partners in planning normally include the community and not only the local government and its business partners. Planning and policy-making should be based on interactive social processes, which the Tsassamba Committee successfully applied in the processes of bulk infrastructure design and construction, despite having to do this simultaneously with spatial planning and land formalisation.

Notes

1 A social and labour plan sets out the applicant's human resources development programmes, which are required under the Mineral and Petroleum Resources Development Act as a prerequisite for granting mining rights (RSA, 2002).
2 The bulk infrastructure projects included a water reservoir, pump stations for sewage, tarred roads and the upgrading of electrical substations.

3 To deliver services more cost effectively, local government in Australia was reformed by amalgamating local councils.
4 Sedibeng is a Water Board providing services in the Free State, Northern Cape and North West Provinces.

References

Arellano-Yanguas, J., 2008. *A Thoroughly Modern Resource Curse? The New Natural Resource Policy Agenda and the Mining Revival in Peru.* IDS Working Paper no. 300. Institute of Development Studies, Brighton, UK.

Ayelazuno, J., 2014. Oil wealth and the well-being of the subaltern classes in sub-Saharan Africa: A critical analysis of the resource curse in Ghana. *Resources Policy*, 40, pp. 66–73.

Bel, G., Hebdon, R. and Warner, M., 2007. Local government reform: Privatisation and its alternatives. *Local Government Studies*, 33(4), pp. 507–515.

Boyd, S., 2002. *Partnership working: European Social Partnership Models.* STUC (Scottish Trades Union Congress). www.gov.scot/resource/doc/25954/0028681.pdf (accessed 27 December 2016).

Chapman, R., Plummer, P. and Tonts, M., 2015. The resource boom and socio-economic well-being in Australian resource towns: A temporal and spatial analysis. *Urban Geography*, 36(5), pp. 629–653.

DME (Department of Minerals and Energy). 1998. *White Paper: A Minerals and Mining Policy for South Africa.* Pretoria: Government Printer.

DMR (Department of Mineral Resources), 2010. *Amendment of the Broad-Based Socio-Economic Empowerment Charter for the South African Mining and Minerals Industry. September 2010.* www.lonmin.com/downloads/send/2-downloads/39-mining-charter-2010 (accessed 30 December 2016).

Dollery, B. and Johnson, A., 2005. Enhancing efficiency in Australian Local Government: An evaluation of alternative models of municipal governance. *Urban Policy and Research*, 23(1), pp. 73–85.

Hamann, R., 2003. Mining companies' role in sustainable development: The 'why' and 'how' of corporate social responsibility from a business perspective. *Development Southern Africa*, 20(2), pp. 237–254.

Healy, P., 1998. Collaborative planning in a stakeholder society. *The Town Planning Review*, 69(1), pp. 1–21.

Healy, P., 2006. *Collaborative Planning: Shaping Places in Fragmented Societies.* Basingstoke: Palgrave.

Hillier, J. and Gunder, M., 2003. Planning fantasies: An exploration of a potential Lacanian framework for understanding development assessment planning. *Planning Theory*, 2(3), pp. 225–248.

ICMM (International Council on Mining and Metals), 2008. *Planning for Integrated Mine Closure: Toolkit.* http://hub.icmm.com/document/310 (accessed 6 November 2016).

IIED (International Institute for Environment and Development), 2002. *Breaking New Ground: Mining, Minerals, and Sustainable Development.* London: Earthscan.

Minnaar, A., 2005. Private-public partnerships: Private security, crime prevention and policing in South Africa. *Acta Criminologica*, 18(1), pp. 85–114.

Ndoni, D.B. and Elhag, T., 2012. *Overcoming the Barriers to Innovation in PPP/PFI Project-Based Environments.* Royal Institution of Chartered Surveyors (RICS) annual Construction, Building and Real Estate Research Conference (COBRA), 11–13 September, Las Vegas.

Osei-Kyei, R. and Chan, A.P., 2015. Review of studies on the critical success factors for public–private partnership (PPP) projects from 1990 to 2013. *International Journal of Project Management*, 33(6), pp. 1335–1346.

Rogerson, C.M., 2011. Mining enterprise, regulatory frameworks and local economic development in South Africa. *African Journal of Business Management*, 5(35), pp. 13373–13382.

Rogerson, C.M., 2012. Mining-dependent localities in South Africa: The state of partnerships for small town local development. *Urban Forum*, 23(1), pp. 107–132.

RSA (Republic of South Africa), 1996. *Constitution of the Republic of South Africa*. Pretoria: Government Printer.

RSA (Republic of South Africa), 2000. *Municipal Systems Act (no. 32 of 2000)*. Pretoria: Government Printer.

RSA (Republic of South Africa), 2002. *Mineral and Petroleum Resources Development Act (no. 28 of 2002)*. Pretoria: Government Printer.

RSA (Republic of South Africa), 2006. *National Spatial Development Perspective*. Pretoria: Government Printer.

Stats SA (Statistics South Africa), 2012. *Census 2011*. Pretoria: Stats SA.

Stats SA (Statistics South Africa), 2016. *Census 2015*. Pretoria: Stats SA.

Straussman, J.D., 2007. An essay on the meaning(s) of 'capacity building': With an application to Serbia. *International Journal of Public Administration*, 30, pp. 1103–1120.

Turner, L., 1994. Social partnership: An organising concept for industrial relations reform. *Workplace Topics*, 4(1), pp. 83–97.

Tsassamba Committee, 2008. *Tsassamba Committee Minutes*, Postmasburg: Tsantsabane Local Municipality.

Tsassamba Committee, 2014. *Tsassamba Committee Minutes*, Postmasburg: Tsantsabane Local Municipality.

Tsassamba Committee, 2015. *Tsassamba Committee Minutes*. Postmasburg: Tsantsabane Local Muncipality.

Tshangana, M., 2015. *Selected Committee Presentation on the Revitalisation of Distressed Mining Towns Programme*. Pretoria: National Department of Human Settlements.

Van Horen, B., 2002. Planning for institutional capacity building in war-torn areas: The case of Jaffna, Sri Lanka. *Habitat International*, 26, pp. 113–128.

Watson, V., 2009. 'The planned city sweeps the poor away . . .': Urban planning and 21st century urbanisation. *Progress in Planning*, 72(3), pp. 151–193.

5 Spatial planning for Postmasburg

*Stuart Denoon-Stevens, Verna Nel
and Thulisile Mphambukeli*

Planning or playing?

> Planning is an unnatural process; it is much more fun to do something. And the nicest thing about not planning is that failure comes as a complete surprise rather than being preceded by a period of worry and depression.

That remark (attributed to businessman and TV presenter Sir John Harvey Jones) may seem flippant, but we feel it encapsulates the concerns we have expressed in this chapter. Many mining towns, like Postmasburg, suffer the consequences of 'having fun' – developing indiscriminately – rather than facing the 'worry and depression' involved in the tough job of planning. We expect planning to be taken seriously, to minimise the possibility of failure. We expect municipalities to produce successes and say 'That's what we planned', not to produce failures and say 'We didn't expect that!'

Planning for a sustainable future is demanding in any circumstances, but for a mining town it is particularly tough. Mining is inherently destructive and the town's narrow economic base makes it vulnerable to change. Episodes of growth and decline cause volatility and uncertainty. Ups and downs in the fortunes of the mine cause surges and declines in population and have drastic effects on mineworkers' incomes. In a town like Postmasburg that has sprung up around a mine, the increasing urbanisation demands housing and infrastructure and social services. Many mining companies contribute generously, and the government is under pressure to do so too, especially in towns where, as is fairly typical in South Africa, more than a quarter of the economically active population are unemployed.

Planning for the future of a mining town is a complex problem with many interdependent variables. The situation is inevitably dynamic, subject to unanticipated changes over time, with multiple, often conflicting, goals and unexpected or novel outcomes. Past trends may not offer any direction for the future, so simple, routine planning will not suffice for a mining town. Given the uncertainty of a mine's future, spatial plans for a mining community must take into account several possible post-mining scenarios.

Undertaking spatial planning while riding the 'resource roller coaster' (Wilson, 2004) has been described as a 'wicked problem' (Rittel and Webber, 1973) or a 'big mess' (Grunau and Schönwandt, 2010; Armson, 2011). A wicked problem is one that has no simple solution, because circumstances and requirements keep changing and efforts to solve one part of the problem bring new problems to light, and the 'solution' becomes the problem of the future. 'Messy' situations arise from the complexity of the socio-economic and ecological system (SES) in which we live. The ability of a SES to adapt to change and retain its functions is one of the hallmarks of its resilience (Elmqvist et al., 2014). A resilient town can recover from setbacks or even disasters.

As a complex adaptable system, a SES can be unpredictable and hence uncontrollable (Anderies et al., 2004). In dealing with such a system planners are obliged to venture into the unknown. This includes planning for possible decline (Martinez-Fernandez et al., 2012; Wiechmann and Pallagst, 2012), whereas most planners have been trained to plan for growth and development (Rydin, 2011). Planning is not easy amidst uncertainty largely generated by external factors (such as changes in demand for or prices of commodities) and under pressure from calls for more sustainable development.

To add to the pressure on South African planners, the Spatial Planning and Land Use Management Act (SPLUMA) (RSA, 2013) requires municipalities to compile a Spatial Development Framework (SDF). SPLUMA lays down detailed specifications for the SDF. It must give expression to five development principles that must inform all spatial planning and land development: spatial justice, spatial sustainability, efficiency, spatial resilience and good administration. It must emphasise social inclusion, redress for past injustices, sustainable socio-economic development and the maintenance of ecosystem services.

This chapter examines and critiques the 2015 SDF compiled for Postmasburg by Tsantsabane Local Municipality. We argue that it will not help the town develop the resilience it needs to cope with an unpredictable future. The concept of resilience has been applied in many disciplines, such as psychology, ecology and economics. The focus of this chapter is on economic resilience, in line with the SPLUMA principle of spatial resilience. This principle pertains to supporting and enabling sustainable livelihoods through the planning process, with specific emphasis on communities most vulnerable to environmental hazards and disasters and economic shocks, which clearly includes mining communities.

We demonstrate that the SDF for Postmasburg is largely based on an extrapolation of past trends. It has thus not really considered the future, nor has it explored the scenarios that could result from the varying fortunes of the mine and reliance on a single economic sector. We argue that, by ignoring the complexity of the SES and not taking a long-term view, the planners have compromised the town's resilience. They are thus not in a position to steer the town successfully through uncertain times and possible mine closure in the future.

Resilience in the face of uncertainty

Mining towns are notable for boom and bust cycles of growth and decline. This volatility may have local causes (such as rising labour costs or labour unrest), but mostly it is caused by changes in demand reflected in international commodity prices (Randall and Ironside, 1996, Veiga et al., 2001; Wilson, 2004). A mining town is thus a subsystem of a global socio-economic system, and it is often the larger system that decides the town's future (Godsell, 2011). The ups and downs make residents' future uncertain, and mine closure is the sword of Damocles that may fall at any moment.

What is 'resilience'?

'Resilience' comes from the Latin *resilire*, meaning 'to spring back'. The concept of resilience has been applied in many contexts, often in a positive sense and hence as a normative goal, but fundamentally it is a neutral term to describe how a system reacts to stress and change, hence negative resilience is also possible (Gunderson and Holling, 2002; Gallopín, 2006; Elmqvist et al., 2014).

The term 'resilience' is used in physics to describe the ability of a material to return to its original form after being distorted, and it is appropriately applied in disaster risk management to describe the ability of people or places to 'bounce back' after a shock. Resilience has also been described as the ability to 'bounce forward', in reference to the ability of natural ecosystems, and later socio-ecological systems, to recover from disasters (Seeliger and Turok, 2013). Both the 'bounce back' and 'bounce forward' interpretations assume a state of equilibrium to which the system returns. However, the definition that is most applicable to a SES is the ability of the system to recover from a disturbance and adapt to changing circumstances while maintaining its function. The adaptive capacity of a SES is intrinsic to its resilience. Gallopín (2006, p. 296) distinguishes between 'coping' and short-term responses to a disturbance or disaster and the longer-term adaptive capacity to achieve a sustainable state. This adaptive capacity arises from the structure and properties of a system that enable it to evolve and produce new structures and novel behaviours.

Useful discussions on the topic of resilience and resilient systems may be found in Gunderson and Holling (2002); Anderies et al. (2004); Gallopín (2006); Walker and Salt (2006); Folke et al. (2010); Geyer and Rihani (2010); Innes and Booher (2010); Simmie and Martin (2010); Burkhard et al. (2011); Martin-Breen and Anderies (2011); Seeliger and Turok (2013); Chandler (2014) and Turok (2014). The following two subsections draw on these sources.

Properties of a resilient system

Properties of resilient complex adaptive systems that enable them to adapt in the face of change and stressors are *diversity, redundancy, stores of resources* for emergencies, and effective *information transmission*. A SES also has the benefit of human agency, which means it can anticipate, plan and learn. *Diversity* is critical to resilience – the greater the diversity (of functions, services and responses), the more options the system has. *Redundancy* refers to alternatives, options, back-ups or duplications that are in place to support the system and enable it to continuing functioning should one part collapse. Closely related to redundancy are the *stores of resources*, or 'capital' held within the system, such as savings in an economy, emergency supplies, institutional knowledge, and social and human capital.

Information transmission occurs through the network of feedback loops. The structure of the network can affect the nature and quality of the information and the speed of transmission. The feedback loops may dampen or amplify the impact of external influences through the system. The dampening effect can even out the highs and lows of the resource roller coaster, while amplification can either make bad times worse or build on good times to increase prosperity. The length of the information network can affect the rapidity of transmission: short pathways speed it up, while long ones may mean that the information is received too late to prevent problems. Thus tight networks with short information pathways enable a system to adjust more rapidly to change, which strengthens resilience. Longer information pathways – usually associated with centralisation of decision making – tend to decrease the likelihood of timeous detection of problems and increase the likelihood of a critical threshold being crossed (Walker and Salt, 2006).

The adaptive cycle

Most systems are part of nested systems that range over multiple spatial or institutional scales and have the ability to influence each other. Thus a reduced demand for commodities in one economy can be the death knell of a mining community halfway around the world. Resilience is thus 'not a fixed quantity that defines a system, but a dynamically varying one' (Gunderson and Holling, 2002, p. 31). Change can be rapid, for example following disasters such as earthquakes or tornadoes, or much slower, such as soil erosion or habitat destruction. Such change can creep up on a SES, undermining its resilience and reducing the distance to the threshold of collapse.

Four phases of 'adaptive cycles' of change over both spatial and temporal scales have been recognised: *exploitation, conservation, release* and *reorganisation*. The *exploitation* phase is one of rapid growth, taking advantage of opportunities within the system, such as technological innovations that generate new industries. During the *conservation* phase, growth slows down and the system becomes more stable but also more rigid. Rigidity locks in available resources, such as human or financial capital, and reduces the flexibility of the system through increased regulation or efficiencies in production (such as better ways of extracting resources), as alternatives are no longer considered. The more rigid the system, the more brittle it becomes, increasing the probability of a collapse. And the longer a system is kept in this phase through artificial means, the smaller are the shocks required to trigger a collapse. The *release* phase is usually a rapid transition of the system that disperses the capital that was amassed during the conservation phase. However, a more gradual, partial shift is possible. As stocks and capital that were previously locked into the system become available, a phase of *reorganisation* may begin, where new possibilities, structures and behaviours can be explored. The 'crisis' of the release phase can provide 'windows of opportunity for improvement even though they are dangerous events that can produce destructive outcomes' Gallopín

(2006, p. 295) or 'creative destructions' (Burkhard et al., 2011, p. 2878). Unsustainable systems can be replaced by more appropriate ones, but the converse is also possible, where the resources of the system have been gradually eroded, leaving little capital for reorganisation.

Understanding each phase of the adaptive cycle helps planners to develop appropriate policy to anticipate and prepare for possible shocks. This demands strategic and integrated planning, including spatial planning, which is our subject in the next section.

Spatial planning amid uncertainty

Spatial planning is concerned with making or shaping places. It can be defined as 'self-conscious collective efforts to re-imagine a city, urban region or wider territory and to translate the result into priorities for area investment' (Healey, 2004, p. 46). It includes social, economic, cultural, political and ecological dimensions of sustainable development. Spatial planners must take a long-range view and recognise the complexity of the SES for which they are planning. Attention to the future – both predicting and shaping it – is at the heart of planning. Planning is about managing the uncertainty of the future, by taking action now or by preparing actions for unforeseen events. Planners need to 'future-proof' towns and cities so that they will be desirable places to live in for decades to come, and this may include 'de-growth'(Rydin, 2011, pp. 137–139).

Planning is by definition about the future, but there have been criticisms that planners have 'lost sight of the future' (Myers and Kituse, 2000, p. 221) and are inclined to be too involved in immediate concerns, perhaps because they lack skills or because they are so overwhelmed by day-to-day responsibilities that they lack energy and resources for long-range planning. The influence of politics – with its short-term focus based on electoral cycles – also limits the time-scale and creativity of planning. Other hindrances to long-range planning are the rapidity of social, technological and economic change and the overwhelming complexity of the future with its 'wicked problems'.

Useful sources to consult on spatial planning are Myers and Kituse (2000); Abbott (2005); Geyer and Rihani (2010); Rydin (2011); De Roo et al. (2012) and Freestone (2012).

Spatial planning in South Africa

One consequence of limited future-vision is the poor quality of the SDFs produced for South African municipalities. Many are too broad or utopian (Todes, 2008, p. 10) or are 'uninformed by theory' (Dewar and Kiepiel, 2012, p. 30). Many are 'mediocre, lacking persuasive statements of how to attain a desired future' (Oranje, 2014, p. 7). They often demonstrate an inadequate comprehension of the complexities of a town's socio-spatial dynamics and a limited ability to deal with them. They seldom take into account the socio-economic and ecological interactions between activities, or the economic potential of the area, or the dynamics of the local economy and how this affects the livelihoods of those who depend on it. They thus have had limited effect in changing spatial patterns or densities or increasing integration (Todes, 2008; Du Plessis, 2013; Du Plessis and Boonzaaier, 2015; Musvoto et al., 2016).

The neglect of local dynamics, let alone the effect of external influences, suggests that many municipal SDFs are myopic, focusing mainly on immediate issues and failing to anticipate possible future problems and plan to manage or mitigate them. They tend to be parochial and ignore the effect of external influences. SDFs are intended to integrate different sectors and stakeholders, but many do not attempt this. Because they disregard both spatial and temporal drivers of change, many SDFs do not promote municipal resilience.

Planning in mining towns

During a town's initial growth phase, the municipality must state in its SDF how it will provide sufficient basic and social infrastructure and affordable housing and manage expansion. However, where there is volatility, it is not easy to anticipate how much growth (or decline) to plan for financially or physically. In a mining town, planners may work on the anticipated lifespan of a mine, but it could be extended by improved technology that enables the extraction of previously uneconomic reserves or shortened by an international recession or a dramatic fall in commodity prices.

However, as the conservation phase of the adaptive cycle sets in, the amount of capital (financial and emotional) invested by the mine, the government and the community may prevent a rational view of the future of the community. Ideally, planning for a post-mining future should happen during the mine's initial planning or at least during this conservation phase, but the need to evaluate and prepare for post-mining circumstances will become increasingly urgent with time.

Communication and cooperation between the mines and the municipality in the planning process are essential for several reasons. As the expansion (or contraction) of mining activities has both direct and indirect consequences for the town, the municipality must be kept informed, as this will affect the provision of housing, social and physical infrastructure. A lack of communication can lead to housing shortages and hence encourage informal settlements, and put a severe strain on key municipal infrastructure during expansion phases. Stakeholder participation in the planning process is required by South African legislation. Several authors recommend that planning for an uncertain future should include considering a variety of possible scenarios in conjunction with all stakeholders, including all local economic sectors (e.g. Healey, 2006; Innes and Booher, 2010; Robinson, 2014).

Planning for decline

Spatial planners over the past century largely had to deal with urban growth and its consequences. Today they are increasingly confronted with the problems of urban decline, but proper management of such decline by controlled reduction of urban populations, economies and territory has been infrequent. Among the reasons for decline have been disease, war and structural economic changes due to globalisation and the transition from manufacturing to service economies or, in the case of resource towns, the depletion of a resource or the changing technology of the industry.

Mining towns are not alone in experiencing decline. Many towns in developed countries have experienced population decline and many more anticipate a loss of population, and consequent reduction of their economic and fiscal base. Most towns view decline pessimistically and seek to reverse or at least limit its consequences through local economic development strategies (Nel et al., 2003), skills development (Plöger and Weck, 2014), tourism (Caravelis and Ivy, 2001; Martinez-Fernandez et al., 2012) or residential attractiveness strategies (Miot, 2015). In China the government is making a concerted effort to restructure the economies of declining single-resource towns by helping them develop substitute industries, particularly those with strong backward and forward linkages or high-tech industries (He et al., 2017). Martinez-Fernandez et al. (2012) note some attempts to develop mining areas as innovation or information technology hubs. However, they point out that global knowledge flows tend to bypass physically remote areas (like Postmasburg), making it difficult for them to attract and retain the required skills.

Some towns have reconceptualised decline as 'creative shrinkage' and sought innovative ways to manage it (Wiechmann and Pallagst, 2012), such as 'de-urbanising' by demolishing vacant houses, increasing the size of stands by consolidating plots, regularly removing litter and clearing up illegal dumping, and creating more green spaces that maintain land values and create an image of stability. The short-term use of vacant areas for sports, community gardens, cultural events and outdoor art can promote tourism and improve the local quality of life, and permitting temporary economic activities on vacant industrial or commercial sites can provide an opportunity for entrepreneurs. Allowing nature to reclaim abandoned areas can help to rehabilitate ecosystems.

Strategies that work for a city may not be appropriate for a mining, town, particularly one as remote as Postmasburg. Some small resource towns are able to survive and reorganise to convert a mining economy to one driven by services. Diversity of local economy and skills, a municipality willing to anticipate, prepare and act, and resources to adapt are vital for such a town's future.

For more on planning for decline, see the following sources on which we drew in this section: Randall and Ironside (1996); Caravelis and Ivy (2001); Nel et al. (2003); Godsell (2011); Martinez-Fernandez et al. (2012); Wiechmann and Pallagst (2012); Plöger and Weck (2014); Miot (2015); Marais and Nel (2016) and He et al. (2017).

Spatial planning and resilience in Postmasburg

According to the SPLUMA principle of spatial resilience, spatial plans should ensure sustainable livelihoods, particularly for those communities most likely to be affected by economic or environmental shocks. Mining towns such as Postmasburg are particularly vulnerable to economic shocks. In this section we assess the degree to which the SDF (Tsantsabane Local Municipality, 2015) provides the basis for resilience within the context of mining growth or decline.

Economic resilience

To evaluate the economic resilience of the 2015 SDF, we first had to assess the current state of the municipality's economy, in particular its economic resilience. To do this we conducted a shift share analysis, a tress assessment and a location quotient analysis.

The shift share analysis indicates three things: the performance of the local economy in comparison to the national economy (the *national growth share*); whether growth in the municipality occurred in sectors that were, at a national level, lagging or growing (the *industry mix share*); and the local shift – the increase (or decrease) in employment in the local economy in a sector which is growing faster (or slower) than the same sector at a national level (the *local share shift*). When employment in a local industry grows faster (or declines more slowly) than its counterpart nationally, we see a positive shift in the net share of national employment (Smith, 2015).

The Tress index[1] indicates the diversity of the economy. A score of 100 indicates that all economic growth occurs in a single economic sector, and a score of 0 indicates perfect distribution of economic activity across all the sectors. A score of around 50 is considered to indicate a relatively diverse economy (Meintjes, 2001). Tsantsabane's tress score is 77.35,[2] indicating a significant lack of economic diversity.

The location quotient analysis indicates in which economic sectors a location's economy specialises. It compares the contribution of the different economic sectors to the total GVA (or total employment) of a location's economy and a reference economy (usually the provincial or national economy within which the location falls). Where the location quotient is greater than 1, this means that this sector contributes more to the location's economy than the comparable reference economy (and vice versa), which indicates a specialisation in this location's economy.

Table 5.1 shows the results of our shift share analysis. The national growth share calculation estimated that the local economy would have increased by R540 million if its growth had followed the same trends as national growth, whereas in fact the local economy had increased by R744 million. This indicates that from 1995 to 2013 Tsantsabane performed better than the average municipality in South Africa; in fact, it outperformed the national economy.

The industry mix share calculation estimated a score of -143. Mining is the largest contributor to the negative result, with a score of -165, followed by central government at -57. The sectors that are in line with national growth are communication, finance and insurance, business services with scores of 31, 34 and 28 respectively. This implies that growth in Tsantsabane has occurred mostly in sectors that are performing poorly at a national level. In other words, Tsantsabane's growth pattern, in terms of the sectors driving this growth, is the opposite of national trends.

Table 5.1 Shift share analysis of the Tsantsabane local economy, 1995–2013

Industry	National growth share	Net	Industry mix share	Net	Local share shift	Net
Agriculture, forestry & fishing	81.13%	11	−16.7%	−2	−50%	−7
Mining & quarrying	**81.13%**	**168**	**−83.0%**	**165**	**157%**	**314**
Food, beverages & tobacco	81.13%	1	−49.7%	−1	5%	0
Textiles, clothing & leather goods	81.13%	0	−59.4%	0	48%	0
Wood, paper, publishing & printing	81.13%	0	−60.8%	0	29%	0
Petroleum products, chemicals, rubber & plastic	81.13%	2	24.8%	1	−16%	0
Other non-metal mineral products	81.13%	2	−83.7%	−2	−31%	−1
Metals, metal products, machinery & equipment	81.13%	7	−26.3%	−2	34%	3
Electrical machinery & apparatus	81.13%	0	−9.0%	0	−72%	0
Radio, TV, instruments, watches & clocks	81.13%	0	−16.8%	0	−64%	0
Transport equipment	81.13%	1	8.3%	0	60%	1
Furniture & other manufacturing	81.13%	2	−55.3%	−1	16%	0
Electricity	81.13%	7	−46.5%	−4	38%	3
Water	81.13%	4	−53.4%	−2	21%	1
Construction	81.13%	8	57.4%	5	−129%	−12
Wholesale & retail trade	81.13%	41	11.9%	6	−57%	−29
Catering & accommodation services	81.13%	4	−28.6%	−1	−63%	−3
Transport & storage	81.13%	36	−4.2%	−2	107%	47
Communication	81.13%	11	233.6%	31	367%	48
Finance & insurance	81.13%	26	105.8%	34	−117%	−38
Business services	81.13%	50	46.6%	28	−98%	−60
Community, social & personal services	81.13%	48	−12.5%	−7	−44%	−26
General government	81.13%	118	−38.8%	−57	−42%	−61
Total		**540**		**−143**		**181**

Source: Authors, using data from Quantec (2016). To guide this analysis, we used the shift share study by Smith (2015) of a locality in the United States, with the obvious shift of focus to Tsantsabane.

Note: The net values in this table have been rounded to the nearest whole number.

The local share shift is 181, showing that the growth in the local economy was in sectors that were lagging in the national economy. This effect was over and above the national growth share and industry mix share, as described in the previous paragraphs. The main contributor to this result is mining, which grew by R310 million in Tsantsabane between 1995 and 2013 (in constant 2005 values), a growth of 261%. In terms of percentage of GVA, in 1995 mining and quarrying made up 25.6% of the total Tsantsabane economy. By 2013 this had increased to 33%. In contrast, the national economy declined by R4 million over the same period, while the percentage contribution of the mining sector to the national GVA declined from 9.97% to 5.57%.

This analysis is further supported by our location quotient (LQ) analysis of the local economy, which provides an easier way of looking at temporal economic trends. Figure 5.1 shows that – unlike the national trend – the mining sector in

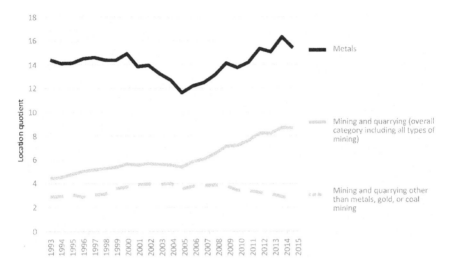

Figure 5.1 Location quotients of mining and quarrying, metals and other mining and quarrying in Tsantsabane, 1993–2015

Source: Quantec, 2016

Tsantsabane grew substantially between 1993 and 2015, with the location quotient of mining and quarrying nearly doubling over this period, probably as a consequence of the declining share of gold mining in South Africa's economy. The location quotient of metals mining is also particularly high (15.39), but instead sees a maintenance of the LQ value from 1993 to 2000, a dip from 2001 to 2006, and recovery from 2007 to 2015. Overall, the growth in the metals mining LQ is small, with only a 7% increase in LQ from 1993 to 2015. Looking at the non-metal mining and quarrying sector, we see it also has a regional advantage in Tsantsabane, with an LQ of 2.7 in 2015, and only very modest growth and decline from 1993 to 2015. In summary, the high LQ indicates a substantial local advantage in the mining sector, and in particular in the metals sector.

Our findings show that Tsantsabane is heavily reliant on the mining sector, with metals mining contributing around 70% of total GVA in this municipality in 2015. It is thus nearly mono-functional in nature, a trend that has worsened over time. This means that any changes in the national and international mining sector, and particularly in the price of iron, will have a serious effect on Tsantsabane. The lack of diversity means it lacks economic resilience – a matter which should be a prime consideration in Tsantsabane's 2015 SDF.

The economic analysis in the SDF reviews the employment status and dependency ratio of the economic sectors in which Tsantsabane's labour force are employed, and GVA by sector, for either the decade 2001 to 2011, using census data, or the decade 2002 to 2012, using data supplied by Global Insight.[3] The SDF concludes that the primary sector, and in particular mining, is crucially important for the Tsantsabane economy. Thus the development objectives are to 'integrate various areas in Tsantsabane Local Municipality to form a well-functioning space economy', and the strategies for achieving this are stated as follows:

- Channel development into a system of nodes and corridors, in accordance with the principles of the National Spatial Development Perspective.
- Do not promote or support developments that are out of context with the desired development directions.
- Development must be localised in specific strategic areas where there can be a focused effort on the provision of engineering services, transportation and land use integration.
- Consolidate existing areas rather than creating new development areas. (Tsantsabane Local Municipality, 2015)

However, none of the standard South African regional economic analyses appear to have been conducted (i.e. shift share, tress index and location quotient). There is no mention whatsoever of the lack of diversity in the economy of Tsantsabane. We found several indications that the authors of the SDF and, possibly, the planning staff at the Tsantsabane municipality, do not fully understand the vulnerability of the local economy and its lack of resilience. This implies an inadequate understanding of the concept of spatial resilience and how to evaluate it within the context of Tsantsabane. An indication of limited understanding of the possibility of the local economy declining at some point in the next 20 years is evident in the land demand projections, as shown in Table 5.2. As this table shows, the SDF assumes that growth will continue in the area until 2035, and that by then the population will have grown to 26,774 households. It should be noted that low, medium and high growth estimates were undertaken and included in the SDF document, but only the high estimate was used in calculating the potential land needed, without any reason being provided for this decision.

The problem with these population growth calculations is, firstly, is it actually possible to reliably predict how many households will be in Tsantsabane in 20 years' time? Historically, even some of the most knowledgeable demographers in South Africa have struggled to calculate a reliable estimate of population growth for municipalities.[4] To expect a planner, who probably has limited training in demography, to undertake such an analysis when there are multiple unknown variables in play, including the uncertainty of future iron prices, including the uncertainty of South African politics, over such a long-time period is likely to produce highly questionable population estimates. At best, Tsantsabane's projection should have been limited to a five-year period.

Secondly, these calculations assume that the economy of the municipality will be able to keep pace with the projected population and create new employment opportunities. But there are not likely to be many new jobs – at least in the mining sector – once the current mine expansions are completed. Furthermore, it is possible that Beeshoek mine will come to the end of its life in the next two decades, leading to a further decline in the number of jobs in the area (African Rainbow

Table 5.2 Extract from 2015 Tsantsabane SDF showing projected growth in number of households in the municipality

	2011	2012	2013	2014	2015	2016	2017	2018	2019	2020	2021	2022	2023	2024	2025	2026	2027	2028	2029	2030	2031	2032	2033	2034	2035
A Current households	8,150	0	0	0	0	0	0	0	0	0	0	0	0	0	0	0	0	0	0	0	0	0	0	0	0
B Transnet	0	0	0	83	45	45	45	45	45	0	0	0	0	0	0	0	0	0	0	0	0	0	0	0	0
C Kolomela	0	0	0	392	392	0	0	0	1,120	0	0	0	0	0	0	0	0	0	0	0	0	0	0	0	0
D Redstone Solar Plant	0	0	0	0	0	0	0	12	0	0	0	0	0	0	0	0	0	0	0	0	0	0	0	0	0
D Subtotal direct new jobs/year (B+C)	0	0	0	475	437	90	45	57	1,165	0	0	0	0	0	0	0	0	0	0	0	0	0	0	0	0
E Secondary (indirect) jobs	0	0	0	366	336	35	35	44	897	0	0	0	0	0	0	0	0	0	0	0	0	0	0	0	0
F Total new jobs/year (D+E)	0	0	0	841	773	80	80	101	2,062	0	0	0	0	0	0	0	0	0	0	0	0	0	0	0	0
G Permanent HHs/year	8,150	0	0	740	681	70	70	89	1,815	0	0	0	0	0	0	0	0	0	0	0	0	0	0	0	0
H Natural growth	318	330	343	343	443	460	478	496	516	536	557	578	601	624	649	674	700	728	756	786	816	848	881	916	951
I Cumulative total households	8,150	8,468	8,786	9,856	10,980	11,510	12,058	12,642	14,973	15,509	16,066	16,644	17,245	17,869	18,518	19,192	19,892	20,620	21,376	22,162	22,978	23,826	24,707	25,623	26,574
J Contractors managerial	0	0	0	18	7	87	7	7	107	0	0	0	0	0	0	0	0	0	0	0	0	0	0	0	0
K Contractors semi/unskilled	0	0	0	166	60	780	60	60	960	0	0	0	0	0	0	0	0	0	0	0	0	0	0	0	0
L Squatter families	0	0	0	200	200	200	200	200	200	200	200	200	200	200	200	200	200	200	200	200	200	200	200	200	200
M Permanent res units required (I+J+L)	8,150	8,468	8,786	10,222	11,240	12,490	12,318	12,902	16,133	15,709	16,266	16,844	17,445	18,069	18,718	19,392	20,092	20,820	21,576	22,362	23,178	24,026	24,907	25,823	26,774

Source: Tsantsabane Local Municipality (2015)

Note: This is a direct extract from the SDF. Over and above the issues raised in the text of this chapter, it appears that there are also calculation errors. For example, in 2014 the total permanent residence units required, based on the figures in the table, should be 10,240 and not 10,222 as stated in the table. Furthermore, the formula for permanent residence units required is stated as I+J+L, whereas it seems it should have been I+J+K+L. The errors cast doubt on the overall reliability of this table.

Redstone Solar Plant is a solar thermal power plant, one of the largest in South Africa, producing around 100 MW of energy.

Minerals, 2016; Synergistics Environmental Services, 2015). As jobs decline, it is likely that out-migration will occur, leading to either decline or stagnation in household growth.

If new jobs are not being created, then immigrants to Tsantsabane are unlikely to find employment other than in the informal economy and may be dependent on social grants. A change in the main source of income of Postmasburg households from mine employment to informal work or social grants will change the nature of the SES, from its current state of prosperity to a less resilient state with lower diversity redundancies (i.e. spares or back-ups) or stores of resources. As the mines reach their peak in investment and expansion they are moving into a consolidation phase where the rigidity of fixed investments and optimising efficiency is the antithesis of the flexibility required for resilience.

Another indication of limited understanding in the 2015 SDF is the lack of awareness of alternative futures. The SDF proposes an extension of about 160 hectares to the industrial areas. As the existing industrial areas cover only about 70 hectares, the proposed expansion nearly triples the industrial footprint of Postmasburg. It could be achieved by the municipality releasing the land (which it owns) to the private sector. However, as manufacturing GVA grew only modestly from 1993 to 2015, by about R3.36 million annually,[5] as shown in Figure 5.2, it is unlikely that such a large area of new industrial land will be developed without substantial incentives. But no mention is made of such incentives in the 2015 SDF.[6] And such incentives appear unlikely, given the declining manufacturing sector in Tsantsabane. When we consider the dismal performance of South African government policies and plans in developing industrial areas that are not driven by the private sector or embedded in the local economy (Nel and Rogerson, 2013), we

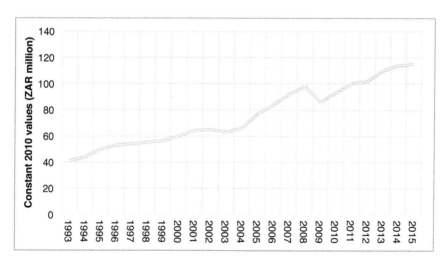

Figure 5.2 Change in manufacturing GVA in Tsantsabane 1993–2015, constant 2010 prices

Source: Authors, using data from Quantec (2016)

can see that the chance of this extra industrial land being developed, or industries remaining once subsidies are reduced, is slim.

It is clear from the above that the authors of the 2015 SDF had a very limited understanding of the local economy and the principles of local economic development and economic resilience. The following section highlights some possible consequences for Postmasburg and Tsantsabane Local Municipality.

How lack of economic resilience affects the housing market and livelihoods

It is useful to undertake a thought experiment to showcase the long-term planning dilemmas. Assume firstly that a middle-class household buys a house in Postmasburg in 2013 for R1.002 million – which was roughly the average house price in this town at that time at constant June 2012 figures (CAHF, 2015). Assume secondly that the property market has the same increase in property value over a 10-year period as an average house in South Africa between 2000 and 2010, as shown in Table 5.3. This would increase the value of the house from R1.002 million to R1.9639 million, a return of R0.9639 million.

Now change the second assumption to suppose that the property value of the house has seen the same change over the 10-year period between 2000 and 2010 as an average middle-class house in Welkom, as shown in Table 5.3. We chose Welkom as a property market affected by mine downscaling (Marais, 2013; Marais and Nel, 2016), which might well be the case for Postmasburg in the future. In this scenario, the value of the house falls from R1.002 million to R0.4208 million, a loss of R0.581 million, and a loss of R1.3828 million when compared to investing elsewhere in South Africa during the same time period.

Table 5.3 Change in average house prices in Welkom and South Africa, 2001–2010 (in constant June 2012 prices)

Year	Welkom (example of a declining mining area)	South Africa
2001	907,258	626,381
2002	906,489	683,458
2003	645,105	758,687
2004	634,711	948,547
2005	734,528	1,146,919
2006	684,543	1,280,798
2007	644,578	1,400,773
2008	654,008	1,361,859
2009	617,907	1,216,686
2010	518,913	1,225,054
10-year change	−43%	96%

Source: Marais, 2013 (Welkom); BusinessTech, 2016 (South Africa)

The point of this exercise is to illustrate the type of impact that economic resilience, or lack thereof, has on an area. For a household making one of the largest financial commitments they will make – buying a house – mine downscaling and economic uncertainty are not merely a matter of academic interest but a real threat to their long-term financial investments and future financial security. Consequently, it is imperative that planners take these issues seriously and draft SDFs in a manner that takes account of such possible threats.

Lack of foresight and resilience will also affect the livelihoods and well-being of lower income households. Better-skilled people have a greater probability of finding new employment than low-skilled people, should the local economy shrink because a mine downscales. Thus households with low skills and a housing investment in the town may become trapped in a declining town with few future prospects and depending heavily on social grants for their livelihoods. This has become the growing, and worrying, trend throughout the rural areas of South Africa (Xuza, 2010). The challenge for municipalities that have an undiversified and fluctuating economic base is to ensure that their intervention in the housing market for low-income households does not lock these households into the area.[7]

It is critical that Tsantsabane Municipality take into account the relationship between Postmasburg's economy and the changing spatial structure of the town. Of the contract mineworkers who completed the survey undertaken for this book, 43% were living in informal dwellings, whereas only 5.4% of mineworkers employed by the mining companies were living in informal dwellings. This indicates that the increasing use of contract mineworkers is partly what is driving the growth of informal settlements in Postmasburg.

The prospect of work in the mines may be encouraging migration into Postmasburg and fuelling the growth of informal settlements. Figure 5.3 shows which years individuals who migrated to Postmasburg moved to the town (46.6% of our survey respondents). It shows that migration into Postmasburg spiked in 2010, around the time that Kolomela mine opened, indicating a possible correlation between the opening of the mine and migration to the town.

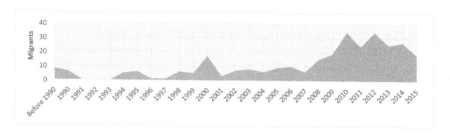

Figure 5.3 Year that individuals living in informal settlements at the time of the survey moved to Postmasburg (excluding individuals who had never lived outside of Postmasburg)

Source: Authors

Looking again at Tsantsabane's Municipality's SDF, once again we see limited consideration of this issue. The only issues it discusses in this regard are the lower income of households living in informal settlements, the poor infrastructure conditions, lack of tenure and so forth. No awareness is shown in this document of the link between mining growth or decline and the growth or decline of informal settlements. Such awareness is crucial. Encouraging the establishment of low-income housing where the economic base is fickle in nature may not be the best course of action. This issue should have been debated in the SDF.

Planning for an uncertain future in Postmasburg

The job of spatial planners is to take diverse possible futures into account, create a long-term vision for a place (as required by South African legislation) and provide strategic direction. The Tsantsabane Municipality's 2015 SDF fails to do this for Postmasburg. It lacks foresight. It assumes that the future will mirror the past, that current trends will persist. Mining towns face uncertainties. They are at the mercy of the resource roller coaster. They need contingency plans for mine decline or closure, and a long-term plan for dealing with shrinkage and building a new economy. This SDF fails to offer either kind of plan.

In this chapter we have argued that this SDF does not address the vulnerabilities related to the narrow economic base of Postmasburg or the reliance on a declining industry that in South Africa is subject to the vagaries of international demand. With little diversity, the local economy – and hence the community – has little resilience to deal with economic shocks. The SDF makes no mention of diversifying the economy by developing other industries or activities to supplement or replacing the existing employment opportunities should the mining sector decline. The SDF does not meet the SPLUMA principle of spatial resilience.

The assumption that the past trends can be extrapolated to the next five or 10 years, with the mine continuing to expand, reveals a lack of communication with the mine, or a limited understanding of its operations or the employment implications. Furthermore, the SDF does not recognise where the region is within the adaptive cycle (the conservation phase) and the possibility of shrinkage (the release phase), with all the environmental, economic and social consequences thereof.

These consequences include the loss of human capital in the form of skilled labour and entrepreneurial talents, leaving Postmasburg with the people least likely to find employment elsewhere in the region. A decline in mining activities and employment will have a knock-on effect on all other economic activities, as demand and purchasing power wane. For the community, the consequences could include loss of the value of their investment in their houses and reduced social and retail amenities as these become less viable because of reduced demand. Some social infrastructure such as schools may no longer be required or viable and have to close, with all the ramifications associated with closure. The municipality may increasingly have to care for indigent households (e.g. providing free basic and health services), placing a growing financial burden on a restricted budget as income decreases. This may mean poor maintenance of infrastructure and deterioration in public services.

Community leadership, vision and strategic planning are critical for mining towns to manage their special circumstances. Instead of run-of-the-mill spatial plans, they need innovative, evidence-based planning, that includes a thorough economic analysis. Attention must be paid to alternative futures. Diversifying the economic base of a remote mining town in an arid environment may not be easy, but the story of Rooiberg (Godsell, 2011) shows it is not impossible. The costs of creating a new trajectory for the town may be high, but failing to plan for decline will exact a much higher social, psychological and economic toll.

Notes

1 The Tress index is a standard tool for analysing a regional economy. It has mostly been used in South Africa, with limited usage in other countries.
2 Note that the Tress index is sensitive to the number of sectors used. The large number of sectors we considered, 23, results in a more nuanced calculation than the conventional analysis which typically uses only 9 or 10 sectors.
3 A company specialising in economic data.
4 For example, see the discussion on projections by Rob Dorrington, one of South Africa's most respected demographers, of Cape Town's population in Figure 3.1 in the Cape Town SDF (City of Cape Town, 2012).
5 Constant 2010 values.
6 It must, however, be noted that the 2014/2015 Tsantsabane Integrated Development Plan mentions an industrial hub, and R1 million set aside for this, but we found no mention of this in any other document to which we had access.
7 The policy for the provision of state-subsidised (Reconstruction and Development Programme) houses permits only one house per applicant. If a household receives an RDP house in Postmasburg, that household will be excluded from receiving another house elsewhere. Thus households are locked into the place where they received the house unless they are prepared to live in an informal settlement or rent elsewhere.

References

Abbott, J., 2005. Understanding and managing the unknown: The nature of uncertainty in planning. *Journal of Planning Education and Research*, 24, pp. 237–251.

African Rainbow Minerals, 2016. *Interim Results for the Six Months Ended 31 December 2015*. www.arm.co.za/im/files/results/interim_31dec15.pdf (accessed 17 May 2016).

Anderies, J.M., Janssen, M.A. and Ostrom, E., 2004. A framework to analyze the robustness of social-ecological systems from an institutional perspective. *Ecology and Society*, 9(1), p. 18.

Armson, R., 2011. *Growing Wings on the Way: Systems Thinking for Messy Situations*. Axminster: Triarchy Press.

Burkhard, B., Fath, B. and Müller, F., 2011. Adapting the adaptive cycle: Hypotheses on the development of ecosystem properties and services. *Ecological Modelling*, 222, pp. 2878–2890.

BusinessTech. 2016. *Average House Prices in South Africa: 1995–2015*. https://businesstech. co.za/news/general/120187/average-house-prices-in-south-africa-1995-2015/ (accessed 15 December 2016).

CAHF (Centre for Affordable Housing Finance in Africa), 2015. *Housing Market Overview for Tsantsabane, Northern Cape: 2008–2013*. Draft report for the Housing Development Agency. CAHF, Parkview, South Africa.

Caravelis, M. and Ivy, R., 2001. From mining community to seasonal visitor destination: The transformation of Sotiras, Thasos, Greece. *European Planning Studies*, 9(2), pp. 187–199.

Chandler, D., 2014. *Resilience: The Governance of Complexity*. London: Routledge.

City of Cape Town, 2012. *Cape Town Spatial Development Framework: Statutory Report*. Western Cape Provincial Gazette, 6994, Friday 18 May 2012, Cape Town.

De Roo, G., Hillier, J. and Van Wezmemael, J., 2012. *Complexity and Planning: Systems, Assemblages and Simulations*. Farnham: Ashgate.

Dewar, D. and Kiepiel, J., 2012. Spatial development frameworks on a broader scale: An integrative approach. *Town and Regional Planning*, 61, pp. 30–35.

Du Plessis, D.J., 2013. A critical reflection on urban spatial planning practices and outcomes in post-apartheid South Africa. *Urban Forum*, 25, pp. 69–88.

Du Plessis, D.J. and Boonzaaier, L., 2015. The evolving spatial structure of South African cities: A reflection on the influence of spatial planning policies. *International Planning Studies*, 20(1–2), pp. 87–111.

Elmqvist, T., Barnett, G. and Wilkerson, C., 2014. Exploring urban sustainability and resilience. In: L.J Pearson, P.W. Newton and P. Roberts, eds. *Resilient and Sustainable Cities: A Future*. London: Routledge, pp. 19–28.

Folke, C., Carpenter, S.R., Walker, B., Scheffer, M., Chapin, T. and Rockström, J., 2010. Resilience thinking: Integrating resilience, adaptability and transformability. *Ecology and Society*, 15(4), p. 20.

Freestone, R., 2012. Futures thinking in planning education and research. *Journal for Education in the Built Environment*, 7(1), pp. 8–38.

Gallopín, G.C., 2006. Linkages between vulnerability, resilience, and adaptive capacity. *Global Environmental Change*, 16, pp. 293–303.

Geyer, R. and Rihani, S., 2010. *Complexity and Public Policy: A New Approach to 21st Century Politics, Policy and Society*. London: Routledge.

Godsell, S., 2011. Rooiberg: The little town that lived. *South African Historical Journal*, 63(1), pp. 61–77.

Grunau, J.P. and Schönwandt, W.L., 2010. Dealing with society's 'big messes'. In: G. De Roo, and E.A. Silva, eds. *A Planner's Encounter with Complexity*. Farnham: Ashgate, pp. 41–62.

Gunderson, L.H. and Holling, C.S. (eds.), 2002. *Panarchy: Understanding Transformations in Human and Natural Systems*. Washington, DC: Island Press.

He, S.Y., Lee, J., Zhou, T. and Wu, D., 2017. Shrinking cities and resource-based economy: The economic restructuring in China's mining cities. *Cities*, 60, pp. 75–83.

Healey, P., 2004. The treatment of space and place in the new strategic spatial planning in Europe. *International Journal of Urban and Regional Research*, 28(1), pp. 45–67.

Healey, P., 2006. *Collaborative Planning: Shaping Places in Fragmented Societies*. Basingstoke: Palgrave Macmillan (2nd edition).

Innes, J.E. and Booher, D.E., 2010. *Planning with Complexity: An Introduction to Collaborative Rationality for Public Policy*. London: Routledge.

Marais, L., 2013. The impact of mine downscaling on the Free State Goldfields. *Urban Forum*, 24, pp. 503–521.

Marais, L. and Nel, E., 2016. The dangers of growing on gold: Lessons for mine downscaling from the Free State Goldfields, South Africa. *Local Economy*, 31(1–2), pp. 282–298.

Martin-Breen, P. and Anderies, J.M., 2011. *Resilience: A Literature Review*. Bellagio Initiative. Brighton: Institute of Development Studies (IDS).

Martinez-Fernandez, C., Chung-Tong Wu, C.-T., Laura, K., Schatz, L.K., Taira, N. and Vargas-Hernández, J.G., 2012. The shrinking mining city: Urban dynamics and contested territory. *International Journal of Urban and Regional Research*, 36(2), pp. 245–260.

Meintjes, C.J., 2001. *Guidelines to Regional Socio-Economic Analysis*. Development Paper 145, Development Information Business Unit, Development Bank of Southern Africa, Midrand, South Africa.

Miot, Y., 2015. Residential attractiveness as a public policy goal for declining industrial cities: Housing renewal strategies in Mulhouse, Roubaix and Saint-Etienne (France). *European Planning Studies*, 23(1), pp. 104–125.

Musvoto, G., Lincoln, G. and Hansmann, R., 2016. The role of spatial development frameworks in transformation of the eThekwini Municipality, KwaZulu-Natal, South Africa: Reflecting on 20 years of planning. *Urban Forum*, 27, pp. 187–210.

Myers, D. and Kituse, A., 2000. Constructing the future in planning: A survey of theories and tools. *Journal of Planning Education and Research*, 19, pp. 221–231.

Nel, E.L., Hill, T., Aitchison, K.C. and Buthelezi, S., 2003. The closure of coal mines and local development responses in Coal-Rim Cluster, Northern KwaZulu-Natal, South Africa. *Development Southern Africa*, 20(3), pp. 369–385.

Nel, E.L. and Rogerson, C.M., 2013. Special economic zones in South Africa: Reflections from international debates. *Urban Forum*, 24, pp. 205–217.

Oranje, M., 2014. Back to where it all began . . .? Reflections on injecting the (spiritual) ethos of the early town planning movement into planning, planners and plans in post-1994 South Africa. *HTS Theological Studies*, 70(3), pp. 1–10.

Plöger, J. and Weck, S., 2014. Confronting out-migration and the skills gap in declining German cities. *European Planning Studies*, 22(2), pp. 437–455.

Quantec, 2016. *Easy Data Regional Database*. Pretoria: Quantec Research.

Randall, J.E. and Ironside, R.G., 1996. Communities on the edge: An economic geography of resource-dependent communities in Canada. *Canadian Geographer*, 40, pp. 17–35.

Rittel, H. and Webber, M., 1973. Dilemmas in a general theory of planning. *Policy Sciences*, 4, pp. 155–169.

Robinson, P., 2014. *Future, Change and Choices*. Westville, Durban: Osborne Porter (2nd edition).

RSA (Republic of South Africa), 2013. *Spatial Planning and Land Use Management Act, 16 of 2013 (SPLUMA)*. Pretoria: Government Printer.

Rydin, Y., 2011. *The Purpose of Planning: Creating Sustainable Towns and Cities*. Bristol, Policy Press.

Seeliger, L. and Turok, I., 2013. Towards sustainable cities: Extending resilience with insights from vulnerability and transition theory. *Sustainability*, 5, pp. 2108–2128.

Simmie, J. and Martin, R., 2010. The economic resilience of regions: Towards an evolutionary approach. *Cambridge Journal of Regions, Economy and Society*, 3, pp. 27–43.

Smith, G.W., 2015. *Shift-Share Analysis of Dickinson County Employment Growth*. http://abilenecityhall.com/documentcenter/view/995 (accessed 31 August 2016).

Synergistics Environmental Services, 2015. *Scoping Report for the Proposed Kolomela Mine Expansion Project*. www.sahra.org.za/sahris/sites/default/files/additionaldocs/Kolomela%20Amendment%202015%20Scoping%20Report%20Final.pdf (accessed 31 August 2016).

Todes, A., 2008. Rethinking spatial planning. *Town and Regional Planning*, 53, pp. 10–14.

Tsantsabane Local Municipality, 2015. *Final Spatial Development Framework*. March 2015. Compiled by Aurecon and Assmang. www.tsantsabane.gov.za/FINAL%20SPATIAL%20DEVELOPMENT%20FRAMEWORK.pdf.

Turok, I., 2014. The resilience of South African cities a decade after local democracy. *Environment and Planning A*, 46(4), pp. 749–769.

Veiga, M.M., Scoble, M. and McAllister, M.L., 2001. Mining with communities. *Natural Resources Forum*, 25, pp. 191–202.

Walker, B. and Salt, D., 2006. *Resilience Thinking: Sustaining People and Ecosystems in a Changing World*. Washington, DC: Island Press.

Wiechmann, T. and Pallagst, K.M., 2012. Urban shrinkage in Germany and the USA: A comparison of transformation patterns and local strategies. *International Journal of Urban and Regional Research*, 36(2), pp. 261–280.

Wilson, L.J., 2004. Riding the resource roller coaster: Understanding socioeconomic differences between mining communities. *Rural Sociology*, 69(2), pp. 261–281.

Xuza, P., 2010. The future of struggling small towns in South Africa. In: R. Donaldson and L. Marais, eds. *Small Town Geographies in Africa: Experiences from South Africa and Elsewhere*. New York: Nova Science, pp. 339–349.

6 Government, mining and community relations

Lyndon Du Plessis and Diane Abrahams

Achieving equitable power relationships

Local government has an important role to play in providing basic services to local communities and promoting their social and economic development. This role is particularly important in a mining town. The 'new natural resource policy agenda' (IIED, 2002; Arellano-Yanguas, 2008) underlines the importance of the social, economic and environmental implications of mining development. It encourages collaborative planning, partnerships and planning for mine closure at the start of the mining operations, and advises that local governments should play important roles in relation to mining development, especially ensuring long-term collaborative planning.

In practice it is difficult to achieve these goals internationally. Owen and Kemp (2013) note an inability to set 'a collaborative developmental agenda' for the sector or to find a way to 'restore the lost confidence' of the affected communities and stakeholders. Hamann (2004) observes that partnerships are difficult to achieve, because the power relationships between mining companies and municipalities are often uneven. He also notes that mining companies tend to shift their collaborative planning responsibilities to corporate social responsibility (CSR), which has short-term goals rather than the long-term goals required for collaborative planning.

Research from Australia shows that local governments are finding it difficult to deal with resource booms in their backyards (CSRM, 2013). Key concerns for local governments are the changing expectations that mining brings to local government and the narrow tax base and legislation barriers that prevent local government from fulfilling its required roles (CSRM, 2013). Municipalities in South Africa are confronted by challenges that see them struggling to fulfil these roles. McKinlay (2012) defines the traditional role of local government as 'a subsidiary tier of government, properly subject to detailed direction and oversight by central government' and 'primarily concerned with service delivery and local regulation' and 'a set of locally owned, but nationally supervised infrastructure companies'. McKinlay (2012, p. 3) argues that 'modern societal issues cannot only be addressed by central governments' and that there is a need for 'a partnership approach to tap into the local knowledge, networks and support and resources which local government is uniquely placed to provide'. Boyle (2016, p. 5) argues that 'local governments need to take a more strategic view of their operations', which we take to mean they should adopt a developmental agenda that is broader than just providing basic services and regulating local communities.

The presence of a mine in its jurisdiction increases a local government's development responsibilities. New mining legislation introduced in South Africa in 2002, the Mineral and Petroleum Resources Development Act, (No. 28 of 2002), requires mining companies to contribute to local development through what are called social and labour plans (SLPs). The aim of this government intervention was to change the practices by which the minerals economy had 'developed essentially without undue state intervention, with the result that market forces largely dictated the pattern of its evolution' (Rogerson, 2011, p. 5405). The Act requires mining companies to submit SLPs as a prerequisite for the granting of mining or production rights. The aim of this requirement is to:

- Promote economic growth and mineral and petroleum resources development;
- Promote employment and advance the social and economic welfare of all South Africans;
- Ensure that holders of mining or production rights contribute to the socio-economic development of the areas in which they are operating; and
- Utilise and expand the existing skills base for the empowerment of historically disadvantaged communities and serve the community. (DMR, 2010)

Rogerson (2011, p. 5412) emphasises the importance of SLPs by arguing that. by adopting 'appropriate local economic development interventions', the mines can not only bring 'direct opportunities to local communities' but also build sustainable capacity in various spheres of such communities.

The extended development of Postmasburg through Kolomela mine and the relocation of workers from Beeshoek to Postmasburg have placed pressure on the local government. This chapter is based on in-depth interviews conducted between November 2016 and January 2017 with five senior municipal representatives (elected councillors and appointed officials) and three senior mining representatives from Beeshoek mine (2) (owned by Assmang) and Kolomela (1) (owned by Kumba). The purpose was to gain insight into how the mining activities influenced governance activities in the municipality and the relationship between the mines and the municipality. We consider how far the imperatives of the new natural resource policy agenda are being applied in Postmasburg. We look at how the mining fraternity in Postmasburg, the Tsantsabane Local Municipality and the community of Postmasburg experience one another and to what degree there is long-term collaborative planning between them, including planning for mine downscaling. We consider how far the mines and the municipality cooperate in planning for service delivery and development in the area, what factors favour or hamper cooperative planning, and what steps the mines and the municipality are taking to ensure a working relationship that is in the best interests of the local community.

Stakeholder relations

The Constitution of South Africa places a responsibility on all municipalities to 'promote social and economic development' and on national and provincial governments to 'support and strengthen the capacity of municipalities', implying a strong emphasis on cooperative effort to render basic services and promote development in the best interest of local communities (RSA, 1996, sections 152(1)c and 154(1)). But although the notion of cooperative governance is a constitutional imperative, the Twenty Year Local Government Review 1994–2014 (DPME, 2015) cites a lack of coordination in intergovernmental relations as a major reason for local government's inability to fulfil its constitutional mandate. The Review says a reason often cited for poor cooperation is that 'powers, functions and responsibilities of local government are not always clear' and can 'be adjusted between district and local municipalities, and delegated and assigned from provincial and national government to local government'. Thus, although the various spheres of government have a regulatory responsibility to work in partnership to make municipalities more effective at community level, the difficulty in clearly defining the role of each sphere leads to delay and frustration instead of progress.

Creating a favourable environment for local development in Postmasburg

Some obstacles to the ideal of inclusive and participatory local governance, according to the Review, are 'patronage politics, weak leadership, weak capacity (both human and financial), mismanagement and corruption'. To improve community governance and perform better as 'corporate entities', municipalities need to function constructively within the constitutionally determined regulatory framework and address institutional issues of governance. The National Development Plan: Vision for 2030 (RSA, 2012) says the following aspects need to be addressed:

- Improving the intergovernmental system, including strengthening intergovernmental protocols between district and local municipalities, where there is conflict over the allocation of responsibilities and resources.
- Stabilising the political-administrative interface, including moving away from the practice of making 'politically motivated' appointments in the administration so that there is clear separation between political representatives and officials.
- Strengthening local government by improving systems of active support and monitoring by provincial and national government for local government, including improvements to mainstream citizen participation.

In addition to dealing with the above structural and institutional challenges faced by local government, municipalities have to implement legislative measures to promote service delivery and development at community level. The primary planning tool for municipalities in South Africa is the integrated development plan

(IDP) (see also Chapter 5). Section 25 of the Local Government: Municipal Systems Act, 32 of 2000, obliges all municipalities to create an IDP that 'links, integrates and co-ordinates plans and takes into account proposals for the development of the municipality' (RSA, 2000). The municipality's budget is to be linked to this plan. De Visser (2009, p. 22) says the IDP 'is expected to integrate the planning of all municipal departments under the umbrella of a united strategy', but that this should 'go beyond planning rhetoric and be the basis for the municipality's annual budgets and its spatial planning'.

The Tsantsabane Local Municipality's review of its 2014/2015 IDP highlights the area's dependence on the mining sector. The review mentions the limited economic opportunities in terms of sectors such as agriculture, manufacturing, retail and services, but states that 'mining activities have been rapidly on the increase in the last few years' (Tsantsabane Local Municipality, 2014, pp. 10–11). It proposes the following main aims for its local economic development (LED) strategy:

- To position the local municipality and its development partners to create a good climate for private sector investment, including the provision of infrastructure, household services, good communication and investment promotion and facilitation.
- To encourage the local private sector and the larger investment community to identify and build on opportunities in the local economy, depending on the availability of capital and a favourable investment environment.

The local economic development (LED) strategy thus emphasises the municipality's responsibility for creating a favourable environment that will maximise the benefit the mines can bring to the area and in turn encourage the private sector to expand its investment in the area.

Stakeholders' opinions

The representatives of the Tsantsabane Local Municipality that we interviewed all agreed on the opportunity value that mining brought to the area. They mentioned the ways the mines have helped the municipality, financially and in infrastructure development, such as the installation of pre-paid water meters – for many scholars a neoliberal management practice (Von Schnitzler, 2008). They said the expansion of mining in the area had also brought opportunities for employment and skills development, and increased revenue generation for the municipality.

On the negative side, they said they thought the municipality had become too dependent on the mines for funding various activities emanating from the municipality's individual plans or its IDPs or the mines' SLPs. There was for instance a view that the municipality did not capitalise on the opportunity of raising the levels of basic services provided to the local community. Furthermore the municipality did not deal effectively with the influx of people into Postmasburg and the pressure on service delivery. Some expressed concern about the municipality's inability to regulate, through a registration or licencing process (which is standard for businesses in the formal sector), informal business in the townships, such as spaza shops, and argued that this paved the way for illegal activities such as drug smuggling. Several were of the opinion that the increased mining activities led to social evils such as alcohol and drug abuse, drug smuggling and prostitution. Although the mines have attempted to address these problems through their social upliftment programmes, they have been a major challenge for the municipality. Furthermore, although it can be argued that the illegal activities referred to represents a policing matter, the station commander had indicated that the police service in Postmasburg did not nearly have the personnel capacity to deal with the increased crime levels effectively.

Interestingly, some interviewees said the municipality was not thoroughly prepared for the impact the mining boom would have on its organisational and strategic planning capacity. One interviewee said the municipality had failed to lead the process of Postmasburg's development in the midst of the mining boom, because it did not have the strategic capacity to do so, referring specifically to the fact that planning processes largely excluded the municipality and thus prevented it to integrate the mining sector in its planning activities from a short, medium and long-term perspective. Two respondents made reference to a skills mismatch, meaning that the municipality did not have enough employees with the right skills to deal with the impact of the mining upswing.

Our interviewees from the municipality expressed various concerns about the cooperative relationship from a government perspective. One of them said the initial discussions about the establishment of the Kolomela mine had been between the mining company and the provincial government and the Tsantsabane Municipality had not been involved. This left an immediate gap in terms of cooperative planning between the mine and the municipality. The provincial government is further accused of not communicating effectively with the district and local municipalities, thus acting in direct contradiction of the constitutional and legislative principles regulating cooperative governance and planning. Besides these flaws in the planning phase, the municipal interviewees also thought intergovernmental cooperation had been weak during the developments that took place in the town during the mining boom. They said the provincial departments had been largely reactive in dealing with community issues, especially when it came to social ills. One of them said the police have been totally 'overwhelmed by the increase of crime levels' and there had been little support from provincial government to increase capacity. As far as social services were concerned, the municipal interviewees were all of the opinion that the municipality should rely more on initiatives from the mines to deal with drug and alcohol abuse and other social problems than on assistance from the provincial department of social welfare.

From an institutional management perspective, the municipal interviewees also expressed dissatisfaction with the level of cooperation between government departments. The municipal respondents mentioned the lack of support from the provincial treasury as far as control and planning were concerned. One official expressed serious concern over council decisions that lacked proper financial controls, financial viability planning and financial discipline. The municipal officials felt that the provincial treasury should lend more support to the municipality's finance division to rectify the institutional flaws. Another municipal interviewee described provincial sector departmental support as 'horrendous' (The interviewee referred to here, expressed a general opinion on support by provincial sector departments and at no stage named a specific department. Had he done so, as was the case in earlier reference to treasury support, we would have named the department) and said there was 'too much political consideration in decision-making'.

It was clear from our interviews that although the municipality has the strategic planning tools to enable it to capitalise on the development of Postmasburg that has resulted from the mines and to act as an important partner, a number of negative spin-offs have been experienced. The question is how the mines and the municipality and other government sector stakeholders can collectively ensure that all activities have the best interests of the Postmasburg community at heart.

According to Jenkins and Yakovleva (2006), to achieve sustainable development in the vicinity of large industries like the Postmasburg mines requires progress in three areas: economic development, environmental protection and social cohesion. This agrees with the earlier view of Hilson and Murck (2000, p. 227) that 'sustainable development (in the mining context) is the combination of enhanced socioeconomic growth and development, and improved environmental protection and pollution prevention'. Walker and Howard (cited in Jenkins and Yakovleva, 2006, p. 272) note that sustainable development in the mining sector has been under particular scrutiny, firstly because the public has a poor opinion of the sector and is generally concerned about environmental and social performance rather than such issues as pricing, quality and safety, that would be of concern to the mines themselves, and secondly because the financial sector focuses on the mining sector from the perspective of social responsibility rather than risk management.

Humphreys (2001) argues that as far as the social responsibility of mines for sustainable development is concerned, the question is not necessarily whether the mines can afford to pay attention to it, but rather how they will respond to the pressures of ensuring that they comply with their responsibility to do so. Hamann (2004) refers to the requirements and ensuing challenges that local government and partnerships must deal with in South Africa. Municipalities no longer just provide basic services; they now have to facilitate development. They must therefore ensure participatory preparation of IDPs, which link the municipal budget to proactive planning for land use and the prioritisation of development needs. Hamann (2004, p. 286) says that 'in much of the country, this shift has been impeded by human resource and funding constraints'.

Municipal respondents suggested that although the mines initially injected funds into Postmasburg and the municipality itself, more recently they have done little to assist the municipality. Currently the mines are complying with the legislative requirements in terms of what they are required to give to the municipality, but doing no more than complying. In fact one municipal respondent said that the current difficulties in the relationship between the mines and the municipality result from a failure to consider thoroughly all the effects that mining expansion or, particularly, downscaling could have on the area. One of the interviewees said that 'maybe there should have been a more thorough analysis of the positives *and* potential pitfalls that would come with the boom'. However, the three interviewees from the mining companies claimed that this thorough analysis *had* been done and that in fact the company represented by one of these interviewees was continuing with socio-economic impact studies every three years. Representatives from the mining companies argued that advice had been given to the municipality on developing other sectors of the town's economy into sustainable business development opportunities instead of focusing exclusively on the benefits to be drawn from the mines.

Hamann (2004, pp. 278–279) says South African mines have a history of not always complying with their responsibility to employees and local communities. He therefore stresses the importance of mining companies' corporate responsibility and their partnerships with local stakeholders, particularly because mining is a transitory industry, with major social and environmental effects that must be measured and monitored. He says provision must be made for the effects of possible mine downscaling or closure on the local community. Jenkins and Yakovleva (2006, p. 272) point out that CSR obliges a company to respond 'not only to its shareholders, but also to other stakeholders, including employees, customers, affected communities and the general public'.

An interviewee from the municipality said the mine's interaction with the municipality and the local community was 'merely compliance based' and the mines were 'mostly not fully disclosing information outside of their legislative responsibility'. Another view expressed by a municipal interviewee was that there was no communication or coordination between the mines and the municipality and that their expectations were not the same as far as the development of the town was concerned. What we found interesting, but not necessarily surprising, was that both sets of interviewees, from the municipality and the mines, claimed to be doing their bit. The interviewees from the mines claimed that they were in fact 'doing more than expected' but that the municipality was not making use of the platform created by the mines. An example cited was the serviced erven provided by one mining company, initially for its employees, but subsequently also for other residents in Postmasburg. Respondents from the mining companies argued that while these erven have been made available to the municipality and residents are occupying them, the municipality has failed to issue service accounts efficiently and thus generate revenue for the municipality. This corroborated the view expressed by interviewees from the mines and by those from the municipality that the municipality lacked capacity and was unable to appoint adequately skilled officials. Reasons for this are complex. It is partially related to the lack of local skills but can also be attributed to employment practices within the ruling party.

The literature we have cited in this chapter makes it clear that cooperation and participatory planning between the municipality and the mining sector is essential to ensure that the local community ultimately benefits. In Postmasburg we heard opposing views on the relationship between and how it is unfolding. Both sets of interviewees were satisfied that they had done what was required in order to establish a constructive cooperative relationship that would bring sustainable development to the community of Postmasburg. Both sets blamed the lack of success on shortcomings on the part of the other, and the municipal interviewees blamed it on an institutional factor over which they had little or no control, namely undue political influence in the municipality's administration. Clearly both sets need to perceive and interact with one another differently if Postmasburg is to gain the maximum benefit from the relationship, especially given the recent problems on the mines in South Africa and the resultant downscaling.

Mine-municipal relations and possible decline

Mining has declined in many developed countries since the 1960s and international experience shows that mining companies and local communities are often not well prepared to deal with it. Most of the literature on mine decline or closure focuses on the environment, but awareness is increasing of the need to consider the social and economic aspects too. It has become clear that the planning for decline or closure must not be left to the mining companies but must be shared by government and civil society. Decline and closure of a mine are often traumatic for local communities, especially in remote areas like Postmasburg and especially if they have weak local government, low labour productivity, low non-mining income and minimal labour mobility. Useful recent accounts and discussion of the problems South Africa has experienced may be found in Marais (2013a, 2013b) and Marais and Cloete (2013).

During the interviews, several questions and ensuing discussions concerned the impact of the mine downscaling as a result of the drop in the price of iron ore. According to a report in the Mail and Guardian (2016), this has been caused by the slowdown of growth in China reducing the demand for steel, with a resultant drop in the price of iron ore from $187 a tonne in 2011 to below $40 a tonne in December 2015. The interviewees from the mining companies in Postmasburg said that although the retrenchment of permanent employees has been limited to Kumba Iron Ore's Sishen mine at Kathu at the time of the interviews, the mines in Postmasburg had started suspending the contracts of certain contractors with whom they were doing business – an ominous indication of downscaling to come.

Questioned about the potential impact of mine downscaling or closure, the interviewees were in agreement that it would be detrimental to the town on many levels. The lifespan of the mines was estimated at between 30 and 40 years, and one municipal interviewee was of the opinion that Postmasburg would become a 'ghost town' without the mines. Another spoke of the negative effects on the municipality if the mines downscale or close: loss of revenue, and the pressure from the large labour force who came to Postmasburg specifically to work on the mines, now unemployed and remaining in the municipality's jurisdiction. The municipality would have to provide more free basic services, and overcrowding in informal settlements would probably lead to an increase in social ills. As regards the increased pressure on the municipality to provide services, another municipal interviewee foresaw problems with revenue collection. In this regard one municipal official said that there was a proposal to the council to consider alternative methods of revenue recovery, such as a flat rate for services in the informal settlement of Postmasburg. This was still under consideration in council and at the time of writing a decision was being delayed by the upcoming elections and the ensuing transition, with a new council starting its five-year term.

Our interviewees complained of the lack of clear vision in dealing with the issue of development beyond the mining boom. One of the municipal officials said no planning had been done for the best use of infrastructure after the boom and that the municipality would not be able to manage and maintain the infrastructure without the assistance of the mines. Both mining and municipal respondents were concerned about how to develop the capacity for such long-term planning. It was, for example, mentioned that structures to support community and municipal cooperative relations such as ward committees were malfunctioning and that more effort needed to be put into strengthening civil capacity in this regard. One of the municipal interviewees said that ideas about re-using the infrastructure that came with the mining upswing were often fragmented because people saw no need to think about it at this stage because it was 'too far in the future'.

From our interviews we became aware that signs of downscaling had recently been noticed and that Postmasburg was about to become volatile socially and economically. The general feeling was that stakeholders must understand their respective roles and, more importantly, take responsibility for them, and that they must do their bit to ensure that the environment is protected and that economic and social cohesion are maintained and strengthened, as per the earlier definition of sustainable development (Hilson and Murck, 2000). If this is not done, the reputational and functional risk will increase for both the mines and the local government and in the end communities will suffer.

Conclusion

The purpose of this chapter was to integrate the literature on participative local planning, mining CSR and mine downscaling with the current events in Postmasburg, based on the evidence of approximately six years (2011 to 2016). The chapter reviewed worldwide trends in the mining literature and regulatory mechanisms for mining in South Africa. We considered an ideal environment in which the government, the mining industry and the local community could collaborate in order to make mining as beneficial as possible to Postmasburg.

The chapter provided an overview of the mining boom that started in 2011 and the downscaling as a result in the drop of the world price of iron ore in 2015 and its implications for the mines, the municipality and ultimately the local communities. It became evident to us that the economic injection as a result of the mining boom was fundamental for Postmasburg in many respects. From a socio-economic perspective, the boom provided opportunities for the local municipality and the community. Full advantage does not seem to have been taken of these opportunities, partly because of a lack of institutional capacity to deal with the changes, and partly because of a lack of support for the municipality from the other spheres of government. Representatives from the municipality whom we interviewed also complained of a lack of optimal support from the mines, although our interviewees from the mines denied this and blamed the problems on the shortcomings of the municipality.

The initial cooperative planning between the mines and the municipality seems to have been positive, although it became apparent to us that the municipality, in the view even of some within their own ranks, had become too dependent on the mines. This has subsequently resulted in a less cooperative relationship and the problem has been exacerbated by the downscaling that has taken place recently. Although the primary mines, Beeshoek and Kolomela, do not seem to be under immediate threat, the economic and social effects of the downscaling are a reality and have already affected the community of Postmasburg.

References

Arellano-Yanguas, J., 2008. *A Thoroughly Modern Resource Curse? The New Natural Resource Policy Agenda and the Mining Revival in Peru*. IDS Working Paper no. 300. Institute of Development Studies, Brighton, UK. http://dev2.opendocs.ids.ac.uk/opendocs/handle/123456789/4104 (accessed 12 March 2017).

Boyle, R., 2016. *Reshaping Local Government: Overview of Selected International Experience with Local Government Reorganization, Mergers, Amalgamation and Coordination*. Local Government Research Series no. 10, January 2016, Institute of Public Administration, Dublin.

CSRM (Centre for Social Responsibility in Mining), 2013. *Local Government, Mining and Resources Development in Regional Australia*. Australia: University of Queensland.

De Visser, J., 2009. Developmental local government in South Africa: Institutional fault lines. *Commonwealth Journal of Local Governance*, 2, pp. 1–9.

DMR (Department of Mineral Resources), 2002. *Mineral and Petroleum Resources Development Act, 2002 (No. 28 of 2002)*. Pretoria: Government Printer.

DMR (Department of Mineral Resources), 2010. *Revised Social and Labour Plan Guidelines*. Pretoria: Government Printer.

DPME (Department of Department of Planning, Monitoring and Evaluation), 2015. *Twenty Year Review South Africa 1994–2014, Background Paper: Local Government*. Pretoria: Government Printer.

Hamann, R., 2004. Corporate social responsibility, partnerships, and institutional change: The case of mining companies in South Africa. *National Resources Forum*, 28, pp. 278–290.

Hilson, G. and Murck, B., 2000. Sustainable development in the mining industry: Clarifying the corporate perspective. *Resources Policy*, 26, pp. 227–238.

Humphreys, D., 2001. Sustainable development: Can the mining industry afford it? *Resources Policy*, 27, pp. 1–7.

IIED (International Institute for Environment and Development), 2002. *Breaking New Ground: Mining, Minerals, and Sustainable Development*. London: Earthscan.

Jenkins, H. and Yakovleva, N., 2006. Corporate social responsibility in the mining industry: Exploring trends in social and environmental disclosure. *Journal of Cleaner Production*, 14, pp. 271–284.

Steyn, L. 2016. Iron ore takes Kathu from boom to bust in five years. Mail and Gaurdian. 29 April 2016, p. 7.

Marais, L., 2013a. The impact of mine downscaling on the Free State Goldfields. *Urban Forum*, 24, pp. 503–521.

Marais, L., 2013b. Resource policy and mine closure in South Africa: The case of the Free State Goldfields. *Resources Policy*, 38, pp. 362–372.

Marais, L. and Cloete, J., 2013. Labour migration settlement and mine closure in South Africa. *Geography*, 98(2), pp. 77–84.

McKinlay, P., 2012. *International and New Zealand Trends influencing Change in Local Government: Thoughts for Waikato*. Paper presented at conference on Rethinking Local Government, 10 August 2012, New Zealand Institute of Public Administration, Karapiro.

Owen, J. and Kemp, D., 2013. Social licence and mining: A critical perspective. *Resources Policy*, 38, pp. 29–35.

Rogerson, C.M., 2011. Mining enterprise and partnerships for socio-economic development. *African Journal of Business Management*, 5(14), pp. 5405–5417.

RSA (Republic of South Africa), 1996. *Constitution of the Republic of South Africa, 1996 (Act 108 of 1996)*. Pretoria: Government Printer.

RSA (Republic of South Africa), 2000. *Local Government: Municipal Systems Act, 2000, Act 32 of 2000*. Pretoria: Government Printer.

RSA (Republic of South Africa, Department of the Presidency), 2012. *National Planning Commission, 2012: National Development Plan: Vision for 2030*. Pretoria: Government Printer.

Tsantsabane Local Municipality, 2014. *IDP 2014/15*. Postmasburg: Tsantsabane Local Municipality.

Von Schnitzler, A., 2008. Citizenship prepaid: Water, calculability, and techno-politics in South Africa. *Journal of Southern African Studies*, 34(4), pp. 899–917.

7 Mining and municipal finance

Chris Hendriks and Lochner Marais

How can Postmasburg's municipality cope financially?

The presence of a mine places extraordinary pressure on a town's finances. Land must be made available and infrastructure provided for migrants seeking work. It also brings financial risks: if the mine closes, expensive settlement infrastructure becomes redundant. The local municipality must find funds to manage not only mine-related growth but also decline. In this chapter we look at what the mines have meant for Postmasburg financially (revenue and expenditure).

South Africa's original mining towns were mostly managed and financed by the mining company (see Chapter 1 of this volume). The resource slump that began in the mid-1980s meant that many towns were transferred to local governments – along with the risks and the opportunities (Littlewood, 2014). It also meant that the responsibility for financing these towns shifted from the company to the local government. In many cases the towns required substantial intergovernmental transfers because their lack of a tax base, rates system and reserve funds made it hard for them to cope.

The constraints that mining places on local government have been noted in the international literature (Rolfe et al., 2007; Pick et al., 2008). Other chapters in this book also cover this (see Chapters 6 and 10). In Australia researchers have expressed concern about local governments' inability to deal with pressures, and often they associate this with neoliberalism in government planning (e.g. Pick et al., 2008). The literature in general criticises the overemphasis on finding local solutions to problems created by multinational mining companies. Much research has been done on ways to find additional income, and intergovernmental funding arrangements are emphasised (Rolfe et al., 2007; Argent, 2014). Chapter 10 of this volume describes how a public-private partnership can help to provide and fund the required infrastructure.

However, little research has been done on the impact of mining growth and decline on municipal finance per se. The study described in this chapter goes some way to fill that gap. We examined the National Treasury's audited annual financial statements for Tsantsabane Local Municipality (of which Postmasburg is the main town) for 10 years (2004/05–2014/2015), with the aim of answering four questions about the financial effect of the mines:

- What are the implications of mining for municipal revenue?
- What are the implications of mining for municipal expenditure?

- To what extent have intergovernmental financing systems succeeded in supporting the municipality?
- What are the implications of increased property rates for various types of households in this municipality?

We argue that despite some ongoing concerns about cash flow, municipal own revenue has grown rapidly, expenditure has mostly been brought into alignment with income, and intergovernmental grants are responsive to the pressure that mining exerts on a small town municipality. However, it was worrying to find that increases in property rates seem to be having a heavier impact on non-mining households than on those employed by or contracted to the mines.

International research on mines and local government

'Resource curse' research has devoted much attention to the relationship between governance, institutions and mining at the national level, but we did not find many case studies at the regional or local level. Local studies are important because it is often the local government that has to deal with the local consequences of mining although it has little control over the extraction processes because mining is usually a national function (see for example Kabamba, 2012). In a study of Zambian mining towns, Negi (2014, p. 1007) notes that in contrast to 'the mining companies' projection of grandness and permanence', the towns seemed to be struggling 'in the face of social and spatial changes induced by the mining boom'. In Australia, Pick et al. (2008) found that local governments in resource towns were weak in three essential areas: they were unable to meet local needs, ensure trust or coordinate the different spheres of government. Also in Australia, Rolfe et al. (2007) noted that the vulnerability associated with global resource markets and the difficulty in finding skilled employees for local government functions was placing severe pressure on local governments in many mining towns. Because many mining towns are in remote locations, they do not offer the lifestyle that would attract the professionals who are needed to build flourishing communities. Wasylycia-Leis et al. (2014) note that despite recent attempts at regulating mining companies in Brazil, mining developments continue to disturb local communities and cause difficulties for local governments.

In many countries worldwide, local needs go unmet because local governments cannot earn property tax from mines and are thus 'weak and marginal' (Pick et al., 2008, p. 516). Some case studies, however, indicate that local government revenues do benefit from royalties. For example, a case study based in Brazil shows that royalty revenues are 'matched to a very large extent by reported spending increases, particularly in the areas of urban infrastructure and housing, education and health services' (Caselli and Michaels, 2013, p. 30). In Western Australia the royalties for the region's programme managed to redistribute income from mining at the national level to local governments to address their social, economic and planning concerns (Argent, 2014).

Some researchers have looked at local governments' financial concerns against the historical development of mining towns. In a study of the Namibian mining industry, Littlewood (2014) notes that the late 1980s saw responsibility for these towns being dumped onto local government structures and mine housing being privatised. The financial implications of infrastructure originally put in place by mining companies being transferred to local governments are serious, particularly when infrastructure generated during a boom has to be maintained during periods of decline (Christopherson and Rightor, 2011; Littlewood, 2014). Many towns did not have reserve funds, the local property tax systems were poorly developed and privatisation of housing units increased the risk of non-payment.

Christopherson and Rightor (2011) observe that shale gas drilling appears to be even more problematic for local governments than other kinds of mining because the construction and mining periods may be much shorter. Concerns have also been also expressed in the literature about the way fly-in-fly-out arrangements affect mining towns and their local governments. Christopherson and Rightor (2011) argue that these shift workers contribute little towards the roads, water, sewerage, health and leisure infrastructure that they use, and seldom pay property taxes in the towns where they work although some would contribute to service charges.

Some studies suggest that mining improves local revenue. More problematic is how these funds have been used to mitigate the adverse effects of the resource industry. Pick et al. (2008) note the importance of intergovernmental arrangements and coordination. They say the absence of policy coordination between different spheres of government severely reduces the effectiveness of government institutions. They note that tensions between different spheres of government have been reported in Australia. Rolfe et al. (2007, p. 149) argue that these tensions have arisen because local governments are required to provide essential services 'but often have little prior information, a limited funding base and little guarantee that the population base will remain in future'.

Pick et al.'s (2008) research suggests that very few residents of mining towns in Australia believe that government is in fact serious about addressing the plight of mining towns; rather, they often feel let down by government. Chapman et al. (2015) observe that, in general, policy is inadequate to deal with the implications of an industry that depends heavily on international capital, and government (on various levels) is mostly too slow in reacting to resource extraction developments.

The quest for more responsive and financially sound local governance has given rise to ideas about alternative governance structures, partnerships and hybrid models of local governance. Even if there is some potential in these ideas, the international literature remains on the whole rather sceptical because mining companies tend to dominate such processes and commonly use their corporate social responsibility programmes to fund activities of this kind. Joint planning seems still to be an unattainable ideal (see Chapter 4).

South African research on mines and local government

Research into how mining towns manage municipal finance is underdeveloped in South Africa. Where it has been done, it is usually reported in papers on a wider set of issues. Some reference has been made to the impact of mine downscaling or decline on municipal finance (Marais et al., 2005; Marais, 2013; Van Rooyen and Lenka, 2016). Common concerns are that mine downscaling increases the municipality's risk of bad debt, increases its administrative burden and reduces its cash flows. Historically, as mentioned above, mining companies owned large portions of the housing stock in mining towns. They paid the rates and taxes, often well in advance of payment deadlines, which was good for municipalities' cash flows (Marais, 2013). With downscaling or closure, the companies privatised their housing stock, transferring the risk to the individual households and the municipality and thus reducing the cash flow and increasing the administrative burden associated with collection (Marais, 2013).

Assessment of Tsantsabane Local Municipality's financial statements, 2014/15

As elsewhere in the world, local governments in South Africa provide basic services such as water, electricity, sanitation, refuse removal, municipal transport and roads. They fund a large part of the cost of these services from user charges and property rates within the municipality's own tax base. However, the South African situation and the international situation differ in two ways. Firstly, the municipalities in South Africa commonly subsidise large numbers of poor households. The national fiscus provides municipalities with an 'equitable share'. This is an unconditional transfer to supplement the revenue that municipalities are themselves able to raise (including the revenue from property rates and service charges). It enables municipalities to deliver free basic services to indigent households and also subsidises the cost of administration and other core services for the municipalities that are least able to recover these costs from their own revenues (National Treasury, 2016). Secondly, South Africa has developed over the years an intergovernmental transfer system that distributes funds to municipalities for infrastructure. Unlike many neoliberal financing systems, this South African system is very effective in boosting the flow of revenue to local municipalities.

Revenue

South African municipalities have two basic sources of revenue: their own sources, which include user charges and property rates, and grants from the provincial or national government. Figure 7.1 shows the main categories of revenue received by Tsantsabane Municipality in the 2015 financial year. Own revenue is derived mainly from the sale of water and electricity, property rates and taxes, and service charges for refuse removal, sewerage and sanitation. In 2015, own revenue accounted for 62% of municipal income in Tsantsabane. Figure 7.2 shows the proportions these contributed to Tsantsabane's own revenue in the 2014/15 financial year, according to its financial statements for that year.

   Up to the 2010/11 financial year, Tsantsabane's own revenue increases kept pace with inflation (see Figure 7.3). However, since then Tsantsabane Municipality's own revenue has increased enormously. Its highest per annum growth, 89%, was in the 2012/13 financial year. The average annual growth from 2010/11 to 2015/16

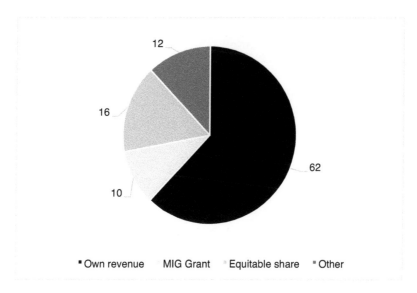

Figure 7.1 Share of municipal income per source, 2015 (percentages)
Note: MIG is the Municipal Infrastructure Grant.

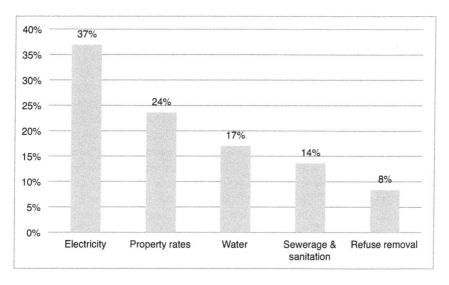

Figure 7.2 Contribution of own sources of revenue in Tsantsabane, 2014/15

was 38%. This increase was mainly due to higher collection rates (for services and property taxes) that increased own revenue sources due to the increase in the housing stock provided by the mines. From 2014/15 to 2015/16, own revenue virtually stagnated as the mines did not create new mining stock.

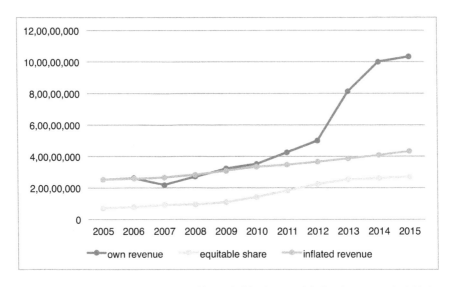

Figure 7.3 Own revenue compared with equitable share and inflated revenue, 2004/15–2014/15 (rand)

Figure 7.3 further shows that, as a result of mining development in the Tsantsabane Municipality, much higher revenue was collected from own sources than from the national government. Kolomela mine, for instance, which had been operating at full capacity since 2013, built 718 houses for employees as part of an integrated approach that made the houses part of the existing community without creating a separate mining town (Kumba, 2015). Beeshoek mine also built about 400 houses for their employees and added a large number of private houses to the town's housing stock (see Chapter 9). The result was more revenue from the sale of electricity and water, property rates and taxes, and charges for refuse removal, and sewerage and sanitation. Figure 7.4 shows the differences between the annually collected revenue in 2012/13 and 2015/16. The big increases in revenue from property rates reflect the contribution the new houses were making to municipal finance.

Interestingly, one of the participants in the survey on which this book is based said the municipality could well have sourced this revenue earlier and that for long periods some mining companies did not pay property rates. Furthermore, Figure 7.2 shows that the equitable share did indeed react to the rapid population increase Tsantsabane experienced from 2009 to 2015. This suggests a responsive system. Chapter 9 of this volume describes how mining has contributed to the rapid development of informal settlements. A responsive equitable share grant has probably helped to support services to poor households in these settlements. Because they raise much less revenue than the large metropolitans, rural municipalities like Tsantsabane depend heavily on transfers from national government to provide services to their communities. To ensure that they get their fair share, section 227 of the Constitution (108 of 1996) stipulates that local government 'is entitled to an equitable share of the revenue raised nationally to enable it to provide basic

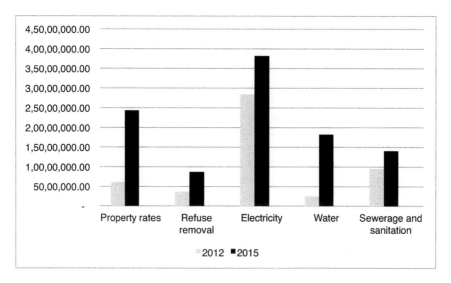

Figure 7.4 Increases in value of own revenue resources, 2012–2015 (rand)

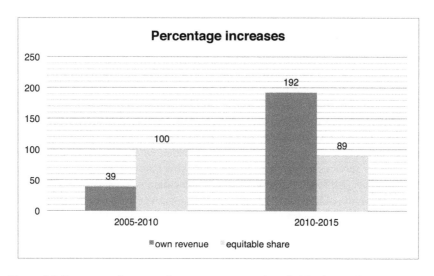

Figure 7.5 Percentage increases in own revenue and equitable share, 2005–2010 and 2010–2015 (rand)

services and perform the functions allocated to it' (RSA, 1996). This equitable share largely depends on the population size and poverty levels in a municipality.

When we compared Tsantsabane's own revenues and equitable share revenues, we found that the latter contributed approximately 16% of the total revenue and grew by 100% from 2005/06 to 2010/11. Own revenue grew by 39% over the same period (see Figure 7.5). From 2010 to 2015, however, the equitable share revenue grew by only 89%, while own revenue grew by 192%. This growth in own revenue was mainly due to increased collection of revenue from the sale of electricity and water, and also property rates and taxes.

Apart from the equitable share, South African municipalities receive other grants that contribute to their total revenue, such as the Municipal Infrastructure Grant (MIG), the Expanded Public Works Programme Grant, the Financial Management Grant and the Municipal Systems Improvement Grant. It is the MIG that contributes most substantially, funding the infrastructure for basic services and roads and social infrastructure for poor households in all non-metropolitan municipalities. The MIG contributes about 10% of Tsantsabane's total revenue. We noted that in the 2012/13 financial year, the financial statements recorded having received grant income from Kolomela mine. This was a one-off occurrence and we suspect the mines have since opted rather to support the public-private partnership (see Chapter 4 of this volume).

Expenditure

Tsantsabane Municipality's main categories of expenditure for 2015/16 were bulk purchases of water and electricity (34%), staffing expenditure (30%), debt impairment (6%) and general expenses (30%). We noted that, despite the mining development that has taken place since 2010, Tsantsabane's total expenditure remains on a par with its total revenue. In several financial years, for instance 2014/15 and 2015/16, its total expenditure exceeded total revenue, leaving the municipality with an operating deficit. This was then made good by selling some assets, which suggests that the Tsantsabane Municipality is struggling to cope financially.

One of the problems is that the proceeds from the sale of water and electricity are lower than the bulk purchasing price, so the Tsantsabane Municipality is actually showing a loss for these two very important sources of revenue. The reasons for this are complex. Municipalities are compelled to provide free basic services to indigent people and the profit Tsantsabane makes on the portion sold to citizens who pay for services has not been sufficient to cover the expenditure on bulk water and electricity. Although the equitable share allocation compensates municipalities for the provision of free basic services, it does not cover increases in the bulk price of electricity that are approved after the budget has been tabled (National Treasury, 2016). Recent increases in the costs of bulk electricity and water have depleted the surpluses municipalities usually generate from these services (National Treasury, 2016). Water has been lost because of leaks in ageing infrastructure and poor maintenance, and illegal connections have led to electricity losses (National Treasury, 2016).

Tsantsabane's second highest single expenditure item, staffing, includes all the current payments to municipal employees – not only salaries and wages but also social contributions such as for pensions and medical schemes. We found there was a steady decrease in the percentage of the total budget that was spent on employee compensation over a ten-year period (2005–2015), from as high as 48% in 2006/07 and 58% in 2007/08 to only 30% in 2015/16 This implies that while the municipality's total revenues increased, the salary bill did not increase proportionally,

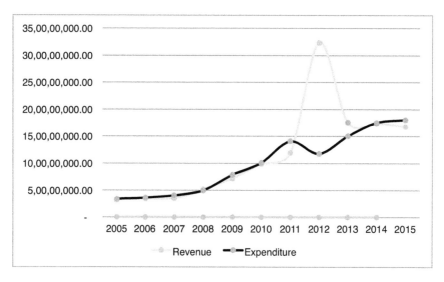

Figure 7.6 Comparison of revenue and expenditure, 2005–2015

which left the municipality with a larger portion of revenue to spend on goods and services. This was probably the result of national guidelines regarding expenditure on staffing.

Our analysis of Tsantsabane's financial systems indicated that what should give the Municipality cause for concern is the amount written off to bad debt. This was as high as 24% of total expenditure in 2010 and although it decreased to 6% (R11,357,221) in 2015, it is still unacceptably high. Many municipalities fail to collect all their rates and taxes, and therefore write off bad debts; in consequence, the National Treasury (2016) has urged municipalities to improve their own revenue collection systems. Many municipalities fail to collect all the money owed to them and their tariffs fail to cover the full costs of the services provided.

Figure 7.6 compares Tsantsabane Municipality's total revenue with its total expenditure. The rapid increase in revenue experienced in 2012 is attributable to a substantial increase in infrastructure grants. We were concerned to see that in 2015/16 expenditure exceeded revenue, which necessitated the selling of municipal assets in that financial year.

Who pays the most for municipal services?

Many mining-town studies point out that the presence of a mine can give rise to new inequalities and particularly inequalities between mining households and those of the host communities (see Chapter 2). Table 7.1 compares the average amounts, and percentages of total expenditure, spent on electricity, water and

Table 7.1 Comparison of Tsantsabane non-mineworker, mineworker and contract mineworker
households' spending on electricity, water and rates as a % of monthly expenditure

Criteria	Non-mining households	Mineworker households	Contract mineworker households
Average total monthly expenditure (rand)	1,517	10,713	7,028
Average monthly expenditure on electricity, water and rates (rand)	182	334	175
% of monthly expenditure on electricity, water and rates	12.0	3.1	2.5

municipal rates by non-mineworker, mineworker and contract mineworker households in Postmasburg. It should be borne in mind that a considerable number of
household heads working at Kolomela are not homeowners. Furthermore, very few
respondents completed questions on expenditure in the survey.

The table shows that increased municipal revenue has probably had the biggest
impact on non-mining households. Non-mining households spend a much larger
proportion of their income on electricity, water and rates than the mining households.
However, the fact that higher-income non-mining households are underrepresented
in these data should be taken into account. If they were included, the percentage
could well prove to be substantially lower. Nevertheless, these are real expenditures
and the data are probably valid for lower-income non-mining households.

Conclusion

Mining development increased the Tsantsabane Municipality's revenue by an average of 31% per annum from 2008 to 2013. This increase was the result of improved
collection of own revenue and an increase in the grants that Tsantsabane received
from the national government, such as the equitable share grant and the Municipal
Infrastructure Grant. This shows that mining-induced growth can boost local revenues
and that intergovernmental transfers are indeed responding to local concerns. However, the increase in total revenues has been offset by the municipality's increases in
expenditure. More bulk water and electricity had to be purchased and the infrastructure for new plots of land had to be financed. Over the ten-year period we studied
(2005–2015), there was a close correlation between revenue and expenditure and in
2015/16 expenditure exceeded income, which is a matter for concern. This might
be the first indication of what mine downscaling could mean for municipal finance.

Although our data on expenditure patterns at the household level are not sufficiently extensive to allow for firm conclusions, indications are that the municipality's increased income from rates and taxes might be particularly detrimental
to low-income, non-mining households. This has relevance for other mining town
municipalities in South Africa, and elsewhere in the world, which may experience
similar effects as a result of mining developments. This requires more detailed
research in future.

References

Argent, N., 2014. Reinterpreting core and periphery in Australia's mineral and energy resources boom: An Innisian perspective on the Pilbara. *Australian Geographer*, 44(3), pp. 323–340.

Caselli, F. and Michaels, G., 2013. Do oil windfalls improve living standards? Evidence from Brazil. *American Economic Journal*, 5(2), pp. 208–238.

Chapman, R., Plummer, P. and Tonts, M., 2015. The resource boom and socio-economic well-being in Australian resource towns: A temporal and spatial analysis. *Urban Geography*, 36(5), pp. 629–653.

Christopherson, S. and Rightor, N., 2011. How shale gas extraction affects drilling localities: Lessons for regional and city policy makers. *Journal of Town and City Management*, 2(4), pp. 350–368.

Kabamba, P., 2012. A tale of two cities: Urban transformation in gold-centred Butembo and diamond-rich Mbuji-Mayi, Democratic Republic of the Congo. *Journal of Contemporary African Studies*, 30(4), pp. 669–685.

Kumba (Kumba Iron Ore), 2015. *Sustainability Report*. www.angloamerican.com/~/media/Files/A/kumba-sustainability-report-2015.pdf (accessed 23 August 2016).

Littlewood, D., 2014. 'Cursed' communities? Corporate social responsibility (CSR), company towns and the mining industry in Namibia. *Journal of Business Ethics*, 120, pp. 39–63.

Marais, L., 2013. The impact of mine downscaling on the Free State Goldfields. *Urban Forum*, 24, pp. 503–521.

Marais, L., Pelser, A., Botes, L., Redelinghuys, N. and Benseler, A., 2005. Public finances, service delivery and mine closure in Koffiefontein (Free State, South Africa): From stepping stone to stumbling block. *Town and Regional Planning*, 48, pp. 5–16.

National Treasury, 2016. *Budget Review*. www.treasury.gov.za/documents/national%20budget/2016/review/FullReview.pdf (accessed 20 August 2016).

Negi, R., 2014. 'Solwezi mabanga': Ambivalent developments on Zambia's new mining frontier. *Journal of Southern African Studies*, 40(5), 999–1013.

Pick, D., Dayaram, K. and Butler, B., 2008. Neo-liberalism, risk and regional development in Western Australia: The case of the Pilbara. *International Journal of Sociology and Social Policy*, 28(11–12), pp. 516–527.

Rolfe, J., Miles, B., Lockie, S. and Ivanova, G., 2007. Lessons from the social and economic impacts of the mining boom in the Bowen Basin, 2004–2006. *Australasian Journal of Regional Studies*, 13(2), pp. 134–153.

RSA (Republic of South Africa), 1996. *Constitution of the Republic of South Africa, (Act No. 108 of 1996)*. Pretoria: Government Printer.

Van Rooyen, D. and Lenka, M., 2016. City of Matlosana. In: L. Marais, E. Nel and R. Donaldson, eds. *Secondary Cities and Development*. London: Routledge, pp. 49–62.

Wasylycia-Leis, J., Fitzpatrick, P. and Fonseca, A., 2014. Mining communities from a resilience perspective: Managing disturbance and vulnerability in Itabira, Brazil. *Environmental Management*, 53, pp. 481–495.

8 Environmental legislation, mining and Postmasburg's ecosystems

Falko T. Buschke, Joost Sommen, Maitland T. Seaman and Richard D. Williamson

Postmasburg as a microcosm of Southern Africa's biodiversity

South Africa is noted worldwide for its extreme biodiversity, reflecting a rich ecological and evolutionary history. Although not as renowned as the country's three global biodiversity hotspots,[1] the Postmasburg region, on the southern outskirts of the Kalahari Desert, has a varied fauna and flora that represent a similar wealth of ecological and evolutionary processes. It is a microcosm of the sub-continent's biodiversity.

Postmasburg also serves as a microcosm of the effects of mining on the African environment. Extraction of the rich metal deposits in the area has shaped the landscape since pre-colonial times. Iron Age settlements here can be dated back to as early as 1650 (Humphreys, 1976). Those early settlers would have affected the distribution of native plant and animal species by hunting, introducing competition from livestock and transforming the land by fire and overgrazing (Beinart, 2003; Boshoff et al., 2016). As metal extraction in South Africa became industrialised during the early 20th century, the human impact increased. Today Postmasburg and Kathu (65 km to the north) are the site of several large-scale open-cast commercial mining operations that have undoubtedly transformed the native ecosystems.

Postmasburg's progression from a small Iron Age settlement to a commercial centre for large-scale international mining operations serves as a case study for understanding the ecological impact of mining throughout Africa. Commercial metal extraction began in early industrialised countries but has shifted to developing economies since 1950. In 2010 only 6% of all metals mined came from Europe and North America; the rest came from the developing south (Schaffartzik et al., 2016). Africa has only recently taken advantage of this shift in metal production, but it promises to be the next great mining frontier. It has 30% of the world's mineral resources, but only 5% has been exploited thus far (Edwards et al., 2014). This seems certain to change, as foreign investment in African mining is skyrocketing. This mining expansion could have devastating effects on natural ecosystems, so there is an urgent need to find ways to minimise them.

More stringent environmental regulation is the first method that governments turn to in an attempt to reduce the negative ecological effects of mining. The mines near Postmasburg serve as a case study for the effectiveness of such policies. Mining activities in this region span the periods before and after South Africa's current environmental policy was introduced. Unlike other countries where environmental policy is incrementally updated and comprises both old and new legislation, South African environmental legislation was mostly promulgated after the first democratic election in 1994 (Kidd, 2008). This makes it some of the most modern globally.

In this chapter we assess whether environmental legislation has changed the impact of mining on the Postmasburg region's ecosystems. To do this we compare the ecological impact of the Postmasburg mines established in the mid-1900s, decades before the current environmental legislation, with the impact of mines established during the early 21st century. The scope of our study did not extend to quantifying all the potential ecological impacts of the Postmasburg mines; rather, in this chapter we synthesise different impressions so as to provide an overview of the general impacts of mining on Postmasburg's ecosystems.

The ecosystems of Postmasburg

Postmasburg's ecosystems are primarily the result of its arid environment. The late-summer rainfall is erratic, varying from 250 to 450 mm a year. Coupled with extremely high temperatures (regularly exceeding 40°C), this dry climate acts as an environmental filter that determines which species can persist in the region (Lovegrove, 1993). We may imagine the current climate as the filter through which species must pass today in order to persist and historical evolution as the process that determined which species got the chance to pass through the filter in the first place (Buschke et al., 2014).

The southern Kalahari has experienced considerable climate change in recent geological history. We would not recognise the Kalahari of 300,000 years ago. Back then, what is now the Kalahari Desert formed the Makgadikgadi Paleolake System, a giant inland water body covering 66,000 km^2 (Burrough et al., 2009). This means that, unlike today, the plants and animals of the Postmasburg region were linked to the Zambezian biogeographical region in present-day Angola, Zambia and Zimbabwe by moist hospitable habitat. This is significant for two reasons: species originating near Postmasburg could expand their distribution ranges to distant territories and species with origins elsewhere could migrate into the Postmasburg region.

These two biogeographical processes are typified by the unique vegetation near Postmasburg, an area known as the Griqualand West Centre (GWC) of Endemism (Van Wyk and Smith, 2001). Certain widespread plant species that thrive in lime-rich soils are likely to have originated in the GWC and later expanded their ranges into adjacent arid ecosystems. In contrast, several other species that originated from the Zambezian or Karoo regions entered the GWC, to which their ranges are now restricted. Overall, the GWC hosts more than 40 plant species found nowhere in the world but in the roughly 450 x 220 km region around the iron-rich modern towns of Postmasburg and Kathu (Frisby et al., 2015). Moreover, the Postmasburg region – and the associated GWC – is uniquely positioned at the interface of three biogeographical regions with distinct evolutionary histories: the Zambian Region, the Southern Kalahari and the Karoo Domains. The Postmasburg environment is thus important not only for its distinctive mixture of species with very different evolutionary backgrounds, but also because it is a transition zone which may be a source of genetic intermingling and, therefore, evolutionary novelty (Smith et al., 2001).

Over the millennia, the climate varied in different areas of southern Africa (Figure 8.1). The area around present-day Postmasburg experienced notable wet and dry cycles during the late Pleistocene and Holocene epochs. By analysing fossilised pollen from the Wonderwerk cave (approximately 70 km north-east of Postmasburg), Brook et al. (2010) deduced that the area had experienced wetter conditions around the last glacial maximum (23,000 to 17,000 years ago). On either side of the transition period between the Pleistocene and the Holocene (11,000 years ago), Wonderwerk cave experienced prolonged dry periods. The past 4,000 years, however, were once again wetter than they are today. This indicates that Postmasburg is currently moving out of a wet cycle into the next dry cycle, which has implications for the possible effects of mining on the ecosystem. In a region that is naturally becoming drier, extracting ground and surface water for mining operations could hasten the onset of prolonged drought, without allowing the natural systems the thousands of years that are needed for it to adapt.

The ecological characteristics of Postmasburg and its surrounds are thus largely due to the long-term expansion of species' geographic ranges during wet spells and contraction during dry spells. The current vegetation in the region is dominated by arid savannah (Figure 8.1.b) but this has not always been the case. Dry spells after the last glacial maximum converted the region to arid Nama Karoo desert conditions (Figure 8.1.c). During wet spells the vegetation of the region would have included more grassland species (Figure 8.1.d) that could support large grazing herbivores.

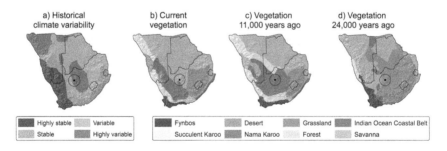

Figure 8.1 Historical climate and vegetation in southern Africa

Source: Data based on simulations by Huntley et al. (2016)

Note: Map (a) shows climate variability in southern Africa over the past 140,000 years, map (b) shows how this variability has shifted the extent of current vegetation biomes. The point is Postmasburg and the circle is a 150 km radius around the town, which includes the areas that constitute the Griqualand West centre of plant endemism.

Wet phases would increase biodiversity, but during dry phases species would persist only if they were specifically adapted to drought conditions or if they happened to occur in narrowly restricted, but climatically stable, refuge habitats. Such refuge habitats around Postmasburg include the Kuruman Hills to the east, the Asbestos Hills to the south and the Korannaberg and Langberg to the west. These mountains provide safe havens for species and thus maintain remarkably high levels of biodiversity. In the 1950s, while producing the first national vegetation map, the pioneering botanist John Acocks produced a list of 302 plant species from a single sampling locality in the Asbestos Hills – the highest number of species from any single locality during his surveys throughout the whole country (Van Wyk and Smith, 2001).

Perhaps the best example of organisms capable of withstanding extreme drought conditions is large branchiopod crustaceans (that include various types of shrimp). These creatures inhabit the temporary waters of rain-filled depressions (called 'pans' in southern Africa). Their drought-resistant eggs can remain dormant in the scorched sediment for decades. The eggs hatch after sporadic rains and the hatchlings embark on a frenzy of growth and reproduction to produce the eggs necessary for withstanding the next phase of drought. These bursts of aquatic life, which only last a few weeks, support many other species higher up the food chain (Allan et al., 1995). The pans around Postmasburg contain high numbers of different branchiopod crustaceans, higher than in much larger territories in Europe, North America or Australia (Hamer and Brendonck, 1997). This example underlines the importance of wet and dry cycles for maintaining high levels of biodiversity in this portion of the southern Kalahari. Human activity that disrupts the natural cycle will inevitably reduce species diversity.

The climate cycles of the Kalahari that produced the range expansion and contraction and the resulting biodiversity of Postmasburg are not unique to this region. Comparable historical processes account for biodiversity patterns in similarly arid parts of Australia. In Africa, range contraction and expansion also explains the biodiversity of very different ecosystems, such as the grassland-forest mosaic of northern South Africa (Breman et al., 2011), the forests of central and eastern Africa, and the Ethiopian Rift Valley lakes.

Because we know that Postmasburg's ecosystems were formed by many of the same historical processes that occurred elsewhere in Africa and the rest of world, we can confidently use Postmasburg as a generalisable case study for the way mining disturbs ecosystems. We ground the study on the notion that today's biodiversity is the result of processes occurring over thousands of years. The biodiversity of one locality, in this case Postmasburg, is due to the cyclical connection and isolation of far-flung biogeographical regions. Therefore, when we investigate possible human disturbance of an ecosystem, we must remember that the ecosystem is embedded in much wider systems across geographic space and geological time.

The ecological impacts of mining at Postmasburg

We created a conceptual diagram to clarify the effects of mining on an ecosystem, by distinguishing four types of impact (Figure 8.2). The first are the *direct impacts* caused by the mining operation, such as clearing of natural habitats, abstraction

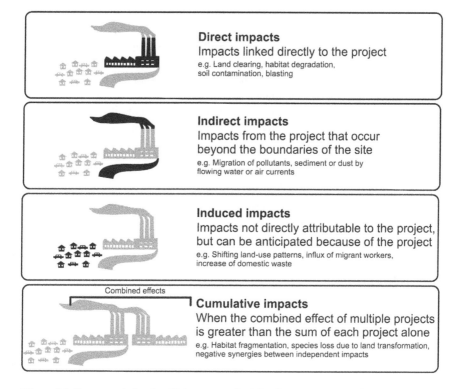

Direct impacts
Impacts linked directly to the project
e.g. Land clearing, habitat degradation,
soil contamination, blasting

Indirect impacts
Impacts from the project that occur
beyond the boundaries of the site
e.g. Migration of pollutants, sediment or dust by
flowing water or air currents

Induced impacts
Impacts not directly attributable to the project,
but can be anticipated because of the project
e.g. Shifting land-use patterns, influx of migrant workers,
increase of domestic waste

Combined effects

Cumulative impacts
When the combined effect of multiple projects
is greater than the sum of each project alone
e.g. Habitat fragmentation, species loss due to land transformation,
negative synergies between independent impacts

Figure 8.2 Framework for classifying types of mining impacts on natural ecosystems

of water, or pollution of land, air and water. The second are the *indirect impacts* – those which extend beyond the boundaries of the mining area or persist after the mine closes, such as the dispersal of pollutants by wind or water, or changes in the water level of downstream rivers. The third are the *induced impacts* – those which are not directly attributable to mining but are expected to occur in the presence of the project, such as changes in land use caused by an influx of workers. The fourth are the *cumulative impacts* – those resulting from the combined impacts of past, current or future impacts of mining. Cumulative impacts are relevant whenever the combined effect of multiple independent impacts do not scale linearly or when different impacts combine to form negative synergies (Damman et al., 1995; Brook et al., 2008; Buschke and Vanschoenwinkel, 2014). The most obvious example of this type is the cumulative loss of biodiversity caused by the initial destruction of natural habitat (He and Hubbell, 2011; Storch et al., 2012). For instance, losing the last 10% of pristine habitat is much more detrimental than losing the first 10% because of the cumulative effect of previous habitat loss.

The impact of mining on the ecosystems at Postmasburg needs to be evaluated in the light of all four types: direct, indirect, induced and cumulative. This is challenging because in many cases like this we have no data for anything other than the most obvious direct impacts (Raiter et al., 2014). Furthermore, we must compare the impacts across two periods in the history of South African environmental management. South Africa developed its commercial mining sector before the promulgation of modern environmental legislation, but during the 1990s it brought in modern and progressive environmental legislation which changed the way the mining sector was regulated.

In the following sections we look at how the impacts of mining at Postmasburg changed with the increased implementation of environmental regulation in South Africa.

The early mines at Postmasburg

Most of Postmasburg's mines today extract iron ore, but one the region's oldest mines, Beeshoek, 7 km west of Postmasburg, was established during the 1930s to extract manganese (Thomaz, 2005). The mine closed during World War II, after which the potential for iron ore extraction was realised. Iron excavation began officially in 1964 after several years of mineral exploration. Mine properties (also called 'leases') generally align with earlier farm boundaries, but the actual excavation footprint is usually made up of a number of smaller areas of operations around the richest ore deposits. This footprint provides a good approximation of the direct impacts of the mining operations on soil, water, air and biodiversity and can be seen from aerial photography (Google Earth Engine Team, 2015) and satellite-derived land-cover data (GeoterraImage, 2015). The iron is mined using open-cast methods, so the direct impacts of mining operations are visible as open scars on the landscape. Today the Beeshoek mine's footprint covers approximately 700 hectares of Kuruman Thornveld and Kuruman Mountain Bushveld. Currently the two savannah vegetation types affected remain largely intact and are considered of low conservation priority (Mucina and Rutherford, 2006).

The direct impact of Sishen mine, 65 km north of Postmasburg, is much bigger than that of Beeshoek when measured as the extent of the mining footprint (Figure 8.3). Sishen mine, founded in 1953 (Taylor et al., 1988), also extracts iron through open-cast methods over an operational footprint of approximately 8,400 hectares of Kuruman Mountain Bushveld, Kuruman Thornveld and Kathu Bushveld, none of which occur elsewhere in formally protected areas. Two additional mines were later founded to the east of Postmasburg: Finsch diamond mine near the village of Lime Acres in 1967 and Indwala lime quarry near Danielskuil in 1975. The entire operation footprint of the diamond mine covers approximately 2,500 hectares of Kuruman Mountain Bushveld and Olifantshoek Plains Thornveld. The lime quarry has a footprint of roughly 475 hectares of Ghaap Plateau Vaalbosveld and Kuruman Thornveld.

All these mines will have increased their size since their first excavations, but it is doubtful that the first miners would have anticipated exactly how they would expand. And even with a clear plan in mind, it is unlikely that they could have anticipated subsequent changes in the mining sector. The expansion of these mines

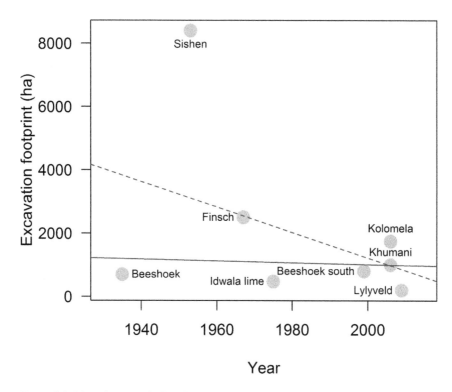

Figure 8.3 Direct impact of mines in Postmasburg region

Note: Dashed line indicates trend in excavation footprint (as estimated from aerial photography and satellite-derived land-cover data) over time when including Sishen mine in the linear regression; solid line indicates trend in excavation footprint over time when excluding Sishen mine. Neither line shows a statistically significant trend (*including Sishen*: slope = -40.16, P = 0.31, R^2 = 0.17; *excluding Sishen*: slope = -2.87, P = 0.83, R^2 = 0.01).

was partly due to improvements in mining technologies. Sishen mine, for instance, benefited from improvements in the explosives used for blasting and the installation of an in-pit crusher (Taylor et al., 1988). These made it possible for the mine to extract more ore at lower costs, which undoubtedly contributed to the growth of the mine. It is unlikely that the expanding mines at Postmasburg would have been much hindered by resistance from the state, especially not because of environmental concerns.

While South Africa had many pieces of legislation that applied to the environment, this legislation differed fundamentally from modern environmental legislation. Early laws were aimed at preserving natural resources so they would remain in a good enough state to be exploited. For example, the South African Water Act of 1956 included provisions for minimising pollution and conserving water, but the underlying purpose was to provide clean resources to agriculture and industry (Kidd, 2008). The integrity of ecosystems was not a priority at the time. Similarly, the notion of 'biodiversity' would have been foreign to the early miners at Postmasburg because the term only gained prominence decades later, during the 1980s (Noss, 1990; Lautenschlager, 1997). Back then, most regulations were aimed more at maintaining grazing lands than preserving biodiversity, and so would have focused on livestock numbers, the ownership and hunting of game and preventing soil erosion (Beinart, 2003).

The early mines at Postmasburg would have had indirect impacts similar to those of modern mines. However, it is not always possible to verify this because they were not required to monitor these impacts. Such impacts would have included the production of dust that could compromise air quality downwind of mining operations or pollutants that could affect downstream water quality in rivers. Rivers near Postmasburg would not experience major indirect impacts because they do not have perennially flowing waters, and open-cast mining is less likely to cause water pollution than other mining methods (coal mining being one notable exception) (Wells et al., 1992). Of more concern would be the lowering of the water-table due to the extraction of ground water, but we may assume that modern mines extract less ground water than the early mines because they have more efficient technologies. Taylor et al. (1988) stated that Sishen mine was situated in a region rich in ground water reserves. Water had to be pumped from the pit at a rate of 1,500 m^3 per hour to drain it for mining, which according to Taylor et al. (1988), is sufficient to meet the mine's water requirements.

It is difficult to speculate on the induced impacts of the early Postmasburg mines because we cannot distinguish them from the induced impacts of other developments, or from the induced impacts of modern mines. The early mines would probably have had much less induced impact than modern mines because the living standards of migrant labourers in those days were much lower. Affluence and improved lifestyles typically worsen environmental impacts (Rosa et al., 2004). Nevertheless, the early mines are still operational today, with all the induced impacts caused by changes in the demographics and infrastructure of the town itself. So, even though the induced impacts of the early mines will have increased less rapidly than those of their modern equivalents, it can be assumed that today they are at least equivalent to those of newer mines.

We face similar difficulties in evaluating the cumulative impacts of early mining at Postmasburg. While their early impacts would have been small, these mines are still operational and contribute to the cumulative impacts of the whole mining sector today.

A transformed industry

Early legislation, as noted above, applied to the environment only indirectly, treating it as a source for human consumption. Global change came in the early 1970s when environmental issues began attracting political and legislative attention. The National Environmental Policy Act was promulgated in the United States in 1970 and this was followed by the Stockholm Conference on the Human Environment in 1972 (Kidd, 2008). The Conference produced a first general text on environmental law and laid the foundations for future global environmental commitments stemming from the United Nations Environmental Programme (UNEP).

Since South Africa was facing its own political challenges at the time, it was only after the first democratic elections in 1994 that the current environmental policy began to take shape. This new policy fundamentally changed the political and legal standing of ecosystems and occasioned major changes in mining procedures at Postmasburg. The most significant of the new policies was Section 24 of Chapter 2 of the National Constitution (Act 108 of 1996), which established the basic right to a clean environment. While this does not grant the environment the intrinsic right to be preserved (as is the case in Ecuador and Bolivia: Humphreys, 2017), it does oblige the state to prevent environmental degradation because citizens have the right to an environment that is not polluted and ecologically degraded. This basic right was the foundation for the National Environmental Management Act 107 of 1998, which outlined the national environmental management principles that guide all other environmental policy in South Africa.

The *Mining and Biodiversity Guideline* issued by the Department of Environmental Affairs and other departments (2013) is a summary document intended to improve environmental compliance by integrating all the biodiversity-related legislation for the mining sector. It lists six principles that mines should be guided by in South Africa. The first is to apply the law. This places the onus on mines to uphold the rights of South African citizens to a clean environment. The second is to use the best available scientific data when assessing how mining will affect ecosystems. This is likely to include the commissioning of baseline surveys by suitably qualified specialists. The third is not to act without engaging with all interested and affected stakeholders. Since citizens have the constitutional right to a clean environment, it goes without saying that they should weigh in on whether mining compromises that right. The fourth is to do an environmental impact assessment (EIA) as part of the application for mining rights. The EIA obliges mines to identify, assess and evaluate all the impacts, both positive and negative, of their activities. The fifth is to apply the 'mitigation hierarchy' (Figure 8.4) when planning mining activities and developing an environmental management programme. This hierarchy helps to evaluate all the impacts identified during the EIA in order to reduce the total impacts of operations. Impacts must be *avoided* wherever possible. If they cannot be avoided they must be *minimised*. If they cannot be avoided or minimised they must be *remediated* after operations and, failing that, they must be *offset*. Remediation is often referred to as either 'restoration' or 'rehabilitation', but Bull et al. (2016) prefer the latter term, as it avoids conflating this stage of the mitigation hierarchy with offsetting. Offsetting is controversial – it requires that the impacts of operations at one locality be compensated by an equivalent improvement elsewhere (either by rehabilitating previously degraded ecosystems or by preventing their imminent destruction). The sixth principle is to ensure that the environmental management programme is implemented effectively and that mining operations proceed as planned.

These new legal and operational considerations have changed the way mines at Postmasburg function. They have ensured that ecosystems are considered during

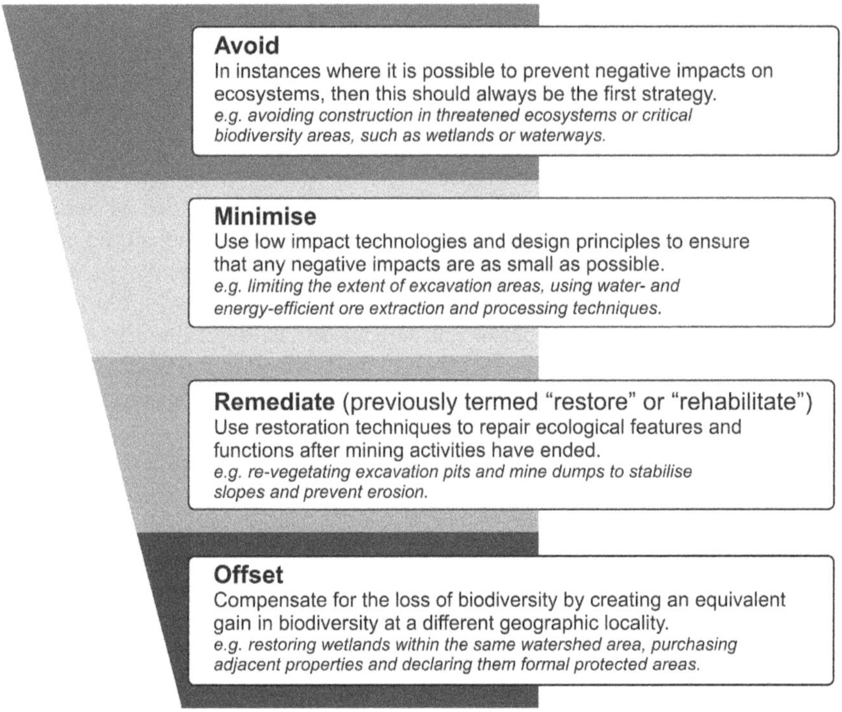

Figure 8.4 Mitigation hierarchy for managing impacts of mining on natural ecosystems
Source: Modified from Department of Environmental Affairs et al. (2013)

all phases of mine development. However, this does not necessarily mean that the impacts on the ecosystems are being reduced. Instead, it is entirely possible that the environmental trade-offs of mining are unavoidable. The following section discusses whether the Postmasburg mining operations initiated during the period of stringent environmental regulation have, in fact, reduced their impacts on ecosystems.

Modern mining at Postmasburg

Four modern mines were developed in the Postmasburg area after the promulgation of modern environmental regulation in South Africa. Unlike the older mines, these four new mines had to apply for environmental authorisation following the six guiding principles described above. The first of these was an extension of the Beeshoek mine in 1999, known as Beeshoek South, whose operation footprint covers roughly 800 hectares of Postmasburg Thornveld, Kuruman Thornveld and Kuruman Mountain Bushveld. In 2006 two new iron mines were established: the Kolomela mine immediately to the west of Postmasburg, with a 1,750 hectare operation footprint in in Postmasburg Thornveld, and the Khumani mine to the south-west of Sishen mine, with a 1,000 hectare operation footprint in Kuruman Thornveld. The fourth new mine was a small extension to Sishen mine in 2009 on the farm formerly called Lylyveld, which now has an operation footprint of approximately 200 hectares in Kuruman Mountain Bushveld and Kuruman Thornveld. The direct impacts of these new mines, as estimated from their footprints, are comparable to those of the older mines, with the obvious exception of the giant Sishen mine (see Figure 8.3).

We found little evidence that modern environmental policy has reduced the direct impacts of the mines near Postmasburg. Some might argue that this is symptomatic of environmental policies that are insufficiently stringent and ambitious (Child, 2009; Noss et al., 2012). However, before drawing conclusions about the effectiveness of the new policies, we must consider three points.

Firstly, there is a 'survivorship bias' (Shermer, 2014) that complicates simple comparisons. Newly formed mines are a subset of all the mines that could have received environmental authorisation and the rights to mine. Although it is very rare for the state to reject mining applications, we cannot know how many potential mines never even reached the application stage because the likelihood of receiving rights was too small to warrant the costly EIA process. So we have no evidence of the 'missing' mines that environmental legislation has prevented or how much direct impact they might have had.

Secondly, environmental regulation could minimise direct impacts if mines simply adhered to the mitigation hierarchy. For instance, new mines visible from aerial photographs are the consequences of several iterations of planning and design to avoid and minimise direct environmental impacts. Moreover, the financial costs involved in meeting the mining licence conditions for remediation mean that companies have an incentive to keep their direct impacts to a bare minimum.

Thirdly, environmental policy plays an important role in ensuring that mines adhere to their original plans. Unlike Sishen mine, which grew in unpredictable ways because of technological advances, new mines must stick to their original strategy in order to comply with the conditions of their mining licence. Although modern legislation has not reduced the *realised* direct impacts of mines, it has probably reduced the *potential* direct impacts by preventing the establishment of unsustainable mines, minimising the impact of mining activities and discouraging the haphazard expansion of operations.

Current environmental regulations place much stricter emphasis on the management of indirect impacts than was previously the case. Mines are now required to monitor specific ecological variables that might be affected by their operations. In most cases, the results from biological monitoring (termed 'biomonitoring') are kept in internal reports by the mining companies. Such reports are not publicised, but are available to state authorities for auditing purposes or to members of the public who request this information under the Promotion of Access to Information Act 2 of 2000. In rare instances, however, the findings from the mine's biomonitoring reports are published in scientific journals.

For instance, Buschke et al. (2012) reported on the invertebrates in temporary pans on the Kolomela mine property. Their study included data that preceded the construction of the mine as well as data collected after the mine had been operational for several years. In this instance, the mine owners had been specifically concerned that dust deposition and ground water extraction would jeopardise the integrity of the aquatic ecosystems, but the authors found no conclusive evidence that this had occurred between 2002 and 2011. This did not, however, completely absolve Kolomela mine from responsibility for any indirect impacts because the effects of such impacts might only materialise after decades. Like many of the ecosystems near Postmasburg, pan ecosystems are the result of processes occurring at much longer time-scales than the mere decade of monitoring data. Only time will tell whether the fragmentation of pan ecosystems by mining activities will result in any long-term damage.

It is unlikely that modern environmental policies affect the induced impacts of the mines at Postmasburg. Put simply, induced impacts fall beyond the mines' sphere of influence and are unlikely to be embedded in the decision-making process. That being said, stakeholder engagement as part of the EIA process might bring to light some concerns about induced impacts. For example, the management of Kolomela holds ongoing focus group discussions with local communities to identify perceived impacts induced by the mine (Kumba, 2014). Although public concern can affect the decision to award mining rights, it is unlikely that mines are held responsible for induced impacts as a condition of their mining licence. It is more likely that they manage these impacts voluntarily to maintain their reputation and preserve their unofficial social licence to operate (UNEP Finance Initiative, 2010).

There is no doubt that the cumulative impacts of modern mines exceed those of older mining operations. This is simply because the impacts of the new mines are in addition to the pioneering operations. Even if the amount of habitat loss caused by modern mines is no larger than that caused by their predecessors, the cumulative effect of the loss is now much higher. Whether late-comers should be held solely responsible for these cumulative impacts, however, remains to be determined; doing so could create perverse incentives (Buschke and Vanschoenwinkel, 2014). For example, developers might flood into pristine areas to avoid being held responsible for cumulative impacts and in so doing create a gold-rush of sorts. This has yet to happen at Postmasburg, probably because environmental authorisation has mostly been handled case by case (Kiesecker et al., 2010) and few, if any, decisions have been made on the basis of future cumulative impacts.

The limits of the possible

The full impact of mining on the ecosystems of Postmasburg will only be realised once operations are ended and the mines are closed. The mitigation hierarchy requires that all impacts that cannot be avoided or minimised must be remediated or offset. Since all of the mines near Postmasburg are still operational, it remains to be seen whether it is even possible to remediate or offset the remaining impacts.

Remediation is a contentious topic among ecologists, who question its real-world feasibility (Zaloumis and Bond, 2011). It is plain that the ecosystems at Postmasburg are the result of the historical wet and dry cycles that periodically connected this region to distant biogeographical regions and then isolated it. We might wonder how it is possible for a system that evolved over tens of thousands of years to be destroyed and then recreated within a single century. Liebenberg et al. (2013) reviewed the outcomes of rehabilitation efforts at Sishen mine, but only quantified vegetation cover as a proxy for rehabilitation success. Recreating vegetation cover is a much more attainable target than re-establishing the natural species composition of the plant community (Lubke et al., 1996; Prober and Thiele, 2005). Liebenberg and colleagues (2013) found that it is possible to re-establish vegetation cover, but their findings do not imply that the natural functioning of ecosystems could be regained. For instance, their study showed that the tailing materials of abandoned mine sites could not support plant growth and had to be enriched with organic material to form a microbe-rich growth medium. Remediation sites also needed to be on gentle slopes and topsoil had to be reshaped to withstand erosion. While it is important to acknowledge these efforts, we must not overlook the fact that most remediation is unlikely to return ecosystems to pre-mining conditions.

Added to the difficulties of habitat remediation is the propensity of large mining companies to sell off their operations to smaller companies once the ore has been almost depleted (CEJ, 2015). This means the purchasing company carries the liability for post-closure mine remediation. However, these smaller companies are prone to going insolvent shortly after the transfer and rarely have the capacity to meet their remediation obligations. In such instances, the areas damaged by mining are never rehabilitated.

One of the biggest mining companies operating in Postmasburg, Anglo American, made headlines in early 2016 for possibly transferring responsibility in this way (Crotty, 2016). Concerned about the struggling commodity markets, Anglo American signalled its intention to sell off its stake in Kumba Iron Ore, the subsidiary company that owns some of Postmasburg's largest iron mines. However, the Centre for Environmental Rights (CER), a non-profit company focusing on environmental justice, has requested that Anglo American publicise all information on the sale of its mining assets (Crotty, 2016). The CER argues that this increased transparency – as required under the 2015 regulations for financial provision for prospecting, exploration, mining or production operations published under the National Environmental Management Act – will prevent future instances of improper transfer of rehabilitation obligations.

Even if mines are kept accountable for remediating their impacts, there will inevitably be some damage that just cannot be repaired. The mitigation hierarchy requires that impacts be offset, but it is doubtful that this will happen. One obstacle is that South Africa has yet to publish a national biodiversity offset strategy, despite various versions being drafted since 2012. There is therefore no overarching policy to guide biodiversity offsets in South Africa. Unless mines choose to implement offsets voluntarily, it seems that lasting impacts on ecosystems will remain unmitigated. Another obstacle is that biodiversity offsetting as a mitigation strategy has developed only in the past 10 to 15 years, which is troubling because these new strategies cannot be applied to the older Postmasburg mines. Successful biodiversity offsets need to be integrated into the design of the mine at the beginning and form part of the environmental authorisation process (Gardner et al., 2013; Bull et al., 2013). It is challenging to offset impacts retrospectively because of the difficulty of establishing the type and quantity of historical biodiversity loss. Moreover, offsets require large amounts of money to ensure lasting outcomes, so unless companies make early financial provisions for offsets (by, for instance, establishing trust funds), the offsets are unlikely to succeed (Jenner and Balmforth, 2015).

Overall, many ecosystem impacts from the mines near Postmasburg will remain unmitigated. While the mitigation hierarchy seems promising on paper, rehabilitation and offsetting are unlikely to deliver the results as promised, and the ecosystems will suffer. Considering the millennia it took for Postmasburg's ecosystems to evolve, it is likely that the scars of the mining industry will remain on the landscape for centuries to come.

Conclusion

The recent history of Postmasburg is inextricably linked to the mining sector. The extraction of metals and minerals has shaped the local landscape. Before mining, however, the ecosystems in the region were fashioned by thousands of years of climate cycles to form the present-day arid environment. All the plants and animals of Postmasburg share the common feature of being adapted to dry conditions, but the evolutionary pathways that led to this point are as varied as the species themselves. Some evolved locally while others migrated from as far away as Zambia or Zimbabwe. Some species found safety in stable climate refuge habitats and some adopted intricate strategies to withstand harsh droughts.

Mining has caused arguably the fastest changes to Postmasburg ecosystems. Natural landscape-scale pressures, which materialised over thousands of years, have been replaced by human-induced impacts that show up within decades. These impacts are wide-ranging and vary from direct impacts such as land transformation to the less obvious impacts induced by, for example, migrant workers' lifestyle changes. More significantly, the mining sector has changed since its beginnings in the mid-20th century. Environmental awareness has blossomed since the early years of mining and this has brought a proliferation of laws and regulations aimed at limiting the negative impacts. While environmental legislation has changed the way mines operate, it is difficult to quantify accurately how much it has actually minimised the impacts of these operations. It seems that modern mines, developed after the birth of modern legislation, cause damage similar to that of their older equivalents. The scars of open-cast mining are as obvious today as they were 50 years ago. What is certain, however, is that modern environmental legislation has effectively prevented much thoughtless destruction of ecosystems. While this alone is insufficient to minimise the negative effects of mining, it does make it easier for us to see the trade-offs that must be made when excavating metals and minerals. Ultimately, it is these trade-offs that will determine the future of Postmasburg and the surrounding ecosystems. Our paper did only assess the mining impacts. But, the impact of mining extends mining operations and includes the settlement of people. Future research should consider this element as well.

Note

1 South Africa has three of the world's 35 biodiversity hotspots: the Cape Floristic Region, the Succulent Karoo and Maputaland-Pondoland-Albany.

References

Allan, D.G., Seaman, M.T. and Kaletja, B., 1995. The endorheic pans of South Africa. In: G.I. Cowen, ed. *Wetlands of South Africa*. Pretoria: Department of Environmental Affairs and Tourism, pp. 75–101.

Beinart, W., 2003. *The Rise of Conservation in South Africa: Settlers, Livestock, and the Environment 1770–1950*. Oxford: Oxford University Press.

Boshoff, A., Landman, M. and Kerley, G., 2016. Filling the gaps on the maps: Historical distribution patterns of some larger mammals in parts of Southern Africa. *Transactions of the Royal Society of South Africa*, 71, pp. 23–87.

Breman, E., Gillson, L. and Willis, K., 2011. How fire and climate shaped grass-dominated vegetation and forest mosaics in northern South Africa during past millennia. *The Holocene*, 22, pp. 1427–1439.

Brook, B.W., Sodhi, N.S. and Bradshaw, C.J.A., 2008. Synergies among extinction drivers under global change. *Trends in Ecology and Evolution*, 23, pp. 453–460.

Brook, G.A., Scott, L., Railsback, L.B. and Goddard, E.A., 2010. A 35 km pollen and isotope record of environmental change along the southern margin of the Kalahari from a stalagmite and animal dung deposits in the Wonderwerk Cave, South Africa. *Journal of Arid Environments*, 74, pp. 870–884.

Bull, J.W., Gordon, A., Watson, J.E.M. and Maron, M., 2016. Seeking convergence on the key concepts in 'no net loss' policy. *Journal of Applied Ecology*, 53(6), pp. 1686–1693.

Bull, J.W., Suttle, K.B., Gordon, A., Singh, N.J. and Miner-Gulland, E.J., 2013. Biodiversity offsets in theory and practice. *Oryx*, 47, pp. 369–380.

Burrough, S.L., Thomas, D.S.G. and Bailey, R.M., 2009. Mega-lake in the Kalahari: A late Pleistocene record of the Palaeolake Makgadikgadi system. *Quaternary Science Reviews*, 28, pp. 1392–1411.

Buschke, F.T., Adendorff, J., Lamprechts, J., Watson, M. and Seaman, M.T., 2012. Invertebrates or iron: Does large-scale opencast mining impact invertebrate diversity in ephemeral wetlands? *African Zoology*, 47, pp. 245–254.

Buschke, F.T., Brendonck, L. and Vanschoenwinkel, B., 2014. Differences between the regional and biogeographical species pools highlight the need for multi-scale theories in macroecology. *Frontiers of Biogeography*, 6, pp. 173–184.

Buschke, F.T. and Vanschoenwinkel, B., 2014. Mechanisms for the inclusion of cumulative impacts in conservation decision-making are sensitive to vulnerability and irreplaceability in a stochastically simulated landscape. *Journal of Nature Conservation*, 22, pp. 265–271.

CEJ (Centre for Environmental Justice), 2015. *Full Disclosure: The Truth about Corporate Environmental Compliance in South Africa*. Cape Town: CEJ.

Child, M.F., 2009. The Thoreau ideal as a unifying thread in the conservation movement. *Conservation Biology*, 23, pp. 241–243.

Crotty, A., 2016. Green lobby group warns Anglo on culling. *Business Times*, 10 April 2016, p. 13.

Damman, D.C., Cressman, D.R. and Sadar, M.H., 1995. Cumulative effects assessment: The development of a practical framework. *Impact Assessment*, 13, pp. 433–454.

Department of Environmental Affairs, Department of Mineral Resources, Chamber of Mines, South African Mining and Biodiversity Forum and South African National Biodiversity Institute, 2013. *Mining and Biodiversity Guideline: Mainstreaming Biodiversity into the Mining Sector*. Pretoria: South African National Biodiversity Institute.

Edwards, D.P., Sloan, S., Weng, L., Dirks, P., Sayer, J. and Laurence, W.F., 2014. Mining and the African environment. *Conservation Letters*, 7, pp. 302–311.

Frisby, A.W., Siebert, S.J., Cilliers, D. and van Wyk, A.E., 2015. Redefining the Griqualand West Centre of plant endemism. *South African Journal of Botany*, 98, p. 178.

Gardner, T.A., Von Hase, A., Brownlie, S., Ekstrom, J.M.M., Pilgrim, J.D., Savy, C.E., Stephens, R.T.T., Treweek, J., Ussher, G.T., Ward, G. and Ten Kate, K., 2013. Biodiversity offsets and the challenge of achieving no net loss. *Conservation Biology*, 27, pp. 1254–1264.

GeoterraImage, 2015. *2013–2014 South African National Land-Cover Dataset. Data User Report and Metadata*. A commercial data product created by GeoterraImage, South Africa.

Google Earth Engine Team, 2015. *Google Earth Engine: A Planetary-Scale Geo-Spatial Analysis Platform*. https://earthengine.google.com.

Hamer, M.L. and Brendonck, L., 1997. Distribution, diversity and conservation of Anostraca (Crustacea: Branchiopoda) in Southern Africa. *Hydrobiologia*, 359, pp. 1–12.

He, F. and Hubbell, S.P., 2011. Species-area relationships always overestimate extinction rates from habitat loss. *Nature*, 473, pp. 368–371.

Humphreys, A.J.B., 1976. Note on the southern limits of Iron Age settlement in the Northern Cape. *South African Archaeological Bulletin*, 31, pp. 54–57.

Humphreys, D., 2017. Rights of Pachamama: The emergence of an earth jurisprudence in the Americas. *Journal of International Relations and Development*, 20, 459–484.

Huntley, B., Collingham, Y.C., Singarayer, J.S., Valdes, P.J., Barnard, P., Midgley, G.F., Altwegg, R. and Ohlemüller, R., 2016. Explaining patterns of avian diversity and endemicity: Climate and biomes of southern Africa over the last 140,000 years. *Journal of Biogeography*, 43, pp. 874–886.

Jenner, N. and Balmforth, Z., 2015. *Biodiversity Offsets: Lessons Learnt from Policy and Practice. Country Summary Report: South Africa*. Business and Biodiversity Programme, Fauna and Flora International.

Kidd, M., 2008. *Environmental Law*. Cape Town: Juta.

Kiesecker, J.M., Copeland, H., Pocewicz, A. and McKenney, B., 2010. Development by design: Blending landscape-level planning with the mitigation hierarchy. *Frontiers in Ecology and the Environment*, 8, pp. 261–266.

Kumba (Kumba Iron Ore), 2014. *Kolomela Mine SEAT Report 2014*. Anglo American PLC. www.angloamericankumba.com/~/media/Files/A/Anglo-American-Kumba/documents/kumba-socio-economic-assesment-tool-report.pdf.

Lautenschlager, R.A., 1997. Biodiversity is dead. *Wildlife Society Bulletin*, 25, pp. 679–685.

Liebenberg, D., Claassens, S. and Van Rensburg, L., 2013. Insights and lessons learned from the long-term rehabilitation of an iron ore mine. *International Journal for Environmental Research*, 7, pp. 633–644.

Lovegrove, B., 1993. *The Living Deserts of Southern Africa.* Cape Town: Fernwood.

Lubke, R.A., Avis, A.M. and Moll, J.B., 1996. Post-mining rehabilitation of coastal sand dunes in Zululand South Africa. *Landscape and Urban Planning*, 34, pp. 335–345.

Mucina, L. and Rutherford, M.C. (eds.), 2006. *Strelitzia 19: The Vegetation of South Africa, Lesotho and Swaziland.* (2 CD set). Pretoria: South African National Biodiversity Institute.

Noss, R.F., 1990. Indicators for monitoring biodiversity: A hierarchical approach. *Conservation Biology*, 4, pp. 355–364.

Noss, R.F., Dobson, A.P., Baldwin, R., Beier, P., Davis, C.R., Dellasala, D.A., Francis, J., Locke, H., Nowak, K., Lopez, R., Reining, C., Trombulak, S.C. and Tabor, G., 2012. Bolder thinking for conservation. *Conservation Biology*, 26, pp. 1–4.

Prober, S.M. and Thiele, K.R., 2005. Restoring Australia's temperate grasslands and grassy woodlands: Integrating function and diversity. *Ecological Management and Restoration*, 6, pp. 16–27.

Raiter, K.G., Possingham, H.P., Prober, S.M. and Hobbs, R.J., 2014. Under the radar: Mitigating enigmatic ecological impacts. *Trends in Ecology and Evolution*, 29, pp. 635–644.

Rosa, E.A., York, R. and Dietz, T., 2004. Tracking the anthropogenic drivers of ecological impacts. *Ambio*, 33, pp. 509–512.

Schaffartzik, A., Mayer, A., Eisenmenger, N. and Krausmnn, F., 2016. Global patterns of metal extractivism, 1950–2010: Providing the bones for the industrial society's skeleton. *Ecological Economics*, 122, pp. 101–110.

Shermer, M., 2014. Surviving statistics. *Scientific American*, 311, pp. 94–96.

Smith, T.B., Kark, S., Schneider, C.J., Wayne, R.K. and Moritz, C., 2001. Biodiversity hotspots and beyond: The need for preserving environmental transitions. *Trends in Ecology and Evolution*, 16, p. 431.

Storch, D., Keil, P. and Jetz, W., 2012. Universal species-area and endemics-area relationships at continental scales. *Nature*, 78, pp. 78–81.

Taylor, D.J.C., Page, D.C. and Geldenhuys, P., 1988. Iron and steel in South Africa. *Journal of the South African Institute for Minerals and Metallurgy*, 88, pp. 73–95.

Thomaz, C., 2005. Beeshoek iron-ore mine, South Africa. *Mining Weekly*, 5 August 2005. www.miningweekly.com/article/beeshoek-ironore-mine-2005-08-05 (accessed 10 May 2016).

UNEP (United Nations Environmental Programme) Finance Initiative, 2010. *Demystifying Materiality: Hardwiring Biodiversity and Ecosystem Service into Finance.* CEO Briefing. UNEP FI, Geneva.

Van Wyk, A.E. and Smith, G.F., 2001. *Regions of Floristic Endemism in South Africa: A Review with Emphasis on Succulents.* Pretoria: Umdaus Press.

Wells, J.D., Van Meurs, L.H. and Rabie, M.A., 1992. Terrestrial minerals. In: R.F. Fuggle and M.A. Rabie, eds. *Environmental Management in South Africa.* Juta: Cape Town, pp. 112–132.

Zaloumis, N.P. and Bond, W.J., 2011. Grassland restoration after afforestation: No direction home? *Austral Ecology*, 36, pp. 357–366.

Section C

To rent or to own?

Many mining towns were originally developed as company towns. Mineworkers rented their houses from the mining companies. The rentals were usually low and often subsidised by the company. By the mid-1980s the mining companies had started to privatise the houses, offering homeownership to their employees and thus saving themselves the long-term costs. The resource slump of the 1980s and the rise of multinational mining companies made it important to focus on core business practices. Shareholders were not keen to continue being responsible for peripheral expenses such as employee housing. But privatised housing is a risk for the employees in periods of mining busts – losing one's job on the mine while still paying a mortgage could be disastrous. A bust would mean market conditions unconducive to selling a house. Owning an unsaleable property could leave a household 'locked into' a mining town with minimal economic prospects.

Fly-in-fly-out arrangements in Australia have mitigated the adverse effects of mining decline or closure. Changing labour regimes have been the main driver of this system, but it has had the effect of reducing household dependence on mining towns. Mineworkers in Australia live mostly in temporary rental accommodation at the mine while owning a house in a large town or city. Fly-in-fly-out is a kind of migrant labour system, though differing from the South African system in not originating in a racial agenda and not being designed for low-income mineworkers. A growing body of literature notes the unintended consequences of Australia's fly-in-fly-out arrangements, such as the very poor housing conditions, but the system itself is unlikely to change because it has the advantage of reducing place attachment at the mine and setting up only temporary settlements.

South Africa's post-apartheid government inherited a mining industry in which black mineworkers had to live in high-density mining compounds (multi-storey buildings with many people per room), while white mineworkers usually had decent low-density housing close to the mine. The mid-1980s saw the first attempts at providing homeownership to black mineworkers in South Africa. But the mining busts at the end of the 1980s made this difficult. Mine closure in the Free State Goldfields, for example, soon put an end to these attempts. By the mid-1990s, living-out allowances had become common for mineworkers. Those who preferred not to live in the compounds could use the allowance to find accommodation elsewhere. We note that there is a dearth of research on this topic. The living-out allowance did not necessarily improve mineworkers' housing conditions; rather, it served to increase the number of mineworkers living in informal housing around the mine.

Overcoming the legacy of apartheid has not been easy. Early policy proposals recommended the dismantling of the derelict and overcrowded compounds, and they were demolished at many mines. Elsewhere they were transformed to provide more congenial rental accommodation (for example, single occupation of rooms). New policies introduced in the mid-1980s began emphasising homeownership for mineworkers at the mine's location. This is in direct contrast to Australian policy and to mining company policy across the globe. Since 2002 the various versions of the Mining Charter have advocated this form of homeownership in mining settlements. This emphasis on ownership was taken further in the Strategy for the Revitalisation of Distressed Mining Towns. This strategy, a direct consequence of the 2012 Marikana massacre, proposed that the problem of poor living conditions in mining areas should be solved by means of homeownership, the assumption being that ownership would bring about stability. The overemphasis on ownership – as opposed to rental housing – is being challenged in the most recent literature. Homeownership has the potential drawback of locking mine employees into locations where long-term economic prospects are dim. In contrast to countries like Australia, South Africa has opted for policies that will encourage permanent settlement in mining areas.

The two main mining companies in Postmasburg have opted for different housing options. Most of the housing provided by Kumba is owned by the company and the employees pay low rentals. There is, however, talk of privatising the housing to Kumba employees. Assmang has opted for an alternative homeownership model in which the property is transferred only once the house has been fully paid for. On this topic the two chapters in this section take opposite views. Chapter 9 (*Mineworker housing*) argues that rental housing is the answer in mining towns. It first assesses the current types of mineworker housing. Two factors, the end of apartheid and increased mechanisation on the mines, have given mineworkers options other than the compounds. The authors assess the effects of the policies of Postmasburg's two main mining companies. They compare the characteristics of contract-worker housing with those of the housing of the town's original inhabitants. Their conclusion is that ownership leads to increased levels of housing satisfaction, but that rental housing reduces the long-term risks associated with mining busts. Promoting ownership can also be seen as the companies' way of shifting their risks to their employees. Chapter 10 (*The Khumani approach to homeownership in Postmasburg*) argues for the benefits of homeownership through an alternative tenure arrangement, based on an instalment sale agreement that ultimately results in ownership. In this model, the mining company actively engages in the development of bulk infrastructure, servicing of stands, construction of houses and facilitation of developer and end-user finance. The approach mimics the conventional registered title and mortgage-bond finance prevalent in South Africa. It both demonstrates and pilots a way of sharing the risks between the company and the employees and adds a further nuance to the complexity of providing mineworker housing.

9   Mineworker housing

Jan Cloete and Stuart Denoon-Stevens

Searching for an appropriate response to mine housing

Early writings on mineworker housing were largely about how inhumane the system was. The system of high-density male compounds that supported the apartheid government's migrant labour system and the mining companies' security is well known. By the late 1980s and early 1990s, a body of research had started considering the potential risks of homeownership for mineworkers and the future of the compound (hostel-style housing for mining companies' black employees) in a post-apartheid environment (Crush, 1989, 1992, 1994; Crush and James, 1991). The early post-apartheid period saw less research interest in mine housing, and post-apartheid policy aimed to phase out the compound system. Unions and mining companies found common ground in promoting living-out allowances, as a means of privatising housing. It was not until the mid-2000s that researchers began to question these allowances. They argued that in many cases the allowances resulted in very poor living conditions for mineworkers and that homeownership was not the ideal form of housing provision for mining settlements (Marais and Venter, 2006; Cloete et al., 2009). In 2012 the Marikana massacre dramatically brought the mineworkers' poor living conditions to the fore. International research (see Chapter 2 of this volume) has shown that the mining booms of the 2000s were also responsible for the poor housing conditions and created potential inequalities between mineworkers and non-mineworkers.

Despite the readily available research findings, government programmes have continued to emphasise ownership models for mining towns (see Chapter 10 of this volume). The initial 2004 guidelines provided by the Mining Charter emphasised balanced approaches to tenure, whereas the more recent guidelines (2010 and 2016) have explicitly emphasised homeownership (DMR, 2004, 2010, 2016). The Strategy for the Revitalisation of Distressed Mining Towns of 2012 builds on the same sentiments (see Tshangana, 2015). However, problems associated with homeownership and concerns about locking people into specific locations after mine closure have been noted in the literature (for example, Marais, 2013). And it has been argued that, ironically, the compound system has eased the problems of mine downscaling in, for example, the Free State Goldfields (Marais and Cloete, 2013). Essentially, it was easier to bulldoze a dysfunctional compound than large numbers of family houses.

In this chapter we look at housing conditions for mineworkers in Postmasburg and the risks associated with the various approaches to mineworker housing. We evaluate the extent to which housing conditions and migration trends are interlinked and we compare company policies, housing conditions, and tenure and housing investments for mineworkers, contract mineworkers and the original inhabitants of Postmasburg. We argue that the open-pit mining system, by paying relatively high salaries, reduces the housing inequalities between different categories of mineworker that are so evident in gold and platinum mining towns. However, new inequalities between mineworkers and contract mineworkers,[1] on the one hand, and the original inhabitants and new mineworkers on the other, cannot be ignored, as Postmasburg has seen substantial increases in informal housing over the past 15 years. Finally, we question the appropriateness of the ownership housing models as applied in Postmasburg.

History of mine housing in South Africa

From the late 1800s to the demise of apartheid in 1994, South Africa had two types of mineworker housing: compounds for the poor black employees, and company housing, or their own house, for the more affluent white employees. The compounds were usually built close to the mine, effectively cordoning off the workers from the rest of the town. The aim was to force the mineworkers' families to stay in one of the labour-sending areas – for example South African areas such as the Transkei or other sub-Saharan African countries such as Lesotho, Zambia, Mozambique and Angola – while the government and the mining companies still benefited from a system of cheap labour. Dire conditions typically prevailed in such compounds: a high room-occupancy rate, lack of hygiene and frequent incidents of violence (Crush, 1994). This system was also detrimental to family relationships (Webster, 1993; Crush, 1994; Harington et al., 2004). Notably, the design of the first compounds in Kimberley, used as a template for compounds throughout South Africa, drew directly on the design of the Brazilian Diamond Field slave lodges, which shows how poor black labourers were typically viewed (Weiss, 2011). Some of these labourers found accommodation in municipal compounds, in squatter camps and in domestic accommodation in white residential areas (Harrison and Zack, 2012).

After World War II many mining towns were established internationally and in South Africa. In most cases, residents rented their accommodation from the mining companies. The resource slump of the mid-1980s did large-scale damage to local economies, forcing many mining companies to rethink their commitment to mining towns. One response was to privatise housing, transferring ownership from the mining company to individual households. Another was to transfer the management of the town to local government. In Australia, the rethinking of policy resulted in more outsourcing, higher salaries and fly-in-fly-out (FIFO) arrangements. FIFO arrangements have, however, caused substantial housing problems in mining towns in Australia (see Chapter 2 of this volume) as no new plans for houses were undertaken.

In many mining towns, particularly from the mid-20th century, the model of housing for the wealthier workers tended to follow a design based on the garden city model (Radford, 1990; Marais, 2013; Marais and Nel, 2016). This model has large suburban houses built on large plots of land, wide pavements, open spaces with plants and trees and, at the centre of the suburb, a small neighbourhood shopping centre. The stark contrast between this model and the housing provided for the black mineworkers was a spatial manifestation of the colonial belief – enshrined in legislation – that cities should be reserved for whites and the black population should be restricted to living in tribal areas and urban compounds (Mamdani, 1996; Huchzermeyer, 2004).

This pattern of housing continued until three changes occurred: an increase in squatter camps as a result of the abolition of influx control in 1986, the downscaling of some mines after the early 1990s, and the promulgation of the Mining Charter in 2004.

While squatter camps had existed in South Africa prior to the end of apartheid, the abolition of influx control caused them to mushroom (see for example Saff, 1996, or Malinga, 2000). By 2001, as many as 17% of all miners were living in informal housing and only 25% were still living in workers' hostels (i.e. compounds) (Stats SA, 2002). This was the first step in a marked shift towards workers being a permanent part of the mining town and not segregated from town life. See Cloete (2009) for a discussion of earlier failed attempts to incorporate miners into mining towns.

The second change in the mineworker housing pattern was the downscaling of a number of the mines, particularly in the Free State Goldfields. The most dramatic decline was in the gold-mining sector, where employee numbers dwindled from 400,000 in 1994 to just over 100,000 in 2014. One effect of the downscaling can be seen in Figure 9.1 – the loss of jobs for mineworkers, which in turn reduced the demand for housing in the affected towns.

The implications of the downscaling have been discussed in a series of publications (Binns and Nel, 2001, 2003; Marais et al., 2005; Marais, 2013; Marais and

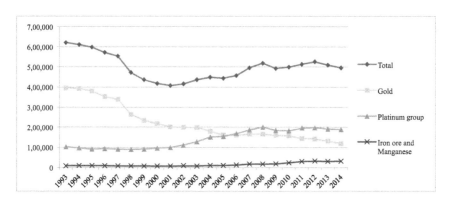

Figure 9.1 Mining employment in South Africa, 1994–2014
Source: Department of Mineral Resources, RSA, 2016

Cloete, 2013; Marais and Nel, 2016). Marais (2013), in particular, highlights the main effects: a declining population in the areas where such downscaling occurs, a lower demand for housing, an increase in unemployment, business closure and a drop in house prices. The depreciation in the housing market is particularly worrying because it means that mining households and other homeowners in mining towns lose a substantial portion of their investments in housing (see Chapter 5 of this volume for more detail). Many retrenched mineworkers in mining towns can neither keep up the payments on their house nor sell it, with the consequence that their house becomes a 'dead asset'. For the municipality, the major effects are an increase in the amount of bad debt because the mines have pulled out of the town and presumably the residents now cannot pay their municipal bills and a decreasing ability to fund the maintenance of municipal infrastructure.

Some mining towns, however, have managed to navigate the pitfalls of downscaling fairly successfully. Matlosana Municipality (formerly Klerksdorp), for example, because of its dual function as a mining town and regional service centre and its strategic location close to economic production hotspots and key transport routes, has survived mine downscaling without too much damage to its economy (Van Rooyen and Lenka, 2016). Rooiberg, in Limpopo Province, is another example of a town that has managed to avoid the full impact of mine downscaling and closure (Godsell, 2011). A first step towards ensuring Rooiberg's resilience was the temporary relocation to the town of former members of a specialised unit of the South African Police Service, the *Koevoet*, which disbanded in 1989. This relocation happened in the latter years of the Rooiberg tin mine downscaling and closure process, and was sufficiently large to fill all available accommodation in the town. More significant was the opening of game farms in the area and the selling-off of mineworker houses to domestic and foreign tourists, coupled with the construction of RDP (Reconstruction and Development Programme) houses and the relocation of farmworkers to the town. These factors created enough of an economic base for the town to continue functioning after the closing of the mine.[2]

The third factor which affected mineworker housing was the promulgation of the Mining Charter in 2004. The Charter committed mining companies to improving the standards of mineworkers' accommodation and also helped miners to own homes either in the mining town or in the labour-sending area (Marais and Cloete, 2013). While these ideas were not new – they had first surfaced in the RDP Policy Framework in 1994 – this was the first time they had been set as specific goals with which mining companies had to comply. These goals were given legislative force by the Mineral and Petroleum Resources Development Act No 28 of 2002, which mandated the Minister of Minerals and Energy, in conjunction with the Minister of Housing, to develop a housing and living conditions standard that would be binding on the minerals industry. Furthermore, the requirement in this Act that mines produce social and labour plans (SLPs) directly stated the need to provide housing for workers (Marais, 2013).

However, progress in implementing this standard proved to be slow. By 2009, only 26% of mining companies had provided housing for employees and 29% had improved the standard of housing. The one notable achievement was a substantial reduction in the number of occupants per unit – from 16 to only four occupants per unit (DMR, 2009).

The most recent milestone, albeit a highly problematic one, was achieved partly because of the Marikana massacre in 2012. After this event, the Presidency established the Special Presidential Package for Distressed Mining Towns, a R18 billion package for the socio-economic development of 15 distressed mining towns in South Africa. What distinguishes this package from previous attempts at providing miners with houses is that previous policies governing state-subsidised public housing had no specific focus on mining areas. Unlike previous policies this package is a specific attempt to deal with mining towns that are experiencing dire socio-economic conditions. It has, however, been criticised for being too focused on housing and on promoting housing expansion in areas that are or could be subject to mine downscaling. If the downscaling does happen, the houses may be abandoned or their occupants could be locked into a location with weak economic prospects (Marais et al., 2017; Ntema et al., 2017).

Housing conditions and trends in Postmasburg

In this section we look at the housing conditions of various types of households and housing in Postmasburg as revealed in the survey. We compare non-mining and mining households, and households with members working at two different mines (Kolomela and Beeshoek).

The two companies that own the Kolomela and Beeshoek mines, Kumba and Assmang, respectively, take different approaches to mineworker housing (although some choice is given to these workers): the former largely provides rental housing; the latter encourages homeownership through its incentive schemes. Ownership means that the long-term risks associated with mining (such as homeownership during downscaling and closure) are transferred to the individual household; rental housing means that the company is responsible for these risks. Furthermore, the intention in Postmasburg by the municipality was to create an integrated town and not a separate mining town, which also caused the long-term risks associated with mining to be transferred to local government.

In assessing the survey data, we distinguished between the following types:

- Formal and informal housing (we made this distinction because of the split between the two groups in the sampling)
- Households in which one or more members are employed by a mine and households with no members employed by a mine
- Households in which one or more members are employed by Kolomela mine and households in which one or more members are employed by Beeshoek mine
- Households in which one or more members are employed directly by a mine ('mine-employed mineworker households') and households in which one or more members are employed by contractors ('contractor mineworker households')

Table 9.1 Housing profile of Postmasburg, 1996, 2001, 2011

Housing category	1996		2001		2011	
	n	%	n	%	n	%
House on separate stand	2679	64.5	3750	74.9	5407	66.6
Traditional dwelling	90	2.2	57	1.1	26	0.3
Flat in block of flats	32	0.8	18	0.4	147	1.8
Town/cluster/semi-detached house	263	6.3	104	2.1	17	0.2
Unit in retirement village	0	0.0	0	0.0	0	0.0
House/flat/room in backyard	181	4.4	113	2.3	75	0.9
Informal dwelling/shack in backyard	113	2.7	260	5.2	287	3.5
Informal dwelling/shack on separate stand	634	15.3	518	10.3	1999	24.6
Room or flatlet on shared property	36	0.9	21	0.4	33	0.4
Caravan/tent	87	2.1	72	1.4	75	0.9
Other	37	0.9	95	1.9	48	0.6
TOTAL	4152	100.0	5008	100.0	8114	100.0

Source: Stats SA (1998, 2002, 2012)

Table 9.1 shows data from the various South African censuses, which provide a good overview of changing trends in housing in Postmasburg. The most prominent trend in Postmasburg's housing profile has been the growth in informal housing between 2001 and 2011. By 2011, nearly one in four houses was an informal shack on a separate stand. If we include the backyard dwelling we find that 28% of the houses in Postmasburg were informal in 2011 (see Figure 9.2). In 2001 only 15% were informal. From 2001 to 2011 the number of households living in informal settlements increased threefold. Statistics South Africa estimated that in 2016 more than 2300 households were living in informal settlements in Postmasburg (Stats SA, 2016), though this is probably an underestimate. While the partnership between mining companies and the municipality has been successful in providing housing to mineworkers (see Chapter 10 of this volume), it has been less successful in dealing with informal settlements.

The general picture we gained from the survey of Postmasburg's informal settlement is of a municipality struggling to provide adequate services to its growing population, especially if we compare our findings (see Table 9.2) with the estimates of Statistics South Africa's 2016 Community Survey for urban informal dwellings across South Africa. Whereas 61% of the South African population have access to water in their yards, 54% of the informal dwellings in Postmasburg not occupied by mine employees and 68% of the mine employee households are forced to use a public tap. And while 69% of the South African population have access to flush or chemical toilets, as many as 56% of the informal dwellings in Postmasburg not occupied by mine employees and 65% of the mine employee households are compelled to use the bucket system (i.e. no acceptable level of sanitation). However, people living in Postmasburg's informal dwellings are less likely than the South

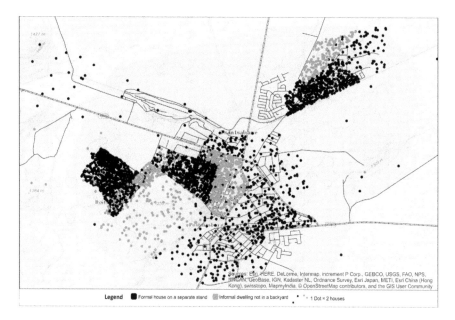

Figure 9.2 Map of informal housing and formal housing in Postmasburg, 2011
Source: Stats SA, 2012

African population at large to share their sanitation with other households – 30% of non-mine employees and 42% of mine employees as compared with 65% of South Africans have to share. Postmasburg's informal settlement dwellers are also less likely to have access to electricity (34% of non-mine employees, 24% of mine employees and 79% of South Africans have access) or to have their refuse removed by the municipality (11% of non-mine employees, 11% of mine employees and 77% of South Africans have refuse removal). All these figures should also be seen against the very high levels of service provision enjoyed by people living in formal dwellings in Postmasburg.

It is interesting to note that, according to the survey (see Table 9.3 later in the chapter), the average income of mine-employed mineworkers living in informal dwellings (R7051 per month) is almost the same as that of contractor mineworkers in formal dwellings (R7013 per month). This – coupled with the relatively lower levels of service provision for mine-employed mineworkers compared with households who do not have a member of their household employed by the mine (see Table 9.2 later in the chapter) – probably indicates that the informal settlements are accommodating late arrivals who are now working on the mines, and who might otherwise have been able to afford formal housing had it been available.

It is not only the informal settlements that have put pressure on the municipality; the number of households in Postmasburg has increased dramatically, nearly doubling between 1996 and 2011. StatsSA's (2016) Community Survey estimated

Table 9.2 Indicators for housing conditions in formal and informal housing in Postmasburg, 2015

| Indicator | | Formal, non-mining | | Formal, mining | | | | | | | | | | | | Informal, non-mining | | Informal, mining | |
| | | | | Total | | Mine-employed | | Contractor | | Kolomela | | Beeshoek | | | | | | | |
		n	%	n	%	n	%	n	%	n	%	n	%			n	%	n	%
Satisfaction	Happy	161	46.0	218	55.5	161	56.5	32	50.8	97	46.6	102	69.4			45	26.6	32	35.2
	Satisfied	103	29.4	124	31.6	99	34.7	14	22.2	85	40.9	29	19.7			33	19.5	11	12.1
	Unhappy	86	24.6	51	13.0	25	8.8	17	27.0	26	12.5	16	10.9			91	53.8	48	52.7
Tenure	Ownership	268	77.2	177	45.2	116	40.7	34	54.0	54	26.0	104	70.7			n/a			
	Rental	79	22.8	215	54.8	169	59.3	29	46.0	154	74.0	43	29.3						
Water source	Piped in dwelling	253	72.3	314	80.1	242	84.9	37	59.7	180	86.5	107	73.3			28	17.4	13	14.3
	Piped on site	77	22.0	65	16.6	35	12.3	22	35.5	24	11.5	32	21.9			44	27.3	16	17.6
	Public tap	20	5.7	13	3.3	8	2.8	3	4.8	4	1.9	7	4.8			89	55.3	62	68.1
Sanitation	Flush	338	96.8	386	98.2	284	99.6	335	96.8	205	98.6	144	98.0			50	29.6	17	19.1
	Pit latrine	3	0.9	1	0.3	0	0.0	3	0.9	0	0.0	1	0.7			25	14.8	14	15.7
	Other	8	2.3	6	1.5	1	0.4	8	2.3	3	1.4	2	1.4			94	55.6	58	65.2
Shared sanitation	Yes	63	18.1	105	26.7	74	26.0	16	25.4	53	25.5	41	27.9			49	29.9	37	41.6
	No	285	81.9	288	73.3	211	74.0	47	74.6	155	74.5	106	72.1			115	70.1	52	58.4
Electricity	Yes	316	91.3	376	95.7	273	95.8	60	95.2	200	96.2	143	97.3			57	34.1	20	23.5
	No	30	8.7	17	4.3	12	4.2	3	4.8	8	3.8	4	2.7			110	65.9	65	76.5
Refuse removal	Yes	281	81.0	356	90.6	265	93.0	55	87.3	197	94.7	128	87.1			18	10.7	10	11.0
	No	66	19.0	37	9.4	20	7.0	8	12.7	11	5.3	19	12.9			150	89.3	81	89.0

that approximately 11,500 households are living in the town. The percentage of households lacking access to water and sanitation increased rapidly between 2001 and 2011. In 2001, 15% of households did not have access to piped water on their stands and 13% had no sanitation; in 2011, these figures had risen to 21% and 17%.

We assessed housing tenure for the different categories in terms of ownership and rental (see Table 9.2). Only 26% of Kolomela employees owned their house, as compared with 71% of Beeshoek employees. Local residents not involved in mining had the largest share of homeownership: 77% of the respondents of the survey said they owned their dwelling they lived in. Of mineworker households living in formal housing, 45% owned their houses. It is important to note that 54% of the contractor mineworker households in Postmasburg said they owned their houses.

Internationally, homeownership is generally associated with higher levels of housing satisfaction (Elsinga and Hoekstra, 2005). In the survey of Postmasburg, respondents were asked to rate their feelings about their housing situation as *happy*, *satisfied* or *unhappy*. Reference has already been made to the different approaches followed by the two mining companies in Postmasburg – ownership in the case of Beeshoek (Assmang) and predominantly rental in the case of Kolomela (Kumba). We found that Beeshoek employees were more satisfied with their housing than their counterparts at Kolomela ($\tau_B = -0.192$, n = 355, p < 0.01): 69% of the former said they were happy with their houses compared to 47% of the latter. This is probably because they the value homeownership. Respondents from households with members employed at a mine and living in formal dwellings generally reported higher levels of satisfaction with their houses than their counterparts who were not employed by the mines ($\tau_B = -0.121$, n = 743, p < 0.01). This is a direct result of the high-quality houses (new and fairly large) provided by the two mining companies (see Chapter 10 for more detail on the size of the houses). These higher levels of satisfaction were reported even though the mining households in formal houses were less likely to own their houses than the non-mining households (45% vs 77%; $\chi^2 = 79.074$, df = 1, p < 0.01).

In the case of mineworker households in formal housing, we compared those with mine-employed members with those with contractor-employed members. We found that the latter were significantly more likely to be unhappy with their housing (27% vs 9%; $\chi^2 = 16.970$, df = 2, p < 0.01), despite the fact that the former were less likely to own their dwellings (41% vs 54%; $\chi^2 = 3.703$, df = 1, p < 0.10).

While we found no other significant differences to account for the level of satisfaction, mine-employed mineworker households did have better access to water ($\tau_B = 0.236$, n = 347, p < 0.01), larger dwellings (5.9 vs 4.6 rooms;[3] t = 3.892, df = 345, p < 0.01) and, on average, earned significantly higher incomes (R15,207 vs R7013; t = 4.142, df = 100, p < 0.01) than contract-employed mineworker households (see Table 9.3). Further, given the intercession of the mining companies in their dealings with the housing market (negotiations with the municipality and private sector and construction of houses for rent, rent-to-buy or sale), the mining households in our sample were in a slightly better position to access satisfactory housing than the non-mining households.

Households in formal mine housing had better access to services than non-mining households in formal housing. The former were more likely to have better access to water ($\tau_B = -0.092$, n = 742, p < 0.05) and to have their refuse removed by the municipality (91% vs 81%; $\chi^2 = 14.191$, df = 1, p < 0.01). Mining households in formal housing also had slightly better access to sanitation than non-mining households in formal housing. Mining households in informal housing were more likely than non-mining households in informal housing to have better access to sanitation ($\tau_B = 0.102$, n = 258, p < 0.10). In formal housing, mining households earned R12,583, compared to R4174 for non-mining households ($t = -5.967$, df = 243, p < 0.01). In informal housing, mining households earned R7051, compared to R2734 for non-mining households ($t = -6.709$, df = 199, p < 0.01). We also found that in formal housing more mining households than non-mining households shared sanitation (27% as compared with 18%, see Table 9.2). In informal housing, more mining households than non-mining households also shared sanitation, probably because mineworkers had to share accommodation as they were less likely to have secured housing of their own.

Housing sizes differed considerably. Formal mine houses (for mine-employed mineworkers) were the largest, with an average of 5.9 rooms per house. Formal houses owned by non-mining households had on average 5.4 rooms per house. The houses where mine-employed mineworkers were living were larger than those of contractor mineworkers (5.9 vs. 4.6 rooms per house; $t = 3.892$, df = 78, p < 0.01). The mostly rental houses of the Kolomela mine (5.9 rooms) were comparable in number of rooms to those of the Beeshoek mine (5.5 rooms). Non-mining households in informal housing had larger houses than mining households in informal housing (2.3 vs. 1.9 rooms; $t = 2.810$, df = 248, p < 0.01), perhaps because mine employees living in informal settlements generally do not expect to be employed long-term by the mine and are therefore less likely to invest in their informal houses.

Kolomela had a larger share than Beeshoek of mining households living in formal dwellings (59% vs 41%), but the two mines had virtually equal shares of mining households living in informal dwellings (49% vs 51%) – differences which are not statistically significant ($\chi^2 = 2.086$, df = 1, p = 0.149). This indicates that neither mine was more likely than the other to house its employees in informal housing. The relatively low numbers of households sampled who were employed by the mines and were living in informal dwellings once again precluded further analysis.

Two important concerns about housing finance in mining towns are the substantial increases in rental fees that result from an influx of mineworkers and especially contract workers, and the long-term consequences of mortgage finance amid the volatility in the mining sector (see Chapter 3 of this volume for literature on these concerns).

The increased rentals, the first concern, make it more difficult for lower-salaried local households to rent houses. We were unable to trace the increase in rentals in Postmasburg with any accuracy, but we were able to discover what rents our sample paid and what percentage of household income this constituted. Our results here are based on small samples (see Table 9.3) due to the small share of those

Table 9.3 Indicators for housing and socio-economic conditions in formal and informal housing in Postmasburg, 2015

Indicator	Formal, non-mining		Formal, mining										Informal, non-mining		Informal, mining	
			Total		Mine-employed		Contractor		Kolomela		Beeshoek					
	n	Avg.	n	Avg.	n	Avg.	n	Avg.	n	Avg.	n	Avg.	n	Avg.	n	Avg.
Number of rooms in dwelling	344	5.4	392	5.7	284	5.9	63	4.6	207	5.9	147	5.5	169	2.3	90	1.9
Income in 2015 ZAR	127	4174	117	12,583	78	15,207	24	7013	53	10,947	54	14,676	135	2734	66	7051
Rent payment in 2015 ZAR	27	1097	147	1071	116	933	21	1839	112	825	25	2184		n/a*		
Percentage of income spent on rent	9	28	44	13	26	13	1	13	29	19	12	15				
Bond payment in 2015 ZAR	4	2000	15	4033	13	4346	2	2000	3	1533	10	4658				
Percentage of income spent on bond	4	11	8	24	7	27	0	0	0	0	7	27				

* Due to a combination of free informal settlement and low reporting, the information is not reported.

renting, those who rent who were willing to report their rental, and those willing to report their income. Though we do not claim that these results are generally applicable to Postmasburg, we nevertheless consider our estimate to be indicative of the reality. Table 9.3 shows that non-mining households who rented a formal house spent 28% of their household income on rent, mine-employed mineworker households spent 13%, and contract mineworker households spent 19%. There was little difference in rent payments by non-mining households (R1097) and mining households (R1071). However, contract workers, at an average of R1839 per month, paid substantially larger amounts than both non-mining households and mining households. Kolomela employees paid an average R825 in rent ($t = -2.407$, df = 24, p < 0.05) and Beeshoek employees who rented their dwellings (a smaller number than at Kolomela) paid R2184. This suggests that while Beeshoek mine employees have to access rental housing on the more expensive open market, company houses are available to Kolomela mine employees.

As with the rental data, we obtained only a small amount of data about housing finance because of a low response rate. In the case of mortgage bonds, the average payment expressed as a percentage of the salary of non-mining households was 11%. The comparative figure for mine employees was 24%, with Beeshoek mine coming in at 27%.

Conclusion

This chapter assessed the 2015 status of housing in Postmasburg and the risks associated with it. The aim of the Mining Charter, the Department of Mineral Resources, national government, Tsantsabane Local Municipality, Kolomela, and Assmang of creating an integrated rather than purely mining town means that the municipality and homeowners will have to bear the long-term risks associated with mining booms and busts. The two main mines have opted for different tenure options, Beeshoek providing mainly ownership housing and Kolomela encouraging rental accommodation, with apparently a long-term plan to transfer ownership of these houses to the occupants (i.e. its mineworkers). These two types of tenure option have different long-term implications. Whereas Kolomela is willing to take long-term risks, Beeshoek has transferred these risks to the individual households. The implications of these different approaches should be evaluated over the long term. It is more than likely that with the closure of one or more of the mines in the area there will be an over-supply of houses (given the lack of diversification in the economy), resulting in a severe depreciation of the market value of these houses and the rentals that can be charged.

While the influx of mine employees does not seem to be displacing resident owners (non-mining families, who have higher levels of ownership), it does seem to be exerting upward pressure on rentals. The result is that, on average, non-mining families do spend a larger share of their smaller incomes on rent. The uptake of informal housing by mine employees seems to be low and they appear to be receiving a lower level of services than their non-mining counterparts in informal housing. Contractor-employed mineworkers were found to be less satisfied with their housing than mine-employed mineworkers. This seems to be largely because they have lower salaries and higher rentals. It may also be a manifestation of a new trend in mining housing, the use of contract labour, which seems to be contributing to the growth of informal settlements (see also Chapter 5).

This phenomenon warrants further scrutiny as it might be a method by which mining companies are attempting to shirk their social responsibilities with regard to their employees. For example, Anglo American (2016) claims that by 2014 they had provided housing for 75% of its employees. However, if we include mine-employed mineworkers (permanent and temporary) as well as contractor-employed mineworkers in this calculation, then Anglo American is apparently supplying housing to only 48% of its workforce.[4]

We found that Beeshoek employees were more satisfied with their housing than employees at the Kolomela mine, although higher levels of ownership and better water access were the only significant differences This may indicate that, at least in the short run, the housing model used by Beeshoek makes employees happier with their housing than the model used by Kolomela (Chapter 10 of this volume elaborates on the housing model used by Beeshoek). But this may change once mining operations decline.

Tsantsabane Municipality seems to be struggling to provide the informal settlements with adequate services (whether the residents are employed by the mines or not) and is lagging behind the South African urban informal sphere in respect of virtually all indicators. The growth of this form of housing surely means that some form of planning is required. The indicator in respect of shared sanitation also requires some attention because previous research showed this was one of the key variables in improving health outcomes (Marais and Cloete, 2014). Formality could, however, prove not to be the desired outcome of such planning, as during bust periods in mining informality might be easier to manage than formality.

However, the municipality does not appear to have the administrative capacity to respond to the demand for housing and services in its jurisdiction, as evidenced by the lagging service provision in the town (see Chapter 5 and Chapter 6). This prompts a question about what role smaller municipalities like Tsantsabane should play in executing the housing function. Possibly, for jurisdictions with limited administrative capacity, this function should be retained by provincial government or the Housing Development Agency where (it is to be hoped) there is greater administrative capacity.

In conclusion two profound questions can be asked: (1) Should municipalities guide mines in determining the type of housing provided? (2) Should mines contribute financially to provide services for informal settlements? These questions form the basis for future research.

Notes

1 In 2014 there were 1082 permanent employees, 135 temporary employees, 672 on-site contractors and 2132 off-site contractor employees and employees of suppliers at Kolomela mine (Anglo American, 2016).
2 Farmworkers were relocated to the town through fear of what might happen after 1994 when new labour and land laws were implemented. Godsell (2011) argues that farmers were scared of possible land claims and uncertain how changes to tenant rights would affect them.
3 Rooms in the survey included toilets and kitchens.
4 This is probably an underestimate, given that this only refers to on-site employees. If off-site employees are also counted, then this figure drops to 23%.

References

Anglo American, 2016. *Kolomela Mine SEAT Report*. www.angloamericankumba.com/~/media/Files/A/Anglo-American-Kumba/documents/kumba-socio-economic-assesment-tool-report.pdf (accessed 16 September 2016).

Binns, J.A. and Nel, E., 2001. Gold loses its shine: Decline and response in the South African goldfields. *Geography*, 86, pp. 255–260.

Binns, T. and Nel, E., 2003. The village in a game park: Local response to the demise of coal mining in KwaZulu-Natal, South Africa. *Economic Geography*, 79(1), pp. 41–66.

Cloete, J., Venter, A. and Marais, L., 2009. Breaking new ground, social housing and mine-worker housing: The missing link. *Town and Regional Planning*, 54, pp. 27–36.

Crush, J., 1989. Accommodating black miners: Home ownership on the mines. In: *South African Review 5*. Johannesburg: Ravan, pp. 335–347.

Crush, J., 1992. The compound in post-apartheid South Africa. *Geographical Review*, 82(4), pp. 388–400.

Crush, J., 1994. Scripting the compound: Power and space in the South African mining industry. *Environment and Planning D: Society and Space*, 12(3), pp. 301–324.

Crush, J. and James, W., 1991. Depopulating the compounds: Migrant labor and mine housing in South Africa. *World Development*, 19(4), pp. 301–316.

DMR (Department of Mineral Resources), 2004. *Broad-Based Socio-Economic Empowerment Charter for the South African Mining Industry*. www.westerncape.gov.za/Text/2004/5/theminingcharter.pdf (accessed 7 January 2017).

DMR (Department of Mineral Resources), 2009. *Mining Charter Impact Assessment Report*. www.dmr.gov.za/publications/finish/108-minerals-act-charter-and-scorecard/126-miningcharterimpact-oct-2009/0.html (accessed 13 September 2016).

DMR (Department of Mineral Resources), 2010. *Amendment of the Broad-Based Socio-Economic Empowerment Charter for the South African Mining and Minerals Industry*. www.gov.za/sites/www.gov.za/files/33573_838.pdf (accessed 7 January 2017).

DMR (Department of Mineral Resources), 2016. *Mineral Economics: Statistics (B1 Stat Tables)*. www.dmr.gov.za/publications/summary/149-statistics/8271-b1-stat-tables-2015.html (accessed 17 October 2016).

Elsinga, M. and Hoekstra, J., 2005. Homeownership and housing satisfaction. *Journal of Housing and the Built Environment*, 20(4), pp. 401–424.

Godsell, S., 2011. Rooiberg: The little town that lived. *South African Historical Journal*, 63(1), pp. 61–77.

Harington, J.S., McGlashan, N.D. and Chelkowska, E.Z., 2004. A century of migrant labour in the gold mines of South Africa. *Journal of the South African Institute of Mining and Metallurgy*, 104(2), pp. 65–72.

Harrison, P. and Zack, T., 2012. The power of mining: The fall of gold and rise of Johannesburg. *Journal of Contemporary African Studies*, 30(4), pp. 551–570.

Huchzermeyer, M., 2004. *Unlawful Occupation: Informal Settlements and Urban Policy in South Africa and Brazil*. Trenton, NJ and Asmara, Ethiopia: Africa World Press.

Malinga, S.S., 2000. *The Development of Informal Settlements around Daveyton on the East Rand, 1970–1999*. Unpublished Doctoral Dissertation, Rand Afrikaans University (now University of Johannesburg), Johannesburg.

Mamdani, M., 1996. *Citizen and Subject: Contemporary Africa and the Legacy of Late Colonialism*. Princeton, NJ: Princeton University Press.

Marais, L., 2013. The impact of mine downscaling on the Free State Goldfields. *Urban Forum*, 24(4), pp. 503–521.

Marais, L. and Cloete, J., 2013. Labour migration, settlement and mine closure in South Africa. *Geography*, 98(2), pp. 77–84.

Marais, L. and Cloete, J., 2014. 'Dying to get a house?' The health outcomes of the South African low-income housing programme. *Habitat International*, 43(1), pp. 48–60.

Marais, L. and Nel, E., 2016. The dangers of growing on gold: Lessons from the history of the Free State Goldfields. *Local Economy*, 31(1–2), pp. 282–298.

Marais, L., Pelser, A., Botes, L., Redelinghuys, N. and Benseler, A., 2005. Public finances, service delivery and mine closure in Koffiefontein (Free State, South Africa): From stepping stones to stumbling blocks. *Town and Regional Planning*, 48, pp. 5–16.

Marais, L., Van Rooyen, D., Nel, E. and Lenka, M., 2017. Responses to mine downscaling: Evidence from secondary cities in the South African Goldfields. *The Extractive Industries and Society*, 4(1), pp. 163–171.

Marais, L. and Venter, A., 2006. Hating the compound, but . . . mineworker housing needs in post-apartheid South Africa. *Africa Insight*, 36(1), pp. 53–62.

Ntema, J., Marais, L., Cloete, J. and Lenka, M., 2017. Social disruption, mine closure and housing policy: Evidence from the Free State Goldfields, South Africa. *Natural Resources Forum*, 41(1), pp. 31–40.

Radford, D., 1990. The architecture of Herbert Baker's mining housing. *South African Journal of Art and Architectural History*, 1(3), pp. 89–97.

Saff, G., 1996. Claiming a space in a changing South Africa: The 'squatters' of Marconi Beam, Cape Town. *Annals of the Association of American Geographers*, 86(2), pp. 235–255.

Stats SA (Statistics South Africa), 1998. *The People of South Africa Population Census, 1996. Report 03–01–30 (1996)*. Pretoria: Stats SA.

Stats SA (Statistics South Africa), 2002. *South African Census 2001. Report No. 03–02–03*. Pretoria: Stats SA.

Stats SA (Statistics South Africa), 2012. *South African Census 2011. Statistical Release P0301.4. (2011)*. Pretoria: Stats SA.

Stats SA (Statistics South Africa), 2016. *Community Survey 2016: Provinces at a Glance, Report 03–01–03*. Pretoria: Stats SA.

Tshangana, M., 2015. *Selected Committee Presentation on the Revitalisation of Distressed Mining Towns Programme*. Pretoria: National Department of Human Settlements.

Van Rooyen, D. and Lenka, M., 2016. City of Matlosana. In: L. Marais, E. Nel and R. Donaldson, eds. *Secondary Cities and Development in South Africa*. London: Routledge, pp. 49–62.

Webster, E., 1993. Rethinking migrant labour. *South African Historical Journal*, 28(1), pp. 292–299.

Weiss, L., 2011. Exceptional space: Concentration camps and labour compounds in late nineteenth-century South Africa. In: A. Myers and G. Moshenska, eds. *Archaeologies of Internment*. New York: Springer, pp. 21–32.

10 The Khumani approach to homeownership in Postmasburg

Thomas Stewart and Ernst Drewes

A different way to managing mineworker housing

The issue of how to house mineworkers continues to raise concern. Internationally, new mining operations lead to worker camps, high rentals, the displacement of locals and 'hotbedding' (see Chapter 2 of this volume). The cyclical nature of mining and the likelihood of eventual closure aggravate the risks associated with housing provision in mining towns. In South Africa, new mining operations have created a housing shortage and caused informal settlements to mushroom.

Historically, high-density compounds were the standard way to house black migrant workers (see also Chapter 9 of this volume). In the mid-1980s and early 1990s, the idea of homeownership for black mineworkers surfaced in policy debates and the future of the compound was debated. The apartheid legacy of racially segregated human settlements further complicated mine housing. Higher income white workers were usually accommodated in low-density, company-owned rental housing. When the mining boom of the 1980s came to an end, many of these housing units were privatised to individual households. However, having a mortgage bond in a town where mining volatility prevails is risky. Useful discussion of these topics may be found in Crush (1989, 1992); Marais and Venter (2006); Cronje (2014) and Marais and Nel (2016).

In an attempt to deal with the consequences of migrant labour and the compounds and the spatial problems left over from settlement planning under apartheid, the government has introduced several policy proposals. Two are crucial in this respect: the Mining Charter (DMR, 2010; 2017) and the Programme for the Revitalisation of Distressed Mining Towns (see RSA, 2013). Government policies assumed that mining companies should be largely responsible for the living conditions of their workers (DME, 2002). Recent policies have emphasised homeownership, integrated settlements (as opposed to mining settlements) and the dismantling of the compound system (DMR, 2010; RSA, 2013). It was within this context that the Khumani housing approach, which in 2009 won the award for housing project of the year in southern Africa, provided ownership housing in Postmasburg (and also in Kathu and Kuruman).

This chapter assesses the Khumani approach's financial and housing delivery models, practical results and remaining challenges, and the possible expansion and replication of the model to other employee housing initiatives. We also look at how far the Khumani approach complies with government guidelines and may be suitable for dealing with the volatility of the mining industry. The authors of Chapter 9 have argued that there is merit in rental housing as a tenure option for mineworkers. In this chapter we present a counter-argument: we agree with Hoekstra and Marais (2016) that alternative homeownership products could well be applied in mining settlements.

Mine housing and South African housing policy

Chapter 1 explained some theories applied to and policies pursued in mining towns and Chapter 2 considered the housing consequences of mining booms and busts. Ways of housing mineworkers have changed since the days when most of them rented their accommodation from the mining company. The rents they paid were usually below market value and service fees for water and electricity were subsidised. The resources bust of the mid-1980s led mining companies to reconsider their costs for employee housing. Many mining companies privatised the housing they had owned to their former tenants, thus shifting the liability of homeownership to households. By the early 1990s, urban planners had started to question the formal provision of permanent housing near mining areas. This went hand-in-hand with a labour regime change (more outsourcing and contract work) and the introduction of fly-in-fly-out arrangements, especially in Australia (see Chapter 1).

South Africa has many company towns or towns dominated by mining companies. Mineworker housing varies from low-density single housing units to high-density single sex hostels. Marais and Cloete (2013) have argued that, ironically, it has been relatively easy to dismantle mining compounds during periods of mine decline. In contrast, low-density formal housing has imposed longer-term constraints and inhibited mobility (Marais and Nel, 2016). Typically, mine downscaling in an environment of homeownership has resulted in the collapse of housing markets (Marais, 2013). The transfer of company housing to individual households has thus also transferred the risk associated with ownership and collapsing markets to individual households. In some case households did experience a capital gain but in general this was not the case.

There is no policy for the provision of housing in the mining sector in South Africa. To transform the mining industry, the initial Mining Charter emphasised human dignity, privacy for mineworkers, enhanced productivity and better housing (DME, 2002). It required mining companies to implement measures to improve standards of housing and living conditions for mineworkers and to facilitate homeownership options. Later, the Department of Mineral Resources published a Housing and Living Conditions Standard with the overall objective of providing 'standards which will enable mineworkers to have a choice in pursuing suitable housing and living conditions for themselves' (DMR, 2010). To achieve this objective, it required mining companies to compile a housing policy that would

- ensure a decent standard of housing for mineworkers;
- develop social, physical and economically integrated housing within or outside the mining areas;

- ensure secure tenure for employees in housing institutions on the basis of the general provision; and
- promote the use of financing schemes in a manner that is transparent and accountable.

The amendment of the Broad Based Socio-Economic Empowerment Charter for the South African Mining and Minerals industry, issued in 2010, again emphasised that since mine communities form an integral part of mining development, mining companies must contribute meaningfully to community development (DMR, 2010). It further called for mining companies, in collaboration with the mining communities, to determine needs and translate them into projects for community development. To do this the companies must implement measures to improve housing standards and living conditions for mineworkers by, among other things, facilitating homeownership options for all mine employees in consultation with organised labour by 2014.

The Department of Mineral Resources set up various monitoring and evaluation measures, referred to as a 'Scorecard'. The Scorecard measures mining companies' contribution to community development and housing in host and labour-sending communities. The Charter specifies that the Minister shall constantly assess progress against plans to establish acceptable living standards for mineworkers. The assessment will be based on an annual report of compliance compiled by the mining company and submitted to the Minister. Non-compliance with the revised Mining Charter will amount to a breach of the Mineral and Petroleum Resources Development Act (RSA, 2002), resulting in the potential suspension or cancellation of mining licences granted under the Mining Charter (DME, 2002).

Besides amending the Charter, the DMR revised the guidelines for social and labour plans to include 'measures to address the housing and living conditions of employees' (DMR, 2010) Accordingly, the mines must consult and cooperate in formulating and reviewing the integrated development plans (five-year strategic plans, known as IDPs) of the local municipalities and mining communities within which they are based. The Programme for the Revitalisation of Distressed Mining Towns also emphasises the provision of more housing and ownership in mining areas (Tshangana, 2015). The available government housing subsidy budgets are hence targeting specific mining areas, signalling closer collaboration between the government and the mining companies.

The call for ownership in mining settlements is largely in accordance with mainstream low-income housing policy since 1994, though rental and social housing is also emphasised to some extent (Venter et al., 2014). South African housing policies that have been adopted and implemented since 1994 are based on a capital subsidy scheme that subsidises low-income families according to their salaries (Marais and Krige, 2000). These one-off subsidies apply to families with a monthly household income of R0 to R7500 and can be used for various types of housing with various forms of ownership. Apart from those in subsidised rental units, all subsidy recipients are supposed to receive full tenure.

A disadvantage of this framework of state support is that it excludes a large per-centage of employed people who earn more than the maximum monthly income to qualify for state assistance, thus obliging their employer to provide them with decent housing. The Department of Housing's comprehensive Breaking New Ground plan advocates, among other things, greater spatial integration of infrastructure and social facilities, accommodating people closer to their places of work, higher densities, and the integration of previously excluded groups into the cities (DoH, 2004). The plan also promotes housing as a catalyst to achieve national socio-economic goals such as social cohesion, economic growth and poverty eradication (UN, 2013).

While the central government is responsible for financing housing provision, provincial and local governments are meant to be the primary agencies for facilitat-ing this provision (RSA, 1994). For higher income households, access to mortgage finance is an additional requirement. However, there are some hurdles to overcome to qualify for a loan. It may be difficult to obtain a home loan unless the applicant can make an upfront deposit of 10 to 30%. The applicant faces a 20- to 30-year repayment period at an interest rate of prime plus 1 or 2%. The applicant must provide evidence of being able to afford the monthly repayments, determined as not more than 30% of gross income. And the house itself may prove a further hurdle, as it has to comply with certain minimum standards, which may make it difficult for the owner to keep up with bond repayments and municipal charges in times of economic hardship (Marais and Cloete, 2015). Affordability was one of the main concerns for households in areas of mining decline in the early 1990s (Tomlinson, 2007).

It is against this background of changing local and global trends in mine hous-ing, government requirements and the financial needs associated with mortgage finance that we now turn to discussing the Khumani approach.

The Khumani housing approach

The Khumani housing approach has been applied by Assmang in the towns of Kathu, Kuruman and Postmasburg. Assmang originally mined iron ore at Bee-shoek outside Postmasburg. However, the original settlement at Beeshoek (a typi-cal company town) extended across the iron ore reserves. This required Assmang to move their workforce to Postmasburg, a move which was in line with the devel-opment of Postmasburg as a regional hub (see Chapter 4). The move also made it possible to facilitate homeownership through the Khumani housing approach, implemented by the Khumani Housing Development Company (KHDC) (see KHDC, 2016). Khumani is an Assmang iron ore mine near Kathu, a small mining town in the Northern Cape Province. The approach to ownership is referred to as the Khumani Housing Model, based on the mining operation near Kathu.

The regional context and response

During 2005 consultants were appointed to compile a unique homeownership model for the South African mining sector. Although initially focused on the requirements of a single mine (Khumani), the project quickly grew to include three other mines (N'Chwaning, Gloria and Beeshoek), spatially representing three different local municipalities. The spatial challenge was severe, as these mines were located between 15 and 80 kilometres from the nearest town, and the time frame for developing approximately 2000 housing units in time to roll out the expanded mining operations was very short.

Various towns (Kathu, Kuruman, Danielskuil) in the region were analysed to determine their sustainability, or 'vitality', in terms of such indicators as welfare, social aspects, satisfaction and space (Drewes and Van Aswegen, 2011). This research aimed to establish the feasibility of developing the relevant housing projects in existing sustainable towns. The regional influence of each town was therefore evaluated and suitable towns for investment (in housing stock as well as physical infrastructure) were scientifically determined. Contrary to the approach used by other mining operations in the region – and the rest of southern Africa, a model was developed where the mining company established sufficient housing stock in the designated areas. By 2014 just over 2000 housing units had been added through this model.

KHDC intended their envisaged housing developments to form an integrated part of existing sustainable towns in the region, which the local authority, Postmasburg, also supported. This approach in itself was an achievement, indicative of a departure from the segregated and isolated nature of most employer-provided accommodation. It required a level of boldness in a conservative rural town that was still firmly embedded in the apartheid legacy. Various zones were identified and bought within Postmasburg specifically, creating a more integrated urban morphology (see Figure 10.1). The planning resulted in the design and development of stands in three neighbourhoods of Postmasburg: Airfield, Postdene and Boichoko.

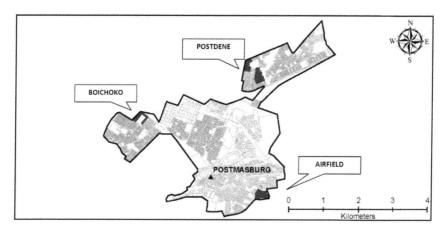

Figure 10.1 Khumani Housing Development Company residential developments in Postmasburg (dark shaded areas)

The Khumani housing approach

African Rainbow Minerals (ARM), owner of Assmang, initiated the Khumani housing approach through Assmang in 2005. This approach was initially to be applied in Kathu and was later also applied in Kuruman and Postmasburg. In identifying land and deciding to develop housing in Postmasburg, ARM evaluated the long-term sustainability of the surrounding settlements, the availability of the necessary engineering services, the affordability of the housing and the investment value for employees (Drewes and Van Aswegen, 2011).

The principles of the Khumani housing approach are that the workforce can live with their families in a secure, healthy, sustainable and protected environment; housing development will be facilitated in a sustainable town near to the mine; and ownership of affordable housing for the workforce will be promoted and facilitated (ARM, 2010). The detailed strategic objectives of this approach are to redress historical social and economic inequalities; integrate mine employees into the local and regional context and society; promote equitable access to land and housing for all permanent employees; facilitate affordable housing and home-ownership; establish an institution to manage housing matters; expand employees' skills and knowledge base; encourage sustainable settlement choices; promote private homeownership and security of tenure for employees; give employees choices and options with regard to housing; help employees learn about homeownership by means of education, training and development; promote the development of family units; and discourage the creation or expansion of informal settlements and mining villages (ARM, 2010).

The mining companies also had to play a facilitating role in acquiring land, installing services and providing houses (Drewes and Van Aswegen, 2011). ARM (2010) further proposed that the mining company should facilitate the financing and construction of the housing by appointing a dedicated 'housing association' to assist and advise employees.

The Khumani housing approach is structured according to the following model (ARM, 2010):

- The first component of the financial assistance qualifies all employees for a one-off capital contribution towards acquiring their own house. The contribution has a maximum of about R290,000 and decreases as income increases, from the full amount for employees in the lowest income band to only 10% for those in the highest band. The second component is a monthly allowance which resembles the traditional housing allowance, and reflects the employee's income band, based on Paterson[1] grading, a system generally used in the mining sector to distinguish between labourers, administrative personnel, technical specialists, professionals and management. Therefore, an employee in the lower income bands will receive a large percentage (up to 100%) of the one-off capital contribution and his monthly allowance will be a percentage of his monthly income. An employee in the high income bands will receive a small percentage (as low as 10%) of the one-off capital contribution, and his monthly allowance will also be a percentage of his income.

- A dedicated housing office in each town provides information such as the layout of the neighbourhoods, available stands or houses, building plan options, and evaluations of employees' affordability levels. This provides a personal interface with which all housing issues are dealt.
- Properties are bought in terms of an instalment sale agreement whereby KHDC remains the co-owner of the property until it is fully paid for. This arrangement ensures that third parties cannot foreclose on a 'company house' if the employee has financial difficulties. It also avoids the cost and administration of a mortgage.
- The instalment sale agreement requires that the loan is paid monthly, directly to the housing company, before any other debts are paid, making it a priority debt. As with a traditional loan from a financial institution, the owner can sell the property only once the loan is redeemed.
- Employees with houses have to take formal responsibility for the monthly rates and taxes, as with private ownership. Every house has pre-paid water and electricity meters and receives monthly rates accounts from the municipality. KHDC is not held liable for paying these accounts, despite effectively being the co-owner.
- Maintenance of the house is the employee's responsibility, although this is not regulated or monitored. KHDC relies on its consumer education programme and its proactive role. Since the houses are at most five to six years old, maintenance is only now becoming relevant and it remains to be seen whether it will be attended to.
- A crucial component of the housing model is the 'right of first refusal', in favour of KHDC, which means that when an employee leaves the employ of the mine, whether by choice or circumstances, the house has to be offered to KHDC at a market-related price, determined by a registered property valuer. KHDC may then exercise its right within a four-month period, or allow the owner to sell the house on the open market. Any profit goes to the employee. This principle applies even if the property has been paid for in full and KHDC is no longer the co-owner. Although this procedure ensures housing stock for the life of the mine, and can be justified given the substantial financial contribution made by the mine, it does to some extent defeat the principle of private homeownership while allowing KHDC flexibility in the number of houses it owns and has available for new employees.
- Loans are granted subject to the purchaser having life and disability insurance cover, sufficient to pay any outstanding debts and subject to the house being insured by means of a homeowner's insurance policy.
- If an employee resigns or is dismissed, the capital contribution is forfeited and the ex-employee must either find alternative finance or sell the house back to KHDC or on the open market within four months.

As an alternative way of facilitating homeownership, the Khumani housing approach largely supports the government's emphasis on providing homeownership, which supposedly provides stability if the housing is located in a normal town rather than a mining village. This stability, however, could lock people into a location that becomes peripheral when the mine declines (Ntema et al., 2017). To some degree, by having KHDC acting as the first buyer, the Khumani approach reduces risks for the employee, though it does not provide much security in the event of mine closure. It does, however, reduce risks for the mining company: Assmang will not be responsible for the long-term liability of owning these housing units after the mine closes. The risk will be with the employees.

Financing and building the houses

The most important component of the Khumani approach is the Khumani Housing Development Company. KHDC is registered as a credit provider and has to deal with all the financial and logistical components of the envisaged approach. The company facilitates all housing matters, included funding the employees' housing loans, for the traditional period of up to 20 years. It also has to raise its own funding and provide end-user funding and development capital to fund bulk infrastructure, municipal services to individual stands, and capital to build the houses. It also facilitates the physical development of the infrastructure and houses.

In 2010 KHDC invested R22 million in bulk services for Postmasburg, broadly in the form of a pro-rata contribution based on the number of housing units to be developed. This bulk infrastructure investment was a joint initiative of the municipality, Assmang (owner of Beeshoek mine) and Kumba (owner of Kolomela mine). KHDC's funding of the bulk infrastructure increased the effectiveness of the model, given that external development funding often hampers development, causing delays that escalate contractors' and developers' costs. It should be noted that it is unusual for a housing developer or financial institution to act as both developer and financier of property. In doing this, the Khumani approach is exposing itself to financial risk on two fronts.

Every Assmang employee has the option to take part in the ownership drive and can apply for both the capital contribution and the housing allowance. Employees can choose to buy a house in any location within the three specified zones, depending on what kind of house they can afford.

KHDC has agreed to an interest rate of prime less 2%, for all grades of employees. This is substantially lower than most commercial banks in South Africa would offer people in these employees' income bands, for the instalment sale agreement. This low interest rate is possible because the loans are financed by the three mining operations (Khumani, Black Rock and Beeshoek), through KHDC.

KHDC contracted a national construction company to install the services (both bulk and internal) and build the top structures. This had the advantage of coupling experience with quality control and adherence to construction protocols. However, we heard criticisms of this from residents we interviewed. One said: 'They brought in construction workers from Gauteng, who did all the work, while the local people were only given limited opportunities.' This is a common complaint in the construction industry and does call for greater sensitivity on the part of an initiative which is perceived to create job opportunities suitable to local skills, especially in areas with high unemployment and few job opportunities. Bringing in external construction workers temporarily inflated and distorted Postmasburg's housing market, which was largely for rental accommodation, creating a secondary boom within the overall mining boom.

The KHDC financing model is probably only applicable within the mining environment. The stability provided to the employees through homeownership is funded twice (by the original capital subsidy and the monthly contribution) by the mining operations. These contributions from the mine reduce the risk of non-payment. According to data presented in Chapter 9 of this volume, Assmang employees spend on average 27% of their income on housing finance, but despite this high percentage they are slightly more satisfied with their housing than people in rental accommodation.

The housing types

It was a challenge to provide housing of all the diverse types required. Most of the smaller houses were built by KHDC, and employees could choose between various designs and finishes. The higher income bands have the option to design and build their own homes using their own service providers. An important support structure for the housing model is the physical availability of the dedicated housing office in each of the towns where the model is applied, providing crucial consumer information, as described above.

A total of 490 stands were developed in the Postmasburg neighbourhoods of Airfield, Postdene and Boichoko, and at the time of writing 341 houses had been built and financed through the Khumani model since 2011 (see Table 10.1). Of these 341 houses, almost all the less expensive ones have been taken up. The fact that some of the more expensive stands and houses are still available may be because the negative economic climate in the iron ore industry worldwide and the general volatility of mining environments have affected affordability. Table 10.2 shows the sizes and prices of the houses provided by the Khumani housing approach in Postmasburg.

Table 10.1 Housing distribution in Postmasburg

Neighbourhoods	Stand size (avg)	House size (avg)	Units built (2016)
Airfield	800m²	230 m²	125
Postdene	600m²	120 m²	165
Boichoko	450m²	60 m²	51

Source: KHDC (2016)

Table 10.2 Housing portfolio

House size	Price range (2012)	% allocation
60 m²	R546,000 – R607,000	15%
80 m²	R629,000 – R708,000	
110 m²	R700,000 – R857,000	48%
135 m²	R767,000 – R957,000	
150 m²	R1,003,000 – R1,148,000	
220 m²	R1,316,000 – R1,444,000	37%
260 m²	R1,367,000 +	

Discussion

In developing its housing approach, KHDC encountered all the complexities of delivering housing in a rural town. Besides building and financing houses, the company had to identify and acquire appropriate land, deal with inexperienced and understaffed municipal officials, install both external and internal municipal services, design a funding model to make the houses affordable to the mine employees and facilitate the entire housing delivery process.

The Khumani housing approach, based on individual homeownership, stands in contrast to international and local employer housing approaches, which mostly reflect the socio-economic stratification of the workplace, are often rental based, result in isolated company housing areas, and inhibit the integration of employees into society. It is also in direct contrast to Kumba Iron Ore's approach – Kumba has largely opted for rental accommodation in Postmasburg (see Chapter 9 of this volume). Like Assmang, Kumba has also developed housing for Kolomela employees in Postmasburg and not in a new mining village adjacent to the mine, but unlike Assmang it has no formal homeownership strategy. It has built houses on a large scale throughout the town (mainly in Postdene and Airfield), but the only tenure option is rental. Kolomela mine has therefore merely shifted the mining sector's traditional housing model to a formal town, and the stock all remains on the balance sheet of the mine.

The value of homeownership is premised on the house being a bondable asset, which is applicable in the normal market situation of supply and demand. Homeownership provided by the Khumani approach has value for both the employee and employer. The former benefits from acquiring homeownership through very favourable financial arrangements in a poor community where there is a housing need; the latter benefits from a more stable workforce and avoids the long-term liability of municipal charges and maintenance and the risks and implications of owning employee houses in the event of mine downscaling. And by offering some housing support, the employer will be more likely to recruit skilled employees who might not otherwise be prepared to work in a remote mining environment.

Applying the Khumani homeownership approach in Postmasburg should be understood against the background of government policies emphasising homeownership. Sadly, the opportunity offered by Assmang has not been embraced by government, either as a concept or as an additional approach that could help deliver housing to the problematic 'gap market', i.e. households whose income is above the level that qualifies for government subsidies but below the level at which the traditional financial institutions will provide a mortgage.

The Khumani housing approach accepts that the beneficiaries are mineworkers who may pursue better employment opportunities elsewhere in the region in the event of being retrenched. Owning a house in a location that suffers a downturn in demand can turn an asset into a liability. The fact that the Khumani approach has a capital subsidy component ensures that the outstanding balance of the loan is covered in the event of a retrenchment. Postmasburg's regional function also means that housing is likely always to be needed – an obvious benefit of locating the housing in a regional centre rather than closer to the mines.

A drawback of the application of the Khumani approach in Postmasburg was the engagement of a national construction company to assure quality and speed up development. This temporarily distorted the local rental market and caused discontent among local job seekers. The economic diversification opportunity of engaging local contractors, builders and developers, who could have gained valuable experience, was largely forfeited by this decision. But this would have taken much more management time and effort, and expensive mistakes could have been made.

Conclusion

The Khumani housing approach is an alternative form of homeownership that can be described as shared ownership. The capital subsidy reduces the risks associated with mine downscaling and the potential decline in the market value of properties, and the housing allowance makes housing more affordable for the employees. The company's right to buy back the house provides the employee with a safety net and the employer with housing stock available in the long term should it be required. Homeownership via the Khumani housing approach spreads the long-term risks to the mine employees and local government, leaving the mining company with fewer risks. Furthermore, although the Khumani housing approach has been described here as applied by a big employer, a mining company, its principles could be applied to a much wider market and possibly induce smaller employers to take a similar approach. The Khumani housing approach is a useful model for providing employee housing in an environment where employees and financial institutions are reluctant to invest. The fact that only a few of the smallest houses (costing less than R500,000) have been taken up (in Boichoko) is a reflection of the relatively high income levels of mining employees, and not the affordability of the houses.

Yet some concerns remain. For example, questions can be asked about the emphasis that both Assmang and the government place on ownership and on creating so-called integrated settlements. The question of who will pay for the long-term consequences in an industry known for its volatility remains unanswered. Despite the problems associated with mining or company towns, the long-term consequences remain the responsibility of the mining company.

Note

1 The grading system is used in the mining industry to grade employees.

References

ARM (African Rainbow Minerals), 2010. *African Rainbow Minerals Housing Policy.* Sandton: ARM.

Cronje, F., 2014. *Digging for Development: The Mining Industry in South Africa and its Role in Socio-Economic Development.* Johannesburg: South African Institute for Race Relations.

Crush, J., 1989. Accommodating black miners: Home ownership on the mines. In: *South African Review 5.* Johannesburg: Ravan Press, pp. 335–347.

Crush, J., 1992. The compound in post-apartheid South Africa. *Geographical Review,* 82(4), pp. 388–400.

DoH (Department of Housing), 2004. *Breaking New Ground: A Comprehensive Plan for the Development of Sustainable Human Settlements.* Pretoria: Government Printer.

DME (Department of Minerals and Energy), 2002. *Broad-Based Socio-Economic Empowerment Charter for South Africa's Mining Industry.* Johannesburg: Government Printer.

DMR (Department of Mineral Resources), 2010. *Publication of the Amendment of the Broad-Based Socio-Economic Empowerment Charter for the South African Mining and Minerals Industry.* Pretoria: Government Printer.

DMR (Department of Mineral Resources), 2017. *Review of the Bbroad-Based Black Economic-Empowerment Charter for the South African Mining and Minerals Industry.* Pretoria: Government Printers.

Drewes, J.E. and Van Aswegen, M., 2011. Determining the vitality of urban centres. In: C.A. Brebbia, ed. *The Sustainable World.* Southampton: WIT Press, pp. 142–155.

Hoekstra, J. and Marais, L., 2016. Can Western European home ownership products bridge the South African housing gap? *Urban Forum,* 27(4), pp. 487–502.

KHDC (Khumani Housing Development Company), 2016. *Khumani Housing Development Company: Quarterly Housing Report.* Sandton: ARM.

Marais, L., 2013. The impact of mine downscaling on the Free State Goldfields. *Urban Forum,* 24(4), pp. 503–521.

Marais, L. and Cloete, J., 2013. Labour migration, settlement and mine closure in South Africa. *Geography,* 98(2), pp. 77–84.

Marais, L. and Cloete, J., 2015. Financed homeownership and the economic downturn in South Africa. *Habitat International,* 32(3), pp. 346–366.

Marais, L. and Krige, S., 2000. Who received what where in the Free State, 1994–1998: An assessment of post-apartheid housing policy and delivery. *Development Southern Africa,* 17(4), pp. 603–619.

Marais, L. and Nel, E., 2016. The dangers of growing on gold: Lessons from the history of the Free State Goldfields, South Africa. *Local Economy,* 31(1–2), pp. 282–298.

Marais, L. and Venter, A., 2006. Hating the compound, but . . . mineworker housing needs in post-apartheid South Africa. *Africa Insight,* 36(1), pp. 53–62.

Ntema, J., Marais, L., Cloete, J. and Lenka, M., 2017. Social disruption, mine closure and housing policy: Evidence from the Free State Goldfields, South Africa. *Natural Resources Forum,* 41(1), pp. 31–40.

RSA (Republic of South Africa), 1994. *White Paper on Reconstruction and Development No. 1954 of 1994.* Pretoria: Government Printer.

RSA (Republic of South Africa), 2002. *Mineral and Petroleum Resources Development Act. No. 28 of 2002*. Pretoria: Government Printer.

RSA (Republic of South Africa), 2013. *The Presidency. Special Presidential Package.* www.thepresidency.gov.za/content/much-progress-made-revitalisation-distressed-mining-towns.

Tomlinson, M., 2007. The development of a low-income housing finance sector in South Africa: Have we finally found a way forward? *Habitat International*, 31(1), pp. 77–86.

Tshangana, M., 2015. *Selected Committee Presentation on the Revitalisation of Distressed Mining Towns Programme*. Pretoria: National Department of Human Settlements.

UN (United Nations), 2013. *The Dynamics of Informal Settlements Upgrading in South Africa: Legislative and Policy Context, Problems, Tension and Contradictions.* Bratislava: United Nations.

Venter, A., Marais, L., Hoekstra, J. and Cloete, J., 2014. Reinterpreting South African housing policy through state welfare theory. *Housing, Theory and Society*, 32(3), pp. 346–366.

Section D

Working and doing business

Staples theory postulates that isolated mining settlements contribute neither to the development of the region nor to the welfare of the people, and the Dutch disease and resource curse theories further emphasise this. The original research based on these economic theories was mainly at country level, but more recently they have been applied at regional or local level. Social theories have also long argued that mining development can be bad for communities. Social disruption theory was used originally in research in Canada and the United States and has more recently been applied in Australia. A number of points from the Australian work are relevant to the situation in South Africa. As South Africa has one of the most unequal societies in the world, mining should preferably not contribute to further inequalities. The findings of our Postmasburg study were mixed: some findings supported the claims about the negative consequences of mining, but we also found much that was not as bad as the theories predicted.

Increased inequality at the local level is commonly noted in the international literature. The Australian literature describes the effects of mining on communities, one being that it makes access to housing more expensive, especially for aboriginal communities. It also describes inequalities between mineworkers and local residents in mining towns. In South Africa, the divide between mineworkers and the original inhabitants could well have resulted from the way mining towns like Postmasburg developed.

We found a second kind of inequality in Postmasburg, between mineworkers directly employed by the mine and those contracted to the mine by a contractor or labour broker. The contract workers have longer working hours, fewer days of leave, limited access to medical aid, and are less likely to belong to a union. Chapter 11 (*Work, wages and welfare in Postmasburg*) analyses labour market outcomes and the welfare of Postmasburg households. The authors compare wages, hours worked and trade union membership for mineworkers and other workers, and for mine-employed mineworkers and contract mineworkers. To determine the extent of poverty and socio-economic inequality at the household level in Postmasburg, they investigate unemployment and household welfare and socio-economic status. They compare the levels of poverty and inequality of mineworker households (again distinguishing between the two types of mineworkers) with those of other households in Postmasburg. Finally, they compare the spending patterns of mining households with those of non-mining households. They conclude that although some inequalities do exist, they are less pronounced than those found in towns dependent on underground mining.

Living in a remote mining town can have negative implications for people's psychological well-being. The Australian literature notes that this is particularly the case for women. There is an emerging body of work on the mental health consequences for shift workers in Australia's fly-in-fly-out system. Chapter 12 (*Psychological well-being on the mine*) assesses the psychological capital and levels of work engagement of mineworkers in Postmasburg. Labour regime change has been less evident in South Africa than in Australia, but shift work and contract work are becoming more common. The authors argue that the mining industry as a whole should consider how changing labour regimes affect their workforce. However, they report relatively high levels of well-being among Postmasburg mineworkers. Chapter 13 (*Businesses in Postmasburg*) looks at how business has grown in Postmasburg over the past decade and points out the long-term risks associated with this growth. Doing business in a mining town can be difficult. Staples theory claims that the mines' value chains usually bypass local enterprises. As recent examples from Australia show, local businesses usually find it difficult to reduce their dependence on the mining sector and diversify. Mine downscaling is bound to have detrimental effects on a mining-dependent business. The authors found that although many Postmasburg business owners are aware of this and acknowledge the changing trends associated with the mining cycle, they nevertheless grumble about the mines bypassing local businesses when procuring products and services.

Although many concerns remain about the effects of mining on local communities, the three chapters in this section show the realities to be substantially different from what they were two decades ago, and decidedly different from the common conception of mining communities. This may well be because Postmasburg's mines are employing higher-skilled workers, as necessitated by open-cast mining. The findings for mining communities in towns dependent on underground mining could be very different.

11 Work, wages and welfare in Postmasburg

Philippe Burger and Jean-Pierre Geldenhuys

A town of rags and riches

The Marikana killings of August 2012 and the five-month-long platinum miners' strike in 2014 once again thrust into the spotlight the living and working conditions of South African mineworkers. Earnings vary widely in the South African labour market. Mining company executives and directors draw high salaries, receive large bonuses and benefit from share options, while mineworkers complain of receiving less than R5000 a month (Forslund, 2013).The companies contend that mineworkers' earnings are in fact more like R8000 or R9000 a month, when employee deductions and employer contributions to pension funds, medical aid schemes and housing allowances are included. But while this may be true for full-time mining company employees, it is usually not true for the many mineworkers employed by labour brokers, who seldom receive any employer contributions from either the broker or the mining company. And mineworkers are often heavily indebted and have to support numerous dependants. A further grievance is that many mineworkers live in squalid conditions in mining compounds or informal settlements.

In this chapter we analyse mineworkers' labour market outcomes (such as wages, hours worked, trade union membership) and compare them with those of other workers in Postmasburg. We compare the labour market outcomes for mine-employed mineworkers with the outcomes for those employed by contractors or labour brokers (henceforth 'contractor mineworkers': these are workers who are not employed by the mine, but who may or may not perform functions or tasks that are similar to those performed by workers employed by mines). We compare the socio-economic conditions and welfare levels (income and spending, asset ownership, and so on) of households where a mineworker lives with those of households where no employed person lives, and with those of households where at least one employed person (but no mineworker) lives. And we compare these levels in households where at least one mine-employed mineworker lives with those in households where at least one contractor mineworker lives. We also estimate and compare household poverty levels, using a popular class of poverty measures.

We argue that in a mining town like Postmasburg mineworkers will be better off (in terms of labour market outcomes such as wages, hours worked, and contract duration) than non-mineworkers, and that mine-employed mineworkers will be better off than contractor mineworkers. However, we are ambivalent about whether mineworker households will be better off than non-mineworker households, especially if the mineworkers are mostly migrants living in informal housing, with little access to public services.

How mining affects local economic welfare: theoretical mechanisms and empirical findings

In this section we look at the mechanisms by which mining, theoretically, may affect economic welfare (particularly its detrimental effects) and we review the findings of microeconomic studies of the links between mining and the economic welfare of people in mining towns or districts. These local and subnational studies can be contrasted with cross-country macro-economic studies (which are not our topic here) of the links between mining and commodity cycles.

By creating jobs, mining should help to reduce poverty. Proponents of mining expansion as an economic development strategy justify their stance by pointing to increased employment and the spill-over effects of higher spending by high-earning mineworkers (Chapter 2 of this volume). But Gamu et al. (2015) observe that relatively few studies have systematically investigated the links between mining and poverty reduction. They identify six mechanisms by which mining can alleviate poverty: economic growth, fiscal transfers, employment, the creation of forward and backward links throughout the economy, private investment in public goods (notably transport infrastructure) and corporate social responsibility (CSR) initiatives by mining companies. Loayza and Rigolini (2016) further identify labour market effects as a possible poverty-alleviation mechanism.

However, the empirical evidence of the economic effects of mining is mixed, with many studies finding that mining is negatively associated with economic outcomes within and between countries. Marais et al. (Chapter 1 of this volume) identify five theoretical frameworks that have been used to study mining towns: staples theory, social disruption theory, the resource curse, Dutch disease and neo-liberalism. They note that many authors working within each of these frameworks have found substantial negative economic effects associated with mining. Gamu et al. (2015) identify seven mechanisms by which mining can be associated with poverty: low economic performance (due to the resource curse and Dutch disease), the sectoral immobility of local workers (who, lacking the necessary skills, cannot be employed in the mining sector), economic inequality, employment volatility, the creation of enclave economies, rent-seeking and negative environmental and social effects. Marais and Ntema (Chapter 2 of this volume) describe the negative social implications of mining (as identified by social disruption theory), including crime, deteriorating health and well-being, the alienation, exclusion and exploitation of indigenous communities and local citizens, and the pressures that an influx of mining migrants puts on the local housing market and public infrastructure and services.

Gamu et al. (2015) reviewed more than 50 empirical studies that investigated the effects of mining on poverty and found mixed results. They classified the studies into three types: cross-national and subnational studies, and local case studies like the one on which this book is based, examining economic outcomes in one mining town. They found that mining was often associated with exacerbation of poverty in cross-national studies focusing on industrial mining, but with alleviation of poverty in subnational studies, especially those focusing on artisanal mining. But local case studies found no discernible effect of mining on poverty.

Subnational studies that examine the effect of mining on poverty allow researchers to compare poverty rates, income levels and more, between mining and non-mining towns and districts within a country. In a subnational study using census data from the United States to establish whether the share of mining employment in total employment in coal-mining Appalachian counties in the United States is associated, either positively or negatively, with the poverty rate, Deaton and Niman (2012) found positive short-run effects (associated with the current level of mining employment) but negative long-run effects (associated with the 10-year lag of mining employment). In a subnational study comparing Appalachian and non-Appalachian counties and using census data and US county employment data, Betz et al. (2015) found no clear evidence of a resource curse effect associated with coal-mining, but they did find consistently negative associations between the coal-mining employment share and population growth and measures of entrepreneurship. Furthermore, the largest effects associated with coal-mining were driven by the boom-bust nature of the US coal-mining industry for the period 1990–2010. Al Rawashdeh et al. (2016) found evidence of a resource curse effect in southern Jordan, the country's most important mining region: it lagged behind other regions in terms of unemployment, poverty and other human development indicators. Loayza and Rigolini (2016), using district-level household and administrative data (on mining production and local fiscal transfers) for Peru, found that mining communities had higher per capita spending levels and lower poverty rates than communities in similar regions, but also higher levels of consumption inequality. In a subnational study of South African mining districts, Walker (2015) found that these shocks led to increases in mining employment and total employment, lower poverty rates and higher average number of hours worked, but to substantial decreases in employment in agriculture and slight decreases in employment in manufacturing. She notes that these last two findings could have long-run negative economic consequences, as they could indicate (premature) deindustrialisation and a lack of diversification in the South African economy: despite its abundant mineral wealth, the country is plagued by slow growth.

Local case studies like the present study allow researchers to collect detailed socio-economic information about individuals and households in a specific mining town or district. Two local case studies of the effects of industrial mining in developing countries are Bury (2005); and Mwitwa et al. (2012).

Investigating changes in land-tenure institutions, land values and land-use patterns in the Cajamarca region of Peru, Bury (2005) found that gold mining had caused substantial change to household livelihoods. With large-scale commercial mining taking over, some households had to make complete changes to their livelihood strategies because they had lost their access to natural resources. Some managed to offset this loss by increasing their economic resources, but the adaptations they made to their livelihood strategies to do this may not be sustainable because the increased land use may deplete the soil's fertility. The most successful households were those who acquired land in the nearby city and those in which at least one member was a mineworker. Around mining towns in Zambia's Copperbelt and the Democratic Republic of the Congo, Mwitwa et al. (2012) found that deforestation had caused biodiversity reduction, water and air pollution, poor health and loss of timber-dependent livelihoods.

In a cross-sectional local case study of mining settlements in the platinum belt of South Africa's North West province, which included interviews with mineworkers, mine managers and widows of miners killed during the Marikana tragedy, Makgetla and Levin (2016) found that the labour unrest and prolonged strikes between 2012 and 2014 were the result of poor living conditions and oppressive working conditions rather than merely low pay. Using the 2014 Quarterly Labour Force Survey data from Statistics South Africa, they found that median wages in the mining sector were higher than those in all the other sectors of the South African economy. They found that the miners were much more likely than the average South African to live in informal settlements and to have no piped water or flush toilets, and that their poor living conditions were not just the legacy of the apartheid migrant labour system but resulted from the rapid expansion of mining in rural areas of the North West from 1994 onwards.

Both Pilossof and Burger (Chapter 3 of this volume) and Makgetla and Levin (2016) note the way the commodity boom of the 2000s and the bust of 2011 affected the prices and volumes of iron ore and the platinum group metals, and the way this in turn affected employment on the iron ore and platinum mines. However, Makgetla and Levin also note that although both of these mining sectors experienced booms during the 2000s, employment on the more capital-intensive iron ore mines did not increase nearly as much as it did on the platinum mines. It was the influx of workers to the platinum mines, putting pressure on housing and service delivery, which led to the poor living conditions in the platinum mining areas.

During October 2014, Kumba Iron Ore commissioned a door-to-door community survey (Kumba, 2014) in the Tsantsabane Local Municipality, in which Postmasburg is situated. The survey included more than 3300 households (almost 11,500 people) and asked questions about household demographics, labour market activity, access to services and so on – questions which were also asked in the 2001 and 2011 South African Censuses and the 2007 Community Survey (all conducted by Statistics South Africa), and many of which were also included in the household questionnaire used in this study. Where possible, we compare our results to the results obtained in this survey. Interestingly, the Kumba survey found a decrease in unemployment (from 33.9% to 29%) and an increase in nominal household incomes from R40,429 to R135,466 (a real increase from R40,429 to R64,585, or 59.7%) between 2001 and 2014, a period of mine construction at Kolomela mine, ending in 2011 (Kumba, 2014).[1]

Data, method, limitations and cautions

To analyse labour market outcomes and household welfare in Postmasburg we used data from the quantitative household survey used for this book and described by Marais et al. in Chapter 1 of this volume. The fieldwork was conducted between October 2015 and February 2016. This questionnaire was based on questions in the adult and household questionnaires used in the National Income Dynamic Study (NIDS) conducted by the South African Labour and Demographic Research Unit (SALDRU) and in the General Household Survey (GHS) conducted by Statistics South Africa.

In our analysis of labour market outcomes in Postmasburg, we divided workers into two main categories: non-mineworkers and mineworkers, while further sub-dividing mineworkers into two sub-categories: those employed by the mine, and those employed by contractors. We then compared the means and medians of the gross and net wages of these categories of workers, and also compared the means, medians and proportions of other labour market outcomes, such as the number of hours worked per week, trade union membership etc. Meanwhile, to analyse household welfare levels in Postmasburg, we divided households into three categories: households without an employed adult, households with at least one employed adult, but no mineworkers, and households with at least one adult employed as a mineworker. We also differentiated between contractor-employed and mine-employed mineworker households, and then compared the mean and median per capita income, spending and food spending of these households, while also estimating and comparing poverty measures for these households.

It is important to note that our chosen study design, the cross-sectional local case study, has some limitations. It does not allow us to make causal inferences about the effects of mining on economic welfare in Postmasburg, because we do not have other, non-mining districts that could serve as counterfactuals (as we would have in a subnational study). And since the data we use are cross-sectional (collected from different individuals and households at a particular point in time, giving a snapshot of labour market outcomes and household welfare levels), we cannot use them to determine the effect of fluctuations in iron ore mining on employment, income and poverty in Postmasburg (as we could do with longitudinal data).[2] Some cautions also apply. When interpreting the results of this study, it is important to take its context into account. It was conducted during the end of 2015 and the beginning of 2016, a period of falling iron ore prices and production, mine restructuring and looming retrenchments (see Pilossof and Burger, Chapter 3 of this volume). Therefore, caution must be exercised in generalising our results to other mining towns (which may mine different minerals and be subject to different price and output dynamics). The differences between the South African and the international mining industries must also be taken into account – refer to the discussion in Marais and Ntema (Chapter 2 of this volume).

However, as Gamu et al. (2015) note, a cross-sectional local case study like ours, in effect a snapshot of the conditions prevailing in a particular mining town at a particular point in time, is a useful complement to mixed-method (quantitative and qualitative) studies that aim to fully understand all the effects of mining on a town. See other chapters in this volume for discussions of qualitative interviews with town planners, municipal managers, business owners and other important role players in Postmasburg.

Labour market outcomes

In this section we present data, compiled from our questionnaire, on the labour market status and employment outcomes of working-age adults, and draw comparisons between mineworkers and other workers, and between mine-employed mineworkers and contractor mineworkers.[3]

As Table 11.1 shows, the labour force participation rate (according to both broad and narrow definitions of the labour force) exceeds 70%, while the labour absorption rate (the ratio of the number of workers to the number of working-age individuals) is 49%.[4] The broad unemployment rate is slightly more than 33%, while the narrow unemployment rate is 26%. In the 2014 Kolomela SEAT Report (Kumba, 2014), the narrow unemployment rate was 29% for Tsantsabane Municipality. Irrespective of which definition of unemployment is used, more than 40% of the unemployed have never worked, and of the unemployed who have worked previously, more than half are long-term unemployed (having last worked more than one year ago).

Table 11.2 compares employment outcomes (such as wages earned, contract duration and trade union membership) for mineworkers and non-mineworkers, and

Table 11.1 Labour market status indicators, working-age individuals (15–64 years) (n = 2717)

	Number of observations	%
Labour market status		
Not economically active	556	26.55
Non-searching unemployed	149	7.12
Searching unemployed	361	17.24
Employed	1028	49.09
Labour force participation		
Labour force participation rate (broad)	1538	73.45
Labour force participation rate (narrow)	1389	71.41
Unemployment rate		
Broad	510	33.16
Narrow	361	25.99
Time since last job (broad unemployment)		
Less than 3 months	22	7.38
3–6 months	48	16.11
6–12 months	57	19.13
1–3 years	79	26.51
More than 3 years	92	30.87
Time since last job (narrow unemployment)		
Less than 3 months	14	6.67
3–6 months	37	17.62
6–12 months	45	21.43
1–3 years	57	27.14
More than 3 years	57	27.14

Note: n = number of working-age individuals.

Table 11.2 Employment outcomes, by type of worker

	Non-mineworkers (n = 521)		All mineworkers (n = 537)		Mine-employed mineworkers (n = 344, 71.37%)		Contractor mineworkers (n = 133, 28.63%)	
	n	Mean (s.d)	n	Mean (s.d)	n	Mean (s.d.)	n	Mean (s.d.)
Gross wage	189	4716.566 (4977.35)	212	11583.98 (11559.75)	114	15667.92 (12850.66)	83	6106.843 (3818.207)
Median (25pc, 75pc)		2900 (1500, 6000)		9650 (5000, 1500)		14000 (10000, 18000)		5500 (3000, 7372)
Net wage	178	3958.051 (3730.861)	195	8527.036 (6047.939)	108	10965.26 (6717.37)	76	5389.026 (3157.648)
Median (25pc, 75pc)		2650 (1500, 5000)		8000 (4500, 11000)		10000 (8000, 135000)		4900 (3000, 7000)
Years of education	502	10.15 (3.26)	512	11.402 (2.10)	333	11.79 (1.96)	131	10.46 (2.34)
Median (25pc, 75pc)		11 (9, 12)		12 (11, 12)		12 (12, 12)		11 (10, 12)
Hours worked per week	392	30.24 (19.15)	402	32.69 (21.47)	237	35.31 (20.27)	118	25.02 (21.17)
Median (25pc, 75pc)		38 (9, 45)		40 (9, 48)		42 (12, 48)		10 (8, 45)
Union membership (freq, %)	424	152 (35.85%)	514	399 (77.63%)	334	300 (89.82%)	129	60 (46.51%)
Received bonus past 12 months (freq, %)	418	183 (43.78%)	490	354 (72.24%)	316	267 (84.49%)	127	57 (44.88%)
Covered by medical aid (freq, %)	439	143 (32.57%)	520	364 (70%)	339	307 (90.56%)	130	34 (26.15%)
Receives pension (freq, %)	436	244 (55.96%)	520	443 (85.19%)	339	316 (93.22%)	130	88 (67.69%)
UIF is deducted (freq, %)	442	351 (79.41)	524	506 (96.56)	340	329 (96.76%)	133	129 (96.99%)
Contract duration (freq, %)	439		523		341		130	
Limited duration		50 (11.39%)		57 (10.90%)		16 (4.69%)		34 (26.15%)
Unspecified duration		108 (24.60%)		71 (13.58%)		9 (2.64%)		55 (42.31%)
Permanent		281 (64.01%)		395 (75.53%)		316 (92.67%)		41 (31.54%)

Notes: freq = frequency; pc = percentile); s.d. = standard deviation. Due to the presence of outliers, the data for gross and net wages were trimmed at the 1st and 99th percentiles (Devore and Berk, 2011). Gross and net wages in ZAR. Due to refusals or ignorance, employer (mine vs contractor) could be assigned to only 477 of the 537 mineworkers.

for mine-employed mineworkers and contractor mineworkers. As is evident from the table, a substantial proportion of respondents (between 60% and 66%) did not provide any information about their wages.[5] Therefore, care should be taken when drawing conclusions about mean and median wage levels.

Table 11.2 demonstrates that mineworkers (about half of the sample) are much better off than other workers in Postmasburg; they have much higher gross and net wages, and their mean and median net wages are between two and three times greater than those of non-mineworkers. These findings are line with those reported by Makgetla and Levin (2016). Using data from 2014 from Statistics South Africa, they found that workers in the mining sector have higher median wages (R7,000 per month) than the average for workers in all other sectors of the South African economy, while only workers in the social or personal services sector and in the business services sector had higher mean wages They also work slightly more hours per week, are more than twice as likely to be trade union members, much more likely to have received a bonus in the past year, to be members of pension funds and medical aids, and to have unemployment insurance, and more likely to be appointed on a permanent basis (almost three-quarters of them are permanently employed, while almost a quarter of non-mineworkers are temporary). Table 11.2 also reveals that mine-employed mineworkers are much better off than contractor mineworkers: both the mean and the median gross and net wages of the former far exceed those of the latter. This is in line with the finding by Makgetla and Levin (2016) that contract mineworkers earn much less than mine employees. The stark differences between the wages of mineworkers and other workers, and between the wages of mine-employed mineworkers and contractor mineworkers are shown in Figure 11.1. The horizontal axis of Figure 11.1 indicates the monthly wage in rand and the vertical axis, measured as a density, shows the proportion of workers earning at each possible value of the wage.

The top right panel of Figure 11.1, demonstrating the distribution of net wages for mineworkers and non-mineworkers, explains why the mean and median net wages of the former far exceed those of the latter (see Table 11.2): the density distribution of mineworkers' wages lies to the right of that of non-mineworkers' wages – the peak as well as more of the area below the curve for mineworkers lies to the right of the curve for other workers.

The bottom panel of Figure 11.1 indicates the distribution of the net wages of mine-employed mineworkers and contractor mineworkers: the mass of the distribution of the net wages of mine-employed mineworkers lies to the right of the distribution of the net wages of contractor mineworkers, explaining why the mean and median net wages of mine-employed mineworkers far exceed those of contractor mineworkers. Lastly, the top left panel of Figure 11.1 shows the distributions of the gross and net wages for the entire sample of workers.

Table 11.2 illustrates that mine-employed mineworkers work longer hours, and are much more likely to be trade union members than mineworkers employed by contractors. They are also much more likely to receive pensions and be members of medical aids, and to have received a bonus in the past 12 months. More

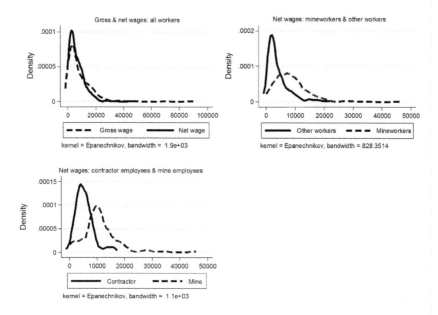

Figure 11.1 Kernel densities: (trimmed) wages

than 90% of them are permanent employees, compared to only 30% of contractor mineworkers. While contractor mineworkers are clearly worse off than mine-
employed mineworkers, more than 70% of mineworkers in the sample reported
being employed by the mine at which they work.

Contractor mineworkers are more likely than non-mineworkers to be trade
union members, to receive pensions and to have unemployment insurance. But
they are less likely to have medical aid, and much less likely to be permanently
employed. Contractor mineworkers also work noticeably fewer hours per week
than non-mineworkers.

Household welfare

In this section we present data, compiled from our questionnaire, on Postmasburg
households' economic welfare, including income and spending, asset ownership
and access to public services like electricity and sanitation. We compare welfare
levels between mineworker households, non-mineworker households and non-
employed households. Mineworker households are households in which at least
one mineworker resides; non-mineworker households are households in which
at least one employed person (but no mineworker) resides; and non-employed
households are households in which no member is employed.

Table 11.3 shows the size and composition of households and basic demographic information about the heads of households. The household head characteristics summarised in this table are for the 909 households for which resident household heads could be identified. Of these 909 households, 886 identified a single (resident) head, 12 identified multiple persons as household heads (with the eldest of these being assigned headship status), and 11 single-person households identified a non-resident as the head of the households). The remaining 23 households were deemed to have non-resident heads, for which no personal characteristics were collected.

Table 11.3 indicates that mineworker households are smaller than non-mineworker households and their household dependency ratio is 20 to 25 percentage points lower than that of non-employed and non-mineworker households. Mineworker households are markedly more likely than non-employed and non-mineworker households to be single-person households, and non-mineworker households by far the least likely. Findings from the 2014 Kolomela SEAT Report are similar to those reported here: the average household size for the Tsantsabane Municipality was 3.46 (Kumba, 2014).

For the sample overall, and for non-mineworker and mineworker households, household heads tend to be male, particularly in mineworker households. Non-employed households are more likely to be headed by females and, as is typical in South Africa, these female-headed households have lower levels of household welfare (Rogan, 2016). The majority of household heads are black (particularly in mineworker households) and about a third are coloured. Seven households reported white household heads and none reported Indian or Asian. About three-quarters of the heads of non-mineworker and non-employed households had lived in Postmasburg in 2005, but less than two-thirds of the heads of mineworker households.

Household heads are predominantly Setswana speakers, particularly in mineworker households. Heads of mineworker households are noticeably younger than the heads of other households, and they also have higher levels of education: about 60% have at least a matric (national senior) certificate, but only about a third of the heads of non-mineworker households and about a fifth of the heads of non-employed households have at least matric. About two-thirds of household heads are employed. Of these employed heads, almost two-thirds are mineworkers, and almost three-quarters of them are employed by mines and not by labour brokers or contractors.

Table 11.3 also demonstrates selected household demographic information, disaggregated by type of mineworker household. We identified two types of mineworker household: those with no resident mine-employed mineworker but at least one contractor mineworker are referred to as contractor mineworker households, and those with no resident contractor mineworker but at least one mine-employed mineworker are referred to as mine-employed mineworker households. Contractor mineworker households are smaller than mine-employed mineworker households, much more likely to be single-person households, and have much lower dependency ratios. Household heads of mine-employed mineworker households are slightly younger than heads of contractor mineworker households, more

Table 11.3 Household size and composition, and characteristics of head, by type of household

Household characteristics	Full sample	Non-employed HHs	Non-mineworker HHs	All mineworker HHs	Contractor mineworker HH	Mine-employed mineworker HH
Household size	(n = 1003)	(n = 199)	(n = 325)	(n = 474)	(n = 120)	(n = 316)
Mean (s.d.)	3.267 (2.07)	3.161 (1.94)	3.787 (2.25)	2.975 (1.92)	2.64 (2.29)	3.11 (1.80)
Median (25pc, 75pc)	3 (2, 4)	3 (2, 4)	3 (2, 5)	3 (1, 4)	2 (1, 3.5)	3 (2, 4)
Household dependency ratio	(n = 932)	(n = 180)	(n = 304)	(n = 445)	(n = 115)	(n = 297)
Mean (s.d.)	46.158 (62.73)	60.037 (78.42)	54.833 (68.41)	34.93 (48.055)	23.07 (41.31)	40.49 (50.76)
Median (25pc, 75pc)	25 (0, 66.67)	33.333 (0, 100)	33.333 (0, 100)	0 (0, 50)	0 (0, 40)	25 (0, 66.67)
Single-person HH (freq, %)	227 (22.6%)	43 (21.6%)	48 (14.77%)	133 (28.1%)	54 (45%)	69 (21.83%)
HH characteristics						
Male	609 (67%)	94 (45.19%)	154 (60.16%)	357 (80.95%)	97 (85.09%)	234 (80.41%)
African	612 (67.33%)	137 (65.87%)	157 (61.33%)	315 (71.43%)	97 (85.09%)	195 (67.01%)
Coloured	285 (31.35%)	69 (33.17%)	95 (37.11%)	120 (27.21%)	25 (21.93%)	112 (38.49%)
Setswana-speaking	441 (48.51%)	96 (46.2%)	115 (44.9%)	228 (51.7%)		
Afrikaans-speaking	350 (38.5%)	86 (41.4%)	113 (44.1%)	149 (33.8%)	60 (52.63%)	150 (51.55%)
Age	(n = 876)	(n = 200)	(n = 249)	(n = 424)		
Mean (s.d)	41.45 (13.04)	45.925 (15.49)	44.157 (12.31)	37.79 (11.01)	39.89 (12.65)	37.05 (10.09)
Median (25pc, 75pc)	38 (31, 50)	45 (31.5, 60)	43 (35, 52)	35 (30, 43)	37 (31, 46)	34 (30, 42)
Lived in P'burg in 2005	622 (68.5%)	172 (82.69%)	191 (74.61%)	258 (58.5%)	58 (50.88%)	178 (61.17%)
Education		(n = 196)	(n = 238)	(n = 418)	(n = 107)	(n = 279)
Mean (s.d)	9.843 (3.58)	7.765 (4.20)	9.315 (3.87)	11.100 (2.37)	10.26 (2.40)	11.44 (2.33)
Median (25pc, 75pc)	11 (9, 12)	9 (5,11)	10 (8, 12)	12 (10, 12)	11 (10, 12)	12 (11, 12)
Employed (freq, %)	597 (66%)	NA	195 (76.2%)	399 (90.5%)	101 (88.60%)	266 (91.41%)

Note: freq = frequency; s.d. = standard deviation; pc = percentile; NA = not applicable. The 25th and 75th percentiles give the middle 50% of the distribution. Dependency ratio = number of dependants (age < 15 or age > 65) to number of working-age adults. Due to refusal or ignorance, only 998 of the 1003 households could be identified as non-employed, non-mineworker or mineworker households, while only 436 of the 474 mineworker households could be identified as contractor mineworker HHs or mine-employed mineworker HHs.

educated, more likely to have lived in Postmasburg in 2005, slightly more likely to be employed, less likely to be black and slightly less likely to be male.

Table 11.4 shows household per capita income, per capita spending levels, ownership of durable assets and access to public services (electricity, water and sanitation).

As was the case for wages (Table 11.2), Table 11.4 illustrates that non-response for household income and household spending was high (about 48% for income, about 50% for spending). However, non-response was extremely low for ownership of household assets, and for household access to public services. As is evident from the table, household access to public utilities or services (electricity, piped water, flush toilet in yard), and household ownership of the durable assets listed in Table 11.4, is widespread (with ownership of a computer and ownership of a car being the two notable exceptions). In the Kolomela SEAT Report (Kumba, 2014), 18% of households sampled in the Tsantsabane Municipality lived in informal dwellings, while 72% had piped water in their dwelling, 86% had access to electricity, and 70% had a flush toilet in their yards.

Table 11.4 also shows values for a count asset index and a principal components asset index. These two indices are often constructed and used as proxies for household welfare in developing countries, where data on household income levels and household spending are often not collected, or unreliable (Booysen et al., 2008). The assets selected for inclusion in the construction of the asset indices correspond to those routinely included in the construction of asset indices for sub-Saharan African countries (e.g. Booysen et al., 2008; Harttgen et al., 2013).

The count asset index was constructed along the lines of Harttgen et al. (2013) by simply counting the number of assets a household owns and the number of public services to which it has access. The minimum value for the count asset index is 0 (household does not own any of the assets and does not have access to any of the public services listed in Table 11.4), and the maximum is 11 (household owns all of the assets and has access to all of the public services listed in Table 11.4).

A drawback of the count asset index is that equal (unitary) weights are assigned to all of the assets included in the calculation of the index, irrespective of their individual importance in explaining household welfare. We therefore used principal components analysis (PCA) to construct a second asset index. In PCA, the weight assigned to each asset in the asset index is estimated as follows. From the set of correlated asset variables, a set of uncorrelated components is created, each consisting of linear, weighted combinations of the asset variables used to construct the asset index. These uncorrelated components are then inverted to obtain the asset indices and the weights for each asset, with the first (principal) component used as the asset index (this is also the component that explains most of the co-variation between the asset variables; see Vyas, 2006; and Harttgen et al., 2013, for a more technical discussion). Because each asset is standardised,[6] the PCA asset index can take on negative values.

While the two asset indices are highly correlated with each other (pairwise correlation coefficient = 0.99), the correlations between both asset indices and household income per capita and household spending per capita are very low (ranging

Table 11.4 Household welfare, by type of household

Indicator	Full sample		Not employed (n = 199)		Employed HH, not mine (n = 325)		All mineworker HH (n = 474)		Contractor mineworker HH (n = 120)		Mine-employed mineworker HH (n = 316)	
	n	mean (s.d.)	n	mean (s.d)	n	mean (s.d)	n	mean (s.d)	n	mean (s.d)	n	mean (s.d)
Income per capita Median (25pc, 75pc)	449	2738.56 (3432.43) 1250 (500, 4000)	116	674.98 (651.98) 500 (265, 750)	150	1900.62 (2337.80) 1000 (450, 2300)	183	4733.47 (4118.67) 3600 (1500, 7000)	67	4072.14 (3129.42) 3500 (1500, 6000)	103	5342.54 (4731.19) 4000 (1400, 9000)
Spending per capita Median (25pc, 75pc)	485	2071.09 (2306.48) 1200 (500, 3000)	116	626.44 (554.26) 479.38 (250, 725)	160	1670.57 (2134.79) 875 (500, 2000)	209	3179.51 (2490.68) 2500 (1333.33, 4500)	75	3001.25 (2277.60) 3000 (1200, 4000)	117	3341.29 (2675.88) 2250 (1400, 5000)
Food spend per cap.Median (25pc, 75pc)	601	585.82 (451.71) 500 (250, 800)	122	312.79 (215.79) 268.33 (150, 400)	198	502.68 (427.44) 375 (200, 700)	281	762.94 (468.73) 700 (500, 1000)	88	650.90 (394.67) 500 (362.50, 800)	169	837.74 (502.11) 750 (500, 1000)
Food share (%) Median (25pc, 75pc)	469	41.10 (25.39) 35.97 (22.22, 53.33)	110	57.14 (25.33) 50.71 (39.13, 71.43)	151	41.81 (23.65) 38.46 (25, 50)	208	32.11 (22.28) 25.32 (16.67, 40.56)	75	30.06 (23.49) 22.86 (14.55, 40)	116	33.76 (23.07) 26.97 (18.75, 42.86)
Asset index: PCAMedian (25pc, 75pc)	946	0.16 (2.32) 1.21 (-0.30, 1.63)	182	-0.69 (2.48) .41 (-2.17, 1.21)	304	0.03 (2.25) 1.20 (-0.46, 1.52)	458	0.57 (2.19) 1.52 (0.64, 1.94)	110	-1.10 (2.85) 0.54 (-4.57, 1.21)	311	1.27 (1.35) 1.63 (1.21, 1.94)
Asset index: CountMedian (25pc, 75pc)	946	8.12 (3.07) 9 (7, 10)	182	6.78 (3.10) 8 (5, 9)	304	7.86 (2.99) 9 (7, 10)	458	8.82 (2.91) 10 (9, 11)	110	6.52 (3.60) 8 (2, 9)	311	9.79 (1.86) 10 (9, 11)
		freq (%)		freq (%)		freq (%)		freq (%)		freq (%)		freq (%)
Uses electricity(cook, light, or heat)	996	808 (81.12%)	198	145 (73.23%)	323	256 (79.26%)	472	404 (85.59%)	119	76 (63.87%)	315	299 (94.92%)
Flush toilet in yard	951	741 (77.92%)	182	123 (67.58%)	305	234 (76.72%)	461	381 (82.65%)	112	63 (56.25%)	312	293 (93.91%)

(Continued)

Table 11.4 (Continued)

Indicator	Full sample		Not employed (n = 199)		Employed HH, not mine (n = 325)		All mineworker HH (n = 474)		Contractor mineworker HH (n = 120)		Mine-employed mineworker HH (n = 316)	
	n	mean (s.d.)	n	mean (s.d)	n	mean (s.d)	n	mean (s.d)	n	mean (s.d)	n	mean (s.d)
Piped water on site	997	804 (80.64%)	198	142 (71.72%)	324	261 (80.56%)	472	398 (84.32%)	119	74 (62.18%)	315	295 (93.65%)
Dwelling is formal	997	737 (73.92%)	198	128 (64.65%)	324	222 (68.52%)	472	384 (81.36%)	119	66 (55.46%)	315	293 (93.02%)
Owns TV	994	783 (78.77%)	197	131 (66.50%)	323	254 (78.64%)	472	397 (84.11%)	119	73 (61.34%)	315	294 (93.33%)
Owns computer	995	328 (32.96%)	198	25 (12.63%)	323	91 (28.17%)	472	211 (44.70%)	119	21 (17.65%)	315	181 (57.46%)
Owns mobile phone	995	949 (95.38%)	198	177 (89.39%)	323	303 (93.81%)	472	467 (98.94%)	119	119 (100%)	315	312 (99.05%)
Owns car	995	448 (45.03%)	198	39 (19.70%)	323	111 (34.37%)	472	298 (63.14%)	119	49 (41.18%)	315	230 (73.02%)
Owns oven or stove	993	851 (85.70%)	197	156 (79.19%)	323	276 (85.45%)	471	417 (88.54%)	118	81 (68.64%)	315	303 (96.19%)
Owns microwave	994	626 (62.98%)	198	89 (44.95%)	323	191 (59.13%)	471	344 (73.04%)	119	48 (40.34%)	314	314 (87.58%)
Owns fridge	994	762 (76.66%)	198	125 (63.13%)	323	243 (75.23%)	471	392 (83.23%)	118	70 (59.32%)	315	295 (93.65%)

Note: freq = frequency; s.d. = standard deviation; pc = percentile; HH = household; PCA = principal component analysis. Due to the presence of outliers, the data for income per capita, spending per capita and food spending per capita were trimmed at the 1st and 99th percentiles (Devore and Berk, 2011). The medians and 25th and 75th percentiles of the untrimmed data are very similar to those reported here, but the means and standard deviations differ noticeably (as expected). The qualitative conclusions drawn from these trimmed data are, however, the same as those drawn from the untrimmed data. The food share in total spending was obtained by dividing reported food spending by reported overall household spending (while an upper limit of 1, i.e. 100%, was imposed on the ratio). Due to refusal or ignorance, only 436 of the 474 mineworker households could be identified as contractor mineworker HHs or mine-employed mineworker HHs.

from 0.05 to 0.10 for untrimmed per capita income and spending, while ranging from 0.01 to 0.08 for trimmed per capita income and spending). However, the pairwise correlations between the asset indices and (trimmed) household income and (trimmed) household spending (unadjusted for household size), are much higher, ranging from 0.29 to 0.36 (the pairwise correlations between the asset indices and untrimmed income and spending range from 0.07 to 0.09, though). Booysen et al. (2008) say low correlation coefficients between asset indices and household income or spending levels are not uncommon, because the discrete nature of the assets comprising the indices makes these indices imperfect approximations for income- and spending-based household welfare measures. They also note that asset indices are slow moving compared to income and spending. The only information captured about the asset is whether the household owns that particular asset, and that it is in working condition: no information is available about the age, quantity and value of the assets that the household owns.

Table 11.4 expresses that mineworker households are much better off (in terms of per capita income and spending, overall asset index scores and ownership of specific individual assets) than non-mineworker households, and non-mineworker households are, in turn, much better off than non-employed households. Mineworker households are 13 and 16 percentage points more likely to live in a formal dwelling than non-mineworker and non-employed households, respectively, and more likely than those households to own of every type of asset listed in Table 11.4, often by a substantial margin. For example, they are 16 and 32 percentage points more likely to own a computer and 29 and 43 percentage points more likely to own a car than non-mineworker and non-employed households, respectively. Mineworker households also devote a smaller portion of total household spending to food than non-mineworker households, who, in turn, devote a smaller portion of total household spending to food spending than non-employed households.

Table 11.4 also illustrates household income, spending and asset ownership by type of mineworker household: contractor and mine-employed. As expected (given the wage results presented in Table 11.2), they differ substantially in asset ownership: mine-employed mineworker households are much more likely to report ownership of all of the assets (with the exception of mobile phones) listed in Table 11.4: the asset ownership rates of these households are mostly at least 30 percentage points higher than the asset ownership rates of contractor mineworker households These higher asset ownership rates translate into much higher asset indices for the mine-employed mineworker households. We also see large differences in the mean and median per capita food spending levels between the two types of household: mine-employed mineworker households spend much more on food per capita than contractor mineworker households.

Surprisingly, given the large difference in wages between mine-employed mineworkers and contractor mineworkers shown in Figure 11.1 and Table 11.2, there are no large differences between the mean and median per capita income and spending levels of the two types of mineworker households. Moreover, contractor mineworker households even have higher median per capita spending levels than mine-employed mineworker households. In contrast to the large differences

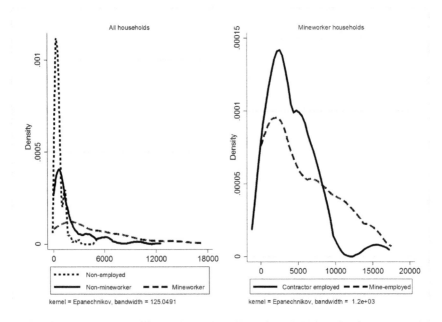

Figure 11.2 Kernel densities: (trimmed) household income per capita

between the wages of mine-employed mineworkers and contract workers (see Figure 11.1), their income and spending distributions also do not differ much (see Figures 11.2 and 11.3). They do, however, differ significantly from those of non-employed and non-mineworker households.

Figure 11.2 shows the distribution of household income per capita, by type of household. The left-hand panel confirms the findings presented in Table 11.4: mineworker households earn higher incomes than non-mineworker households, who, in turn, earn higher incomes than non-employed households (the peak of the income distribution lies furthest to the right for the mineworker households, and also has the longest tail). The right-hand panel shows the difference between the per capita income distributions of the two types of mineworker household: although the income levels at which the two distributions peak are close to one another, the mine-employed mineworker distribution has a fatter right-tail, meaning there are proportionally more such households with higher household income levels. Although the peaks are close, the fatter tail of the distribution of the per capita household income of mine-employed mineworker households raises its mean value somewhat, relative to that of contractor mineworker households. Nevertheless, the median and mean per capita household income are much closer than the median and mean wages of mine-employed and contractor mineworkers (shown in Table 11.2). A very similar picture emerges for household spending (Figure 11.3),

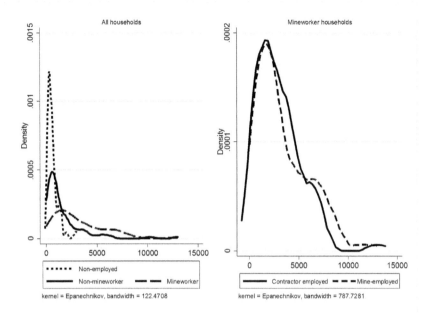

Figure 11.3 Kernel densities: (trimmed) household spending per capita

except in this case the peaks are even closer, while the tail of the distribution of the per capita household spending of mine-employed mineworker households is not very much fatter than the tail of the distribution of the per capita spending of contractor households (implying small differences between the mean and median values, as shown in Table 11.2).

The unexpectedly small differences between the (mean and median) per capita household income and per capita household spending of mine-employed and contractor mineworker households could be attributed to differences in household size and composition and differences in the number of sources of non-wage and non-employment income that these households receive.

As Table 11.3 illustrates, mine-employed mineworker households are on average larger, have higher dependency ratios and are less likely to be single-person households than contractor mineworker households. Furthermore, the ratio of employed household members to household size is substantially lower for mine-employed mineworker households (mean 57.2%, median 50%) than for contractor mineworker households (mean 69.2%, median 77.5%). Therefore, although the total household income for mine-employed mineworkers exceeds that of contractor mineworkers, it also, on average, needs to sustain larger households. Mean and median household income levels, unadjusted for household size, are R12,134 and R10,000 for mine-employed mineworker households and R5899 and R5500 for contractor mineworker households. These values are based on values of per capita income and per capita spending that we trimmed at their bottom 1st and top 99th percentiles. Thus, when adjusted for household size (and therefore expressed in per capita terms), household income and household spending of mine-employed and contractor households are much more closely aligned than the individual wages of mine- and contractor-employed mineworkers.

Mine-employed mineworker households are less likely than contractor mineworker households to receive other, non-employment, forms of income. Specifically, they are slightly less likely to receive an old-age pension (6.4% vs 8.4%) or a disability grant (1.6% vs 2.5%), and much less likely to receive a child support grant (11.7% vs 23.5%). They are also less likely to receive rental income (2.2% vs 3.4%) or income from a private pension (2.2% vs 3.4%). However, they are slightly more likely to receive some form of self-employment income (5.7% vs 3.4%), remittances (4.4% vs 2.5%) or investment income (1.27% vs 0%). However, the effect of grants seems to outweigh the effect of self-employed income, remittances and investment income. We can therefore conclude that the conflicting wage and per capita income and spending results are mainly due to differences in household size and composition, while also possibly reflecting differences in the non-employment sources of income that the two types of mineworker household receive.

Household poverty

In this section we look at the prevalence and acuteness of poverty among workers in Postmasburg. We present a formal measurement of poverty using the Foster-Greer-Thorbecke (FGT) poverty measures (Foster et al., 1984) (Table 11.5). The poverty measure of interest can be then be estimated using $P_\alpha = \frac{1}{N} \sum \left(\frac{G_i}{z} \right)^\alpha, \alpha \geq 0$, where: P_α is the poverty measure of interest, $\alpha = 0$ yields the poverty headcount, $\alpha = 1$ yields the poverty gap, $\alpha = 2$ yields the squared poverty gap, z is the poverty line, $G_i = (z - y_i)$, if $y_i < z$ (and 0 otherwise), and N is the number of households (Haughton and Khandker, 2009).

The poverty headcount (P0) gives the percentage of households that are poor. The poverty gap (P1) shows the extent to which households fall below the poverty line, expressed as a percentage of the poverty line (therefore indicating how much it would cost to lift households out of poverty, as percentage of the poverty line). The squared poverty gap (P2) takes into account inequality among the poor. However, P2, although widely reported (a higher value of P2 for a group of households indicates greater income inequality among poor households), lacks an intuitive interpretation (Haughton and Khandker, 2009).

To construct the FGT poverty measures, we used four separate per capita poverty lines: the upper-bound national poverty line, the national food poverty line, the upper-bound provincial poverty line and the provincial food poverty line (Stats SA, 2015). As the Stats SA prices were for 2011, we converted the poverty lines to 2015 prices using the South African and Northern Cape consumer price indices for urban areas – for the food poverty lines we used the prices in those indices for

Table 11.5 FGT poverty indices, national and provincial poverty lines, spending and income, by type of household

Indicator	Overall (full sample)		Non-employed HH		Non-mineworker HH		Mineworker HH (all)		Contractor mineworker HH		Mine-employed mineworker HH	
HH income	SA line	NC line	SA line	NC line	SA line	NC line	SA line	NC line	SA line	NC line	SA line	NC line
P(0)	0.44	0.42	0.79	0.78	0.49	0.46	0.17	0.16	0.09	0.06	0.23	0.23
P(1)	0.27	0.25	0.47	0.44	0.28	0.26	0.12	0.12	0.04	0.04	0.18	0.18
P(2)	0.20	0.19	0.33	0.30	0.20	0.18	0.11	0.11	0.04	0.03	0.17	0.16
HH spending												
P(0)	0.49	0.47	0.82	0.81	0.58	0.55	0.18	0.17	0.18	0.18	0.15	0.15
P(1)	0.27	0.25	0.50	0.47	0.29	0.26	0.10	0.09	0.08	0.07	0.09	0.08
P(2)	0.19	0.18	0.35	0.33	0.19	0.17	0.07	0.07	0.05	0.04	0.07	0.07
HH food spending												
P(0)	0.47	0.42	0.79	0.71	0.57	0.52	0.26	0.21	0.33	0.28	0.22	0.16
P(1)	0.23	0.22	0.42	0.39	0.28	0.26	0.11	0.10	0.15	0.13	0.10	0.09
P(2)	0.16	0.14	0.28	0.26	0.18	0.17	0.07	0.07	0.10	0.08	0.07	0.07

Note: P(0) = poverty headcount; P(1) = poverty gap; P(2) = squared poverty gap; HH = household. SA line = South African (national) poverty line; NC line = Northern Cape (provincial) poverty line. National line = R965 for HH income and spending and R429 for HH food spending; provincial line = R878 for HH income and HH spending and R399 for HH food spending.

food and non-alcoholic beverages. This gave us the following four poverty lines: R965 (national line, R779 in 2011 prices), R878 (provincial line, R705 in 2011 prices), R429 (national food line, R335 in 2011 prices) and R399 (provincial food line, R310 in 2011 prices).

Table 11.5 demonstrates the results for all three poverty measures (P0, P1 and P2), over all four poverty lines, for the overall sample and disaggregated by type of household.

As Table 11.5 shows, the poverty headcounts (for the overall sample) vary from 0.42 to 0.49 (implying that 42% to 49% of the sampled households lie below particular poverty lines, and are therefore classified as poor), and the poverty gaps vary from 0.22 to 0.27 (implying that an amount equals to 22% to 27% of the poverty line value will have to be spent to lift poor households above the poverty line). Statistics South Africa (2015) found that in 2011 the South African poverty rate (headcount) was 53.8% and the food poverty rate (headcount) was 21.7%. While the poverty rates (headcounts) shown in Table 11.5 are in line with national estimates, the food poverty rates (headcounts) are much higher than Stats SA estimated for South Africa in 2011, and may warrant closer further investigation in future.

As expected (given the household poverty results demonstrated in Table 11.4, all three poverty measures, across both the national and the provincial poverty lines, are highest for the non-employed households (with poverty headcounts from 0.71 to 0.82, implying that, depending on the poverty line and household poverty measure used, from 71% to 82% of non-employed households are poor). Furthermore, also as expected, all three poverty measures, across all the poverty lines, are the lowest for mineworker households (with poverty headcounts indicating that from 16% to 26% of mineworker households are poor, depending on the household welfare measure and poverty line used). Finally, the poverty headcounts indicate that from 46% to 58% of non-mineworker households are poor. These poverty headcounts indicate that there is substantial poverty in Postmasburg, even among households with at least one employed member: working poverty therefore seems to be fairly common. Across all three household poverty measures, the poverty gaps show that, on average, poor mineworker households are not as far below the poverty line as the other types of households, and the squared poverty gaps show that mineworker households' per capita income, per capita spending and per capita food spending are the most equally distributed below the poverty line.

Lastly, Table 11.5 also expresses that mine-employed mineworker households are less likely than contractor mineworker households to be poor, if per capita household spending or per capita household food spending is used as measure of household poverty. However, contractor mineworker households are less likely to be poor when using per capita household income as measure of household poverty. Furthermore, for household income and household spending, the poverty gaps and squared poverty gaps are greater for mine-employed mineworker households, indicating that the per capita incomes and spending of these households lie further below the poverty line on average, and that their income and spending are more unequally distributed below the poverty line. But, using per capita food spending, the poverty gap and squared poverty gap of contractor mineworker households are greater.

These findings confirm the disaggregated analysis of per capita household income and spending shown in Table 11.4 and the kernel densities of per capita household income and spending shown in Figures 11.2 and 11.3. Although the household income and household spending (unadjusted for household size) of mine-employed mineworker households are much higher than those of contractor mineworker households, mine-employed mineworker households are also bigger. Mine-employed and contractor mineworker households also differ in their composition: the former have a higher dependency ratio and a lower ratio of employed members to household size (see Table 11.3). These differences in household size and composition mean that the differences in per capita income and per capita expenditure between mine-employed and contractor mineworker households are much smaller than the differences between their (gross and net) wages (see Table 11.2). Since asset ownership or access to public services is measured at the household level, the large differences in asset ownership or access (Table 11.4) between these two types of mineworker household can be explained by the large differences in household income and spending, unadjusted for household size.

The kernel densities of per capita income (Figure 11.2) are also informative in this regard: they show that, while quite a few mine-employed mineworker households have fairly low per capita income levels (peaking noticeably before those of contractor mineworker households), a large portion of them have per capita incomes greater than those of contractor mineworker households (as evidenced by the fat right-tail of the distribution of per capita income of the mine-employed mineworker households), which serves to drag their mean per capita income level upwards.

The kernel densities of per capita spending (Figure 11.3) also help explain why there is such a small difference in the FGT poverty measures between the two types of mineworker households (again, despite large differences in household spending that is not adjusted for household size). As Figure 11.3 illustrates, there is substantial overlap in the distributions of per capita spending at lower per capita spending levels, which means there are smaller differences between the estimated poverty measures (which focus exclusively on the lower end of the distribution of spending).

For household food spending, both the poverty gap and the squared poverty gap are lower for mine-employed mineworker households than for contractor mineworker households when we use the food poverty lines; but both of these poverty measures are greater for these mineworker households when using income as the household poverty measure. While the poverty headcounts are slightly lower for mine-employed mineworker households when we use household spending as the poverty measure, the poverty gap is greater, indicating that those mine-employed mineworker households that are poor lie further from the (spending) poverty line than contractor mineworker households that are poor. Furthermore, compared to contractor mineworker households, the squared poverty gap for household spending is also greater for mine-employed mineworker households, indicating a more unequal distribution of spending below the poverty line for poor mine-employed mineworker households. But when we compare this with the poverty measures of the non-employed and non-mineworker households shown in Table 11.5, we see that both types of mineworker households are better off, because the two poverty measures of these two types are lower (i.e. better) than the poverty measures of the non-employed and non-mineworker households.

In the survey households were also asked to rank their household income level relative to the income of South African households on a six-step ladder (1 = poorest, 6 = richest) for three periods: the present, 10 years ago and when the respondent was 15 years old. Unsurprisingly, the self-assessed income rankings of non-employed households are lower than those of employed (non-mineworker and mineworker) households (the mean of the current income position of non-employed households was 2.9, compared with 3.0 and 3.1 for non-mineworker and mineworker households). Increases in the self-assessed household income ranking over time were recorded for all three types of household, with the mean self-assessed income ranking increasing by between 0.3 and 0.4 points for all three types. Households were also asked to rank their current household income (on a five-point Likert scale) relative to other households in the area where they live. Once again, the objective measure (Table 11.4) corresponds to the subjective measures of poverty: non-employed households were much more likely (81%) to say their household income lay below the average income level in Postmasburg, while non-mineworker and mineworker households were much less likely (46% and 24%, respectively) to say their household income levels lay below those of other households in Postmasburg.

While mineworker households subjectively rated their households' wealth and income levels above those of non-employed and non-mineworker households, mine-employed mineworker households rated their households' wealth and income levels above those of contractor mineworker households. The mean position on the (six-step) South African household income ladder that mine-employed mineworker households believed they occupied is 3.3 for their current income and 3.0 for their income 10 years ago; compared to 2.5 and 2.30 for contractor mineworker households. Relatively few mine-employed mineworker households (16.6%) believed that their household income was lower than the average household income in Postmasburg, but this was the view of a much higher percentage of contractor mineworker households (44%). These findings are supported to some extent by the summary statistics about household per capita income and household per capita food spending, and more so by the levels of household asset ownership, shown in Table 11.4 (although total household spending per capita was not noticeably different between the two groups). Further support for these findings is provided by the results obtained for household income and household spending (unadjusted for household size), which showed that mine-employed mineworker households have much higher levels of (unadjusted) household income and household spending than contractor mineworker households.

Conclusion

Using data from a household survey conducted between October 2015 and February 2016, in this chapter we discussed the labour market outcomes and household welfare of workers in Postmasburg, distinguishing between mineworkers and non-mineworkers, and further distinguishing between mine-employed mineworkers and contractor mineworkers.

We discussed two sets of findings. The first is that, in Postmasburg, mineworkers have higher wages and work more hours per week than non-mineworkers, while mine-employed mineworkers have higher wages and work more hours per week than contractor mineworkers. In addition, mineworker households are better off than non-mineworker households, who, in turn, are better off than non-employed households. This finding is consistent irrespective of the measure used to compare these three groups of households: their per capita income and expenditure levels differ, their asset ownership levels differ, and their estimated poverty measures differ.

Secondly, although mine-employed mineworkers in general earn much higher wages than contractor mineworkers, we find markedly fewer differences when we compare the per capita income and expenditure levels or poverty levels of mine-employed and contractor mineworker households. The main reasons for this are to be found in the different household sizes and dependency ratios of these two groups of mineworkers, and in their non-employment income sources. Contractor mineworker households are in general smaller, with fewer dependants, and they also receive more grant income.

As discussed earlier, we used a local case study as our study design. Local case studies are context-sensitive, and care should be taken when trying to generalise these results to other mining towns. Also, since we did not compare the economic outcomes in reasonably similar towns that experienced increases or decreases in mining activity (as is done in Loayza and Rigolini, 2016), we cannot use the results from this study to draw causal inferences about the economic effects of mining. Furthermore, in this study our focus is exclusively on money-metric and asset-based economic outcomes, while other authors have noted adverse health, environmental, psychological and sociological effects associated with mining (see Chapter 2 of this volume).

However, between 2001 and 2011, a period characterised by rising iron ore production and prices (see Chapter 3 of this volume), labour market outcomes in the Tsantsabane Local Municipality improved markedly. If we use the 10% samples of the 2001 and 2011 Censuses (Stats SA, 2001, 2011), we find that the share of workers in the mining and quarrying industry increased from 10.7% to 12.7%. At the same time, the labour absorption rate increased by more than 13 percentage points (to 46.9%), the labour force participation rate increased by more than 8 percentage points (to 62.6%), and the official unemployment rate decreased by more than 13 percentage points (to 25.1%). All of these positive labour market developments occurred despite a sharp rise in the number of people living in the Tsantsabane Local Municipality (see e.g. Kumba, 2014). The same labour market dynamics were absent in the Northern Cape as a whole:

the labour absorption rate decreased marginally, the labour force participation rate decreased by more than 6 percentage points, and the official unemployment rate decreased by more than 5 percentage points (to 27.8%).

Longitudinal data, and subnational studies that compare the economic outcomes in well-matched mining and non-mining towns or regions (along the lines of Loayza and Rigolini, 2016) are needed to determine the long-run and causal effects of mining on economic outcomes in small mining towns. But our findings (that those involved in mining are better off than those not involved in mining), and the marked improvement in labour market outcomes in Tsantsabane Municipality between 2001 and 2011, suggest that mining activity in Postmasburg has had both spill-over and trickle-down economic effects. This means that any plans to expand or scale down mining activity and investment should carefully weigh the benefits (which are mostly economic or concentrated in the labour market) against the costs of mining (which are mostly non-economic).

Notes

1 The real increase in incomes was calculated by deflating the 2014 income using the Consumer Price Index for Urban Areas (Statistics South Africa). The 2001 data were taken from the 2001 Census.
2 Cross-section data refers to data collected for a sample of households during a single period. Longitudinal data refers to data collected for a sample of households over multiple periods. For instance, our survey collected data for a single period (from October 2015 to February 2016), which means it is cross-section data of Postmasburg households. Should we repeat this survey annually from October to February of the next year, we will have longitudinal data.
3 Chapter presents basic demographic information.
4 The narrow definitions of unemployed and the labour force participation rate include all those who want to work and are actively searching for work. The broad definitions include all those included in the narrow definition, as well as those who want to work but have given up looking for work (i.e. the so-called discouraged work-seekers).
5 The main reason was refusal. The non-response rate was similarly low for mineworkers employed by mines and non-mineworkers (between 60% and 64%), but much lower (41%) for mineworkers employed by contractors or labour brokers.
6 The standardised value (z) of a variable x is obtained as follows: $z = \frac{x - \bar{x}}{s}$, where x is the value of the variable (0 or 1 for our asset variables), is the sample mean, and s is the sample standard deviation. This standardisation creates a variable with a population mean of zero and a standard deviation of one.

References

Al Rawashdeh, R., Campbell, G. and Titi, A., 2016. The socio-economic impacts of mining on local communities: The case of Jordan. *The Extractive Industries and Society*, 3(2), pp. 494–507.

Betz, M.R., Partridge, M.D., Farren, M. and Lobao, L., 2015. Coal mining, economic development, and the natural resources curse. *Energy Economics*, 50, pp. 105–116.

Booysen, F., Van der Berg, S., Burger, R., Von Maltitz, M. and Du Rand, G., 2008. Using an asset index to assess trends in poverty in seven sub-Saharan African countries. *World Development*, 36(6), pp. 1113–1130.

Bury, J., 2005. Mining mountains: Neoliberalism, land tenure, livelihoods, and the new Peruvian mining industry in Cajamarca. *Environment and Planning A*, 37(2), pp. 221–239.

Deaton, B.J. and Niman, E., 2012. An empirical examination of the relationship between mining employment and poverty in the Appalachian region. *Applied Economics*, 44(3), pp. 303–312.

Devore, J.L. and Berk, K.N., 2011. *Modern Mathematical Statistics with Applications*. New York: Springer.

Forslund, D., 2013. Mass unemployment and the low-wage regime in South Africa. In: J. Daniel, P. Naidoo, D. Pillay, D. and R. Southall, eds. *New South Africa Review 3: The Second Phase–Tragedy or Farce?* Johannesburg: Wits University Press, pp. 141–159.

Foster, J., Greer, J. and Thorbecke, E., 1984. A class of decomposable poverty measures. *Econometrica*, 52(2), pp. 761–766.

Gamu, J., Le Billon, P. and Spiegel, S., 2015. Extractive industries and poverty: A review of recent findings and linkage mechanisms. *The Extractive Industries and Society*, 2(1), pp. 162–176.

Harttgen, K., Klasen, S. and Vollmer, S., 2013. An African growth miracle? Or: What do asset indices tell us about trends in economic performance? *Review of Income and Wealth*, 59(S1), pp. S37–S61.

Haughton, J. and Khandker, S.R., 2009. *Handbook on Poverty and Inequality*. Washington, DC: World Bank.

Kumba (Kumba Iron Ore), 2014. *Kolomela Mine SEAT Report 2014*. Anglo American PLC. www.angloamericankumba.com/~/media/Files/A/Anglo-American-Kumba/documents/kumba-socio-economic-assesment-tool-report.pdf.

Loayza, N. and Rigolini, J., 2016. The local impact of mining on poverty and inequality: Evidence from the commodity boom in Peru. *World Development*, 84, pp. 219–234.

Makgetla, N. and Levin, S., 2016. *A Perfect Storm: Migrancy and Mining in the North West Province*. TIPS (Trade and Industrial Policy Strategies) Working Paper, Pretoria. www.tips.org.za/research-archive/inequality-and-economic-inclusion/item/3099-a-perfect-storm-migrancy-and-mining-in-the-north-west-province (accessed 12 June 2016).

Mwitwa, J., German, L., Muimba-Kankolongo, A. and Puntodewo, A., 2012. Governance and sustainability challenges in landscapes shaped by mining: Mining-forestry linkages and impacts in the Copper Belt of Zambia and the DR Congo. *Forest Policy and Economics*, 25, pp. 19–30.

Rogan, M., 2016. Gender and multidimensional poverty in South Africa: Applying the global multidimensional poverty index (MPI). *Social Indicators Research*, 126(3), pp. 987–1006.

Stats SA (Statistics South Africa), 2001. *South African Census 2001*, 10% sample (version 1.1). Statistics South Africa, Pretoria.

Stats SA (Statistics South Africa), 2011. *South African Census 2011*, 10% sample (version 2). Statistics South Africa, Pretoria.

Stats SA (Statistics South Africa), 2015. *Methodological Report on Rebasing of National Poverty Lines and Development of Pilot Provincial Poverty Lines*. Report No. 03–10–11, Statistics South Africa, Pretoria..

Vyas, S. and Kumaranayake, L., 2006. Constructing socio-economic status indices: How to use principal components analysis. *Health Policy and Planning*, 21(6), pp. 459–468.

Walker, E.R., 2015. *Essays at the Intersection of Environment and Development Economics*. Unpublished PhD thesis, Graduate School of Arts and Sciences, Harvard University, Boston.

12 The work-related psychological well-being of a mineworker

Martina Kotzé and Petrus Nel

How satisfied are Postmasburg's mineworkers with their work life?

People's experiences at work – physical, mental, social and emotional – affect their behaviour and their psychological well-being. The nature of work is changing rapidly and, more than ever, job stress and uncertainty pose a threat to workers' health and well-being. Human resources policies and organisational practices must take into consideration the vital importance of job satisfaction.

In South Africa since the regime change in 1994, several political, economic and labour legislation changes have had repercussions for the work environment. In the mining industry, positive changes have been made through improved health and safety legislation for the workers, but the workplace has become more pressured and insecure (Malherbe and Segal, 2000). The effect of the changes on mineworkers' psychological well-being has not been investigated extensively – several researchers note the level of ignorance about South African employees' mental health and well-being in the mining sector and other industries (e.g. Brand-Labuschagne, 2010; Bowers, 2011). Studies conducted in various industries have found that unhappiness at work damages employees' health and the organisation suffers increased absenteeism, staff turnover and accident rates and decreased commitment and productivity (e.g. Harter et al., 2002; Siu et al., 2004; Schaufeli and Bakker, 2004).

This chapter assesses factors that affect the psychological well-being of mineworkers in Postmasburg. We expected to find that the nature of their work and the demands of their work environment would have a negative effect on their work-related psychological well-being. Contrary to our expectations, however, we found that their overall work-related psychological well-being was fairly good. We also expected to find differences in psychological well-being between those employed by the mine and those employed by a contractor, and we found this was indeed the case: mine-employed mineworkers were more likely than contractor mineworkers to see their employers as trustworthy and to believe that their employer valued their contributions to the mine. We further found that employees tend to be more satisfied with workplace practices when their employers pay bonuses and were more likely to believe that their organisation respected and cared for them.

Changes in the South African mining industry's work practices

From their beginnings in the late 1800s, South African mines were privately owned. During the early years, as Malherbe and Segal (2000) observe, the mines were run like the army, with production conducted in a 'quasi-military' way. At the top of the hierarchy there were the 'commissioned officers' (the mining engineers, geologists and mine managers), at the middle the 'non-commissioned officers' (the artisans, miners and shift bosses), and at the bottom the 'ranks' (the drillers and labourers), who had minimal control over their working and living conditions, did 'repetitive jobs that were easily supervisable', 'were not expected to think about how their activities contributed to the overall success of the enterprise', and were considered 'expendable and exchangeable' (Malherbe and Segal, 2000, p. 21). At this lowest level there was widespread use of migrant labourers. The workers' lives were strictly organised by the mine as control was essential for keeping the system in place. According to Phakathi (2010, p. 181), workplace conditions were 'often characterised by callous management practices' and supervisors were 'racist, bullies, autocratic and abusive'.

Attempts were made to counter the exploitation, manipulation and hazardous working conditions and the repressive capitalist labour regime. Mineworkers often engaged in covert labour protests and resistance, including desertion, output restriction, effort and time bargaining, sabotage and feigning sickness (Cohen, 1980). A 'brotherhood' type of work culture was created to ensure solidarity among black mineworkers. This culture prevented competition, created interpersonal relationships and relieved the pressures of excessive workloads by ensuring that work was equally shared among team members. A worker who 'did not conform to brotherhood norms' was regarded as a 'sell-out' or an 'informer' (Phakathi, 2012, p. 285). Under the colonial and later the apartheid workplace regime, South Africa's mining labour management was characterised by decreased trust and win-lose relationships between white and black mineworkers and in union and management relationships (Phakathi, 2010, 2011).

In 1979, the Wiehahn Commission investigated industrial relations systems in South Africa and their recommendations for the mining industry included a shift away from coercion to negotiation. Black trade unions were beginning to be recognised. In 1982 the National Union of Mineworkers (NUM) was formed. Its aim is to protect its members from health and safety hazards and to negotiate adequate compensation for work-related injuries and accidents (NUM, 2016).

The 1990s marked the start of the journey towards a more democratic South Africa. The country was gradually integrated into the global economy and the workplace conditions typical under apartheid became obsolete. The political and legislative changes in South Africa, the gold price slump and increased production costs, and the consequent losses for many mining operations, led employers to adapt to the new environment by reorganising and relocating production units. Mines started to focus more on their principal business rather than on non-essential services such as hostel management, which was outsourced instead. These changes led to the retrenchment of thousands of employees and an increase in the use of subcontractors.

A breakdown in traditional management practice was inevitable and different workplace and management methods were established to replace the coercive, racial and unsophisticated labour practices. A new labour regime arose where workplace practices were transformed towards increased equity, efficiency and productivity. Novel people-management practices, such as quality circles, self-directed teams, profit sharing, training and performance-based rewards, were introduced to facilitate this process and raise productivity. This led to new models of work in the 1990s which displaced coercive methods in favour of worker participation and consent in the daily management of the production process and also resulted in increased responsibility and productivity. The purpose was to allow labourers to adapt so that they could identify with the goals of the company and expend rather than withdraw effort at the point of production. Management therefore had to relinquish control to a certain extent and allow labour teams to determine the operating methods, team size, bonus systems and most effective ways to work. Unions also adapted their approach as a result of these new management practices. The mining industry made these changes in order to break away from the traditional approaches and create a new workforce for the 21st century.

Some useful discussions of workplace restructuring on South Africa's mines may be found in Malherbe and Segal (2000); Sikakane (2003); Von Holdt (2003); Webster and Omar (2003); Webster and Von Holdt (2005) and Phakathi (2002, 2011). We have drawn on these sources in this section.

As the privately owned mining companies gradually grew into large multinational companies, such as Anglo American, De Beers, Glencor, BHP Billiton, Goldfields, JCI, Anglovaal, Barrick and Rand Mines, the local industry work environment was elevated to a global level and this encouraged further novel ways to manage and operationalise the mines (Nelson and Murray, 2013). New technologies, new mining techniques, more technically sophisticated machinery and remotely controlled and automated processes transformed miners' roles and tasks and their physical work environment. The changes demanded higher technical qualifications, generic skills to replace the traditional 'craftsman-like' skills that were specific to each production process, and more 'process-independent' training (Abrahamsson et al., 2014, p. 39). Workers had to have a more comprehensive understanding of the production process and expectations for teamwork, accountability and autonomy increase.

But despite all the changes in the work environment of the mining industry in general, it seems that most mines are in fact still a long way from achieving optimum workplace and management practices. Managements find it difficult to form work teams. Ali and Hattingh (2014) suggest that change management should be guided by better qualified leaders, principles of trust, greater respect and effective interpersonal conflict resolution. The apartheid legacy still causes linguistic, cultural, ethnic and racial problems and the mines thus remain largely untransformed in their daily activities. Issues of worker development and involvement, benefit sharing, health and safety, housing and racism still present challenges in the post-apartheid mining environment.

The local South African mining industry is currently underperforming, as is evidenced by severe productivity problems (PwC, 2014). The 'transformation conversation' has focused on affirmative action and employment equity in upper management positions, to the neglect of people-management practices (Hartford, 2012). Since the industrial bargaining structures in South Africa are highly centralised (Antin, 2013), personnel management, an integral part of all line functions in all organisations, has become the responsibility of human resources professionals and labour practitioners. Because line management is now separate from personnel management, middle managers and those at supervisory levels (such as team supervisors and shift leaders) are under daily pressure to manage numerous responsibilities, such as monitoring the production cycle and leading production teams, and are sometimes neither equipped nor well prepared for what is required of them (Hartford, 2012; PwC, 2014).

How does mine work affect workers' well-being?

Working conditions in the mining industry can be very tough. Apart from the demands of shift work, safety hazards and increasing pressure due to production demands, for the many migrant workers there is also the difficulty of settling into a remote location. Migrant labour traditionally meant 12 months of work with breaks only at Easter and Christmas. Now there are new forms of migrant work, known by catchy acronyms – FIFO (fly-in-fly-out), DIDO (drive-in-drive-out), BIBO (bus-in-bus-out), SISO (ship-in-ship-out) – where workers travel to their place of work, stay for a period called a 'roster', and then return home for a break (Australian Institute of Management, 2013).

Migrant labour has various consequences that can affect not only the workers themselves but also their families and the local community (Harington et al., 2004). The diversity that an influx of outsiders brings to a town can be positive or negative: it can mean more thriving businesses and better healthcare delivery or it can mean problems such as prostitution, sexually transmitted diseases, hostility and violence. Even without major problems like these, the living conditions and routines on the mines threaten migrant workers' psychological well-being. Working far away from their families, the men are usually housed together in the mine hostels in cramped conditions. They are prone to misuse alcohol and drugs, which contributes to their stress and is likely to have a negative effect on their psychological well-being and their relationships with their families. Although FIFO work has been recommended as a means to mitigate some of the problems of migrant work, it also has several disadvantages. Some studies have shown that a FIFO lifestyle can be bad for workers' physical and psychological well-being, as well as the well-being of their families in general (e.g. Akerstedt, 1990; Takahashi et al., 2006; McLean, 2012).

Shift work is of course a major feature of the mining industry. Internationally, shift patterns in the mining industry are complex and varied. Peets et al. (2012)

identified over 70 distinct patterns of shift work in the Australian coal-mining sector. Shift work and extended workdays, which still total a 40-hour work week but include 10 or 12 hour shifts, are often associated with FIFO, DIDO, BIBO and SISO work schedules and this appears to be an established practice and a popular option for miners (Australian Institute of Management, 2013).

Shift workers report significantly higher levels of psychological and job stress, burnout, emotional exhaustion, depression, anxiety and psychosomatic health problems than workers who do not work shifts (Jamal, 2004; Haines et al., 2008). A significant positive relationship has been found between shift work and excessive tiredness, alcohol abuse to aid sleep (Peets et al., 2012), poor diet and high blood pressure, and a higher incidence of fatigue- and stress-related injuries, including accidents while travelling and working, and occupational injuries (Dembe et al., 2005; Abrahamsson et al., 2014). Chimamise et al. (2013) found that about 73% of serious injuries in a mining company in Zimbabwe occurred during the night shift. Barnes-Farrell et al. (2008) observe that shift work schedules also have implications for employees' well-being outside the work environment, such as strained family relations.

Malherbe and Segal (2000, p. 6) note in the South African context that 'despite the increase in recruitment from within mining communities, the communities of mineworkers remain mainly rural, poor, remote and isolated from other economic opportunities'. These communities often have limited resources and little access to support services, while they are confronted with many challenges that may influence their emotional well-being and mental health. Social connectivity with family, community and co-workers is a key aspect of well-being. When employees are isolated from their friends and families, they find it more difficult to build personal relationships and join supportive networks that are important for psychological health. Mining companies are major sources of employment for local communities. The mental health and psychological well-being of workers and their families are influenced by these employers. Companies operating in isolated areas need to be aware that job satisfaction has a positive influence on employees' life satisfaction, and ultimately on community satisfaction.

The introduction of new forms of work organisation has compelled mining companies to do more with fewer employees in order to reduce working costs, meet production targets and increase mine profits (Phakathi, 2009, 2010, 2011). This has led mines to start subcontracting several ancillary services such as security and cleaning (Malherbe and Segal, 2000). The most controversial form of subcontracting is the subcontracting of normal production activities. These subcontracted workers work alongside the regular workforce, producing tension between the two groups as their job security may be at stake (Sikakane, 2003). Kenny and Bezuidenhout (1999, p. 187) describe various types of labour subcontracting. They define it as casual employment that can take the form of 'gang subcontracting', which implies the arrangement of workers in teams, or 'labour broking', where brokers supply workers in a flexible manner. 'General labour brokers' serve as intermediaries between employers and workers, sourcing labourers who require little formal training for the manual work they undertake, while 'specialisation labour brokers' supply highly trained workers.

Contract mineworkers are often treated differently from permanent employees. Their housing conditions (mostly hostels) may be of a poorer quality. They are sometimes expected to mine in more dangerous areas without concern for health and safety regulations (Bezuidenhout, 2008), while receiving lower wages than permanent employees (Malherbe and Segal, 2000; Sikakane, 2003). Strong correlations between such 'piecework' rates and poor health and safety have been reported for the mining sector. Studies have shown that this piecework has damaging effects on employees' health and safety (e.g. Johansson et al., 2010; Abrahamsson et al., 2014). Furthermore, contractors' active discouragement of trade union membership among their employees is disturbing to organised labourers who perceive this as negating the labour movement's progress over the years (Sikakane, 2003).

Other factors that contribute to stress and may lead to poorer psychological and relationship well-being include dangerous and stressful workplaces (Bowers, 2011). Compared with other sectors, mining has many more inherent risks and thus some of the highest incidences of occupational disease and accidents, including recurring accidents, worldwide (Malherbe and Segal, 2000, p. 24; Kasap, 2011). Accidents decrease workers' confidence and motivation, which leads to poor production outcomes (Akerstedt, 1990; Kasap, 2011). Where workers need to meet production targets in order to qualify for bonuses, this exerts pressure on them to perform and has had serious implications for their health and safety (Chimamise et al., 2013). They and their supervisors take more risks, bypass work rules or take shortcuts by engaging in the informal practice known as *planisa* (which can be translated as 'to improvise') (Phakathi, 2009). Poor psychological well-being has shown to influence mineworkers' safety behaviour, job performance and job satisfaction negatively and make them more prone to accidents (Akerstedt, 1990; Paul, 2009).

Employee health and well-being legislation in South Africa

Stressors affecting employee well-being, such as hazards in the workplace and employers' unreasonable expectations of workers, are addressed fairly adequately in developed countries. But they require urgent attention elsewhere in the world. Sieberhagen et al. (2009) say that employees' safety, health and wellness are given higher priority in industrialised than in developing countries, and that although health and safety are covered by occupational health and safety legislation in developing countries, legislation regarding employee wellness in those countries is still largely lacking.

In 1995 the Leon Commission of Inquiry investigated safety and health in the South African mining industry and its recommendations resulted in the Mine Health and Safety Act No. 29 of 1996 (RSA, 1996). This Act gives workers the right to refuse to do dangerous work. Psychological well-being is addressed in South Africa in the Construction Regulations of 2003 section 15(12)(a), which was included in the Occupational Health and Safety Act No. 85 of 1993 (RSA, 2003). Psychological well-being is referred to in the Construction Regulations 2003 section 15(12)(a) as 'psychological fitness'.

In practice in South Africa today the psychological well-being of employees is still neglected, even though the legislation recognises their needs. Sieberhagen et al. (2009, p. 6) note that whereas 'inadequate safety measures usually have an immediate effect, inadequate attention to psychological health may take considerable time before it manifests as an occupational disease'. Brand-Labuschagne (2010) suggests that the mining industry make use of psychological evaluations of their employees' occupational well-being, to see whether they act in a health- and safety-conscious manner and then deal with any identified weaknesses.

Research on South African employees' psychological well-being has concentrated more on white-collar than blue-collar workers. As mentioned earlier, there is much ignorance about mental well-being in various sectors in South Africa, including mining (Brand-Labuschagne, 2010; Bowers, 2011). Although some psychological well-being problems appear to be inherent in the mining profession because of the nature of the work, employees' well-being and workplace experiences can be influenced in a positive manner if they perceive management and organisational support as being in place.

The work environment of Postmasburg mines

We used Postmasburg's Kolomela and Beeshoek mines to conduct our investigation of the mineworkers' psychological well-being. Both are iron-ore open-pit mines. As open-pit mining is extensively mechanised, these mineworkers' salaries are fairly high and Kolomela offers employee-share ownership that has brought considerable dividends in the past (Kumba, 2014). The work is done in shifts at both mines, with 12-hour shifts being the norm. Kolomela employs approximately 2000 workers indirectly via contractors and 1200 directly with permanent employment contracts (Kumba, 2014). Beeshoek employs 389 workers indirectly via contractors and 633 directly with permanent employment contracts (personal communication, Mine Planning Officer, Assmang Beeshoek Iron Mine, 24 October 2016). Those employed indirectly also have permanent contracts with their contractors and are referred to as permanent contract workers. The survey we conducted between October 2015 and February 2016 showed that these permanent contract workers are paid less than the permanent mineworkers employed by the mine (R6106.84 per month as compared with R15,667.92) and have poorer housing conditions. On salaries and housing, see Chapters 4, 6, 7 and 11 of this volume). Nearly 85% of the directly employed mineworkers at Kolomela who took part in our survey were trade union members, compared to 37% of the contract mineworkers. At Beeshoek 92% of the directly employed mineworkers were union members. The mine could not provide information on the union membership of mineworkers indirectly employed via contractors.

How the study was done

As part of a larger survey, fieldworkers collected data from 238 individuals working at Kolomelo and Beeshoek mines. Just over half (51%) worked at Kolomelo. Most of the participants were black (74%), and 25% were coloured. Almost half of the sample (49%) had Grade 12 (Matric). Just under half (45%) said they had not always lived in Postmasburg. Well over half (59%) were employed directly by the mine and 32% were employed by a contractor. Over 90% said they had not been involved in any major accidents or incidents resulting in an injury related to their work.

The constructs 'burnout' and 'work engagement' are used to indicate levels of psychological well-being in the workplace (Schaufeli et al., 2002; Schaufeli and Bakker, 2004). We measured job burnout according to the Maslach Burnout Inventory (Maslach, 1982; Maslach et al., 1996). Maslach et al. (2001, p. 397) define 'burnout' as 'a prolonged response to chronic emotional and interpersonal stressors on the job, and is defined by the three dimensions of exhaustion, cynicism, and inefficacy'. We used items from the Utrecht Work Engagement Scale to measure workplace engagement (Schaufeli and Bakker, 2004). Bakker (2009, p. 54) defines workplace engagement as 'a positive, fulfilling, work-related state of mind', and says that 'engaged employees have high levels of energy and are enthusiastic about their work'.

We used the Work Well-Being Questionnaire (Parker and Hyett, 2011) to measure the participants' satisfaction with their organisation's workplace practices and to determine their level of workplace well-being. The questionnaire has four components:

> *Work satisfaction:* This indicates the extent to which employees 'view their work as fulfilling', and whether they think it improves 'their sense of self-worth', leads to a 'life with some purpose and meaning' and 'advances their skills'.
>
> *Organisational respect for the employee:* This indicates whether employees judge their superiors to be 'trustworthy' and 'having ethical values', and whether they think the organisation treats them with due regard.
>
> *Employee care:* This indicates how well employees feel their employers and managers treat them, whether the superior is 'caring', truly pays attention, is 'understanding about work concerns' and treats employees the way they would like to be treated.
>
> *Intrusion of work into private life:* This indicates whether employees are 'stressed and pressured at work to meet targets', struggle to relax during non-working hours, and feel their work affects their personal affairs or decreases their self-esteem.

Our findings

Table 12.1 shows that the components of the various constructs have acceptable reliabilities exceeding .7, except for *Intrusion of work into private life*. Reliability estimates equal to or above .7 indicate good reliability. Nevertheless, exploratory research requirements allow for estimates as low as .6 (Hair et al., 2006). Our results show that the participants are fairly satisfied with their work as an average score of 2.5 was obtained. On average, these employees also feel that their employers care about them and show the necessary respect for them, and do not

Table 12.1 Descriptive statistics and reliabilities

Variable	Average	Standard deviation	Reliability	Maximum score
Work satisfaction (workplace practices)	2.5	.79	.87	4
Organisational respect for the employee (workplace practices)	2.4	.77	.86	4
Employee care (workplace practices)	2.4	.85	.84	4
Intrusion of work into private life (workplace practices)	.98	.67	.60	4
Work engagement (psychological well-being)	5.6	1.45	.88	7
Burnout (psychological well-being)	2.3	1.37	.91	7

Table 12.2 Correlations between work satisfaction and workplace practices

	Work satisfaction
Organisational respect for the employee	.78
Employee care	.77
Intrusion of work into private life	−.38

experience much intrusion into their private lives when it comes to work demands. On average, they do not experience any serious burnout and seem to be strongly engaged with their work.

Table 12.2 shows that all three of the workplace practices are significantly correlated with *Work satisfaction* and two of the practices are strongly positively correlated with it. The more the organisation respects the employees by being trustworthy and treating them well, the more satisfied they are with their job and the same reasoning applies to *Employee care*. In contrast, there is a negative correlation (although not very strong) between the perceived *Intrusion of work into private life* and *Work satisfaction*. Hence, when employees experience less stress and pressure at work, they are likely to be more satisfied with their job.

Table 12.3 shows there is a significant negative correlation between *Work satisfaction* and *Burnout*, but a positive correlation between *Work satisfaction* and *Work engagement*. This implies that employees who are satisfied with their work (i.e. who view their work as fulfilling and purposeful) are more likely to be engaged with their work and less likely to experience burnout.

Although all the workplace practices are significantly correlated with burnout, we also needed to determine which of these practices were most important for predicting an employee's level of burnout. The results of our stepwise multiple regression, presented in Table 12.4, show that *Intrusion of work into private life* and *Work*

Table 12.3 Correlations between psychological well-being and workplace practices

	Burnout	Work engagement
Work satisfaction	−.45	.42
Organisational respect for the employee	−.38	.34
Employee care	−.34	.31
Intrusion of work into private life	.49	−.45

Table 12.4 Stepwise multiple regression (criterion: burnout)

Variable	Beta coefficient	t	p
Constant	26.261	8.945	.000
Intrusion of work into private life	.388	6.859	.000
Work satisfaction	−.529	−5.611	.000

Table 12.5 Stepwise multiple regression (criterion: work engagement)

Variable	Beta coefficient	T	p
Constant	29.516	13.619	.000
Intrusion of work into private life	−.343	−5.820	.000
Work satisfaction	.302	5.135	.000

satisfaction are the most important workplace practices that influence employees' levels of burnout: the former explains 24% of the variance in burnout, and the latter 9%. The regression model was statistically significant ($F = 59.386$; $p = .000$). This implies that when employees feel pressured by expectations and deadlines, and find it difficult to relax after work, there is a strong possibility that their work will affect their private life and ultimately their work-related psychological well-being.

We also used a stepwise multiple regression to determine the significant predictors of work engagement. Table 12.5 shows that *Intrusion of work into private life* and *Work satisfaction* are the most important workplace practices that influence employees' levels of work engagement. *Intrusion of work into private life* explains 20% of the variance in work engagement and *Work satisfaction* explains 7%. The results of the regression model were statistically significant ($F = 45.697$; $p = .000$). In other words, both *Intrusion of work into private life* and *Work satisfaction* explained a significant amount of the variance in work engagement.

We investigated the effect of permanent employment on employees' psychological well-being. Most of the sample (59%) said they were employed by the mine. On the basis of a Mann-Whitney U-test (which is used to test for significant differences between two groups) (Field, 2005),[1] we found statistically significant differences between those employed by a mine and those employed by a contractor for the variables *Organisational respect for the employee*, *Burnout* and *Work engagement*. The first variable is related to workplace practices, while the other two are indicators of psychological well-being. Those directly employed by a mine appeared to experience more burnout (mean rank = 125.95 vs 93.32; p = .000) and were less engaged in their work (mean rank = 107.70 vs 127.08; p = .034). However, it should be noted that according to Table 12.1 these employees are not severely 'burnt out' or seriously 'disengaged'. One possible reason for this is that these employees are also more likely to perceive that their employers show respect for them (mean rank = 120.92 vs 102.63; p = .045). This implies that the mine-employed workers in our sample were more likely than those employed by a contractor to view the mines as governed by ethical values, trustworthy and valuing their staff and treating them well. However, we found it noteworthy that there are no statistically significant differences between either of these employee groups with regard to work satisfaction (mean rank = 119.76 vs 104.76; p = .101).

Almost 70% of the participants said they had received a bonus from their employers. To determine whether or not there were statistically significant differences between this group and those who had not received a bonus, we again conducted a Mann-Whitney U-test. Overall, the employees who had received a bonus had significantly higher levels of satisfaction with workplace practices (mean rank = 121.94 vs 93.88; p = .003). They were also significantly more satisfied with their work (mean rank = 122.91 vs 91.65; p = .001), and more likely to perceive that the organisation showed respect for them (mean rank = 120.71 vs 96.74; p = .011) and that their employers cared for them (mean rank = 122.34 vs 92.96; p = .002). The practice of paying a bonus to employees is therefore a relevant factor in their well-being (see Brown et al., 2008).

Discussion and conclusion

Given the level of ignorance about mental health in South Africa's mining sector and concerns about employees' psychological well-being in this context (Brand-Labuschagne, 2010; Bowers, 2011), we thought it important to investigate levels of psychological well-being among a group of employees working at the Kolomelo and Beeshoek mines outside Postmasburg.

We found that the employees in the sample were strongly engaged in their work and fairly satisfied with several workplace practices (employee care, respect from the organisation and not unreasonable intrusion of work into private life). Although issues of worker development, worker participation, benefit sharing, health and safety, housing and racism still remain a cause for concern in the post-apartheid mining regime (Phakathi, 2011; PwC, 2014), we found encouraging results pointing to a more enlightened approach by the mines in Postmasburg. It is evident that most of the employees receive benefits (such as bonuses, medical aid and pension). Our results show that employees receiving benefits have higher levels of satisfaction with workplace practices. They interpret the receipt of a bonus as an indication that the organisation cares about and respects them. These higher levels of satisfaction with workplace practices are also correlated with higher levels of work engagement and a decrease in burnout.

It has been argued that employees working in rural and remote mining operations often have problems with their mental health and emotional well-being (Bowers, 2011), but we found, in contrast, that our sample of mineworkers had fairly high levels of psychological well-being (as evident from their low scores on burnout). Our findings were similar to those of Iverson and Maguire (1990), who found that job satisfaction positively and directly influences one's overall life satisfaction, which indicates the important role of work-related psychological well-being in life and ultimately community satisfaction.

McLean (2012) states that despite the argument that psychological well-being problems are inherent in the mining profession, mineworkers' psychological well-being can be improved by management and organisational support. In corroboration of this, we found that several workplace practices (work satisfaction, organisational respect for the employee, employee care and no unreasonable intrusion of work into private life) are related to mineworkers' psychological well-being. We found strong correlations between these variables. Our findings support a previous study that investigated the effects the work environment has on employees' psychological well-being (Bahrami et al., 2013).

We explored in particular the effect of permanent employment on our participants' psychological well-being. Most of our participants (59%) were employed by a mine on a permanent basis; the rest were employed by a contractor. Both groups were satisfied with their work, but there were some interesting differences. Although being directly employed by a mine may be financially beneficial to the employees, they may experience additional stressors related to production targets that must be met to qualify for bonuses (Chimamise et al., 2013). Being directly employed by a mine on a permanent basis may have some benefits. We found that such employees believe their employers are ethical and trustworthy and value their employees and treat them well. However, it seems that they also experience significantly more burnout than contractor workers and are less engaged in their work. It may be that being employed directly by a mine is a double-edged sword when it comes to psychological well-being.

Mining companies need to ask themselves: 'What should we do to improve the psychological well-being of our employees?' Although it may not be possible to implement all of the various workplace practices (employee care, respect from the organisation and no unreasonable intrusion of work into private life) at once, our study suggests two crucial improvements: reducing the negative influence of the intrusion of work into employees' private lives and striving to improve workplace satisfaction. The latter can be improved by giving employees a sense of self-worth and opportunities to enhance their skills. This will ultimately lead them to view their work as fulfilling and meaningful, whereas requiring them to work overtime often and meet overly high targets will encroach upon their private lives and negatively affect their psychological well-being (Parker and Hyett, 2011).

Previous research has found that because their workplace is dangerous and stressful, mineworkers are more susceptible to damaging levels of stress and recurring incidents and accidents (Malherbe and Segal, 2000; Bowers, 2011; Kasap, 2011). But we found that 90% of our study participants had not been injured in the workplace and in general had high levels of psychological well-being. They were less burnt out than we had expected. They were also fairly engaged with their work. One possible explanation for this may be that the mines in Postmasburg have been through a boom period that enabled them to pay their employees relatively large salaries. Also, 70% of the participants had received a bonus. These factors may well have boosted their psychological well-being. Our findings in future studies of Postmasburg may be very different if this boom ends.

Note

1 Full results not shown.

References

Abrahamsson, L., Segerstedt, E., Nygren, M., Johansson, J., Johansson, B., Edman, I. and Akerlund, A., 2014. *Gender, Diversity and Work Conditions in Mining, Mining and Sustainable Development*. Luleå, Sweden: Luleå University of Technology Press, pp. 43–67.

Akerstedt, T., 1990. Psychological and psychophysiological effects of shift work. *Scandinavian Journal of Work Environment Health*, 16(1), pp. 67–73.

Ali, S.M. and Hattingh, T.S., 2014. *Analysis of Sustainability and the Investment Crisis in South African Platinum Mining using the A3 Problem-Solving Process*. The 6th International Platinum Conference, 'Platinum–Metal for the Future'. Southern African Institute of Mining and Metallurgy. www.platinum.org.za/Pt2014/Papers/159-Ali.pdf (accessed 7 December 2016).

Antin, D., 2013. *The South African Mining Sector: An Industry at a Crossroads*. Hans Seidel Foundation, Johannesburg. www.hss.de/fileadmin/suedafrika/downloads/Mining_Report_Final_Dec_2013.pdf (accessed 20 May 2016).

Australian Institute of Management, 2013. *FIFO/DIDO Mental Health Research Report*. www.miningiq.com/human-resources-talent-recruitment-and-fifo/white-papers/fifo-dido-mental-health-research-report (accessed May 2016).

Bahrami, M.A., Taheri, G., Montazeralfaraj, R. and Tafti, A.D., 2013. The relationship between organizational climate and psychological well-being of hospital employees. *World Journal of Medical Sciences*, 9(1), pp. 61–67.

Bakker, A.B., 2009. Building engagement in the workplace. In: R.J. Burke and C.L. Cooper, eds. *The Peak Performing Organization*. Oxon, UK: Routledge, pp. 50–72.

Barnes-Farrell, J., Davies-Schrils, K., McGonagle, A., Walsh, B., Di Milia, L., Fischer, F.M., Hobbs, B.B., Kaliterna, L. and Tepas, D., 2008. What aspects of shiftwork influence off-shift well-being of healthcare workers? *Applied Ergonomics*, 39(5), pp. 589–596.

Bezuidenhout, A., 2008. New patterns of exclusion in the South African mining industry. In: A. Habib and K. Bentley, eds. *Racial Redress and Citizenship in South Africa*. Pretoria: Human Sciences Research Council (HSRC) Press, pp. 179–208.

Bowers, J., 2011. *Mental Health is Critical to Safety and Productivity in Australian Mining Operations*. Paper presented at the First International Seminar on Social Responsibility in Mining, 19–21 October, Santiago, Chile.

Brand-Labuschagne, L., 2010. *Development and Validation of New Scales for Psychological Fitness and Work Characteristics of Blue Collar Workers*. Unpublished Masters Dissertation (MA in Industrial Psychology), North-West University, Potchefstroom, South Africa.

Brown, G.D.A., Gardner, J., Oswald, A.J. and Qian, J., 2008. Does wage rank affect employees' well-being? *Industrial Relations: A Journal of Economy and Society*, 47, pp. 355–389.

Chimamise, C., Gombe, N.T., Tshimanga, M., Chadambuka, A., Shambira, G. and Chimusoro, A., 2013. Factors associated with severe occupational injuries at mining company in Zimbabwe, 2010: A cross-sectional study. *Pan African Medical Journal*, 14(5), pp. 1–5.

Cohen, R., 1980. Resistance and hidden forms of consciousness amongst African workers. *Review of African Political Economy*, 7(19), pp. 8–22.

Dembe, A.E., Erickson, J.B., Delbos, R.G. and Banks, S.M., 2005. The impact of overtime and long work hours on occupational injuries and illnesses: New evidence from the United States. *Occupational and Environmental Medicine*, 62, pp. 588–597.

Field, A., 2005. *Discovering Statistics Using SPSS*. Thousand Oaks, CA: Sage.

Haines, V.Y., Marchand, A., Rousseau, V. and Demers, A., 2008. The mediating role of work-to-family conflict in the relationship between shiftwork and depression. *Work and Stress*, 22(4), pp. 341–356.

Hair, J.F., Black, B., Babin, B., Anderson, R.E. and Tatham, R.L., 2006. *Multivariate Data Analysis*. Upper Saddle River, NJ: Prentice Hall.

Harington, J.S., McGlashan, N.D. and Chelkowska, E.Z., 2004. A century of migrant labour in the gold mines of South Africa. *Journal of the South African Institute of Mining and Metallurgy*, 104(2), pp. 65–72.

Harter, J.K., Hayes, T.L. and Schmidt, F.L., 2002. Business-unit-level relationship between employee satisfaction, employee engagement and business outcomes: A meta-analysis. *Journal of Applied Psychology*, 87(2), pp. 268–279.

Hartford, G., 2012. *The Mining Industry Strike Wave: What are the Causes and What Are the Solutions?* www.groundup.org.za/article/mining-industry-strike-wave-what-are-causes-and-what-are-solutions/ (accessed 29 April 2016).

Iverson, R.D. and Maguire, C., 1990. The relationship between job and life satisfaction: Evidence from a remote mining community. Working Paper No. 14, Department of Management, University of Melbourne, Australia.

Jamal, M., 2004. Burnout, stress and health of employees on non-standard work schedules: A study of Canadian workers. *Stress and Health*, 20, pp. 113–119.

Johansson, B., Rask, K. and Stenberg, M., 2010. Piece rates and their effects on health and safety: A literature review. *Applied Ergonomics*, 41(4), pp. 607–614.

Kasap, Y., 2011. The effect of work accidents on the efficiency of production in the coal sector. *South African Journal of Science*, 107(5–6), pp. 1–9.

Kenny, B. and Bezuidenhout, A., 1999. Contracting, complexity and control: An overview of the changing nature of subcontracting in the South African mining industry. *The Journal of the South African Institute of Mining and Metallurgy*, July/August (4), pp. 185–192.

Kumba (Kumba Iron Ore), 2014. *Integrated Report*. Johannesburg: Kumba Iron Ore.

Malherbe, S.A. and Segal, N., 2000. *A Perspective on the South African Mining Industry in the 21st Century*. An independent report prepared for the Chamber of Mines of South Africa. Graduate School of Business and Genesis Analytics, University of Cape Town. http://pmg-assets.s3-website-eu-west-1.amazonaws.com/docs/segal.pdf (accessed 12 December 2016).

Maslach, C., 1982. *Burnout: The Cost of Caring*. Englewood Cliffs, NJ: Prentice Hall.

Maslach, C., Jackson, S.E. and Leiter, M.P., 1996. *Maslach Burnout Inventory: Manual*. Mountain View, CA: Consulting Psychologists Press.

Maslach, C., Schaufeli, W.B. and Leiter, M.P., 2001. Job burnout. *Annual Review of Psychology*, 52, pp. 397–322.

McLean, K.N., 2012. Mental health and well-being in resident mine workers: Out of the fly-in-fly-out box. *Australian Journal of Rural Health*, 20, pp. 126–130.

Nelson, G. and Murray, J., 2013. Safety and health in mining in South Africa. In: K. Elgstrand and E. Vingard, eds. *Occupational Safety and Health in Mining: Anthology on the Situation in 16 Mining Countries*. Gothenburg, Sweden: University of Gothenburg, pp. 105–117.

NUM (National Union of Mineworkers), 2016. Homepage. www.num.org.za (accessed 14 October 2016).

Parker, G.B. and Hyett, M.P., 2011. Measurement of well-being in the workplace: The development of the work well-being questionnaire. *Journal of Nervous and Mental Disease*, 199(6), pp. 394–397.

Paul, P.S., 2009. Predictors of work injury in underground mines: An application of a logistic regression model. *Mining Science and Technology*, 19, pp. 282–289.

Peets, D., Murray, G. and Muurlink, O., 2012. *Work and Hours amongst Mining and Energy Workers: Australian Coal and Energy Survey*. First phase report. Griffith University, Queensland, Australia. www.griffith.edu.au/__data/assets/pdf_file/0005/472595/Executive-summary-Work-and-hours-in-M-and-E-ACES-report-no-1-Nov-2012.pdf (accessed 5 May 2016).

Phakathi, T.S., 2002. Self-directed work teams in a post-apartheid gold mine. *Journal of Workplace Learning*, 14(7), pp. 278–285.

Phakathi, T.S., 2009. Planisa! Gold miners' underground practices. *South African Labour Bulletin*, 33(5), pp. 13–15.

Phakathi, T.S., 2010. Workplace change and frontline supervision in deep-level gold mining: Managerial rhetoric or practice? *Transformation: Critical Perspectives on South Africa*, 72(73), pp. 181–204.

Phakathi, T.S., 2011. *Worker Responses to Work Reorganisation in Deep-Level Gold Mining Workplace: Perspectives from the Rock-Face*. DPhil Thesis, University of Oxford, England.

Phakathi, T.S., 2012.Worker agency in colonial, apartheid and post-apartheid gold mining workplace regimes. *Review of African Political Economy*, 39(132), pp. 279–294.

PwC (PricewaterhouseCoopers), 2014. *SA Mine: Highlighting Trends in the South African Mining Industry* (6th edition). November www.pwc.co.za/en/assets/pdf/sa-mine-2014-6th-edition-21-nov.pdf (accessed 3 May 2016).

RSA (Republic of South Africa), 1996. *Mine Health and Safety Act (No. 29 of 1996)*. Pretoria: Government Printer.

RSA (Republic of South Africa), 2003. *Construction Regulation R. 7721 in Terms of the Occupational Health and Safety Act (No. 85 of 1993)*. Pretoria: Government Printer.

Schaufeli, W.B. and Bakker, A.B., 2004. Job demands, job resources and their relationship with burnout and engagement: A multi-sample study. *Journal of Organizational Behaviour*, 25, pp. 293–315.

Schaufeli, W.B., Salanova, M., Conzález-Romá, V. and Bakker, A.B., 2002. The measurement of engagement and burnout: A two sample confirmatory factor analytic approach. *Journal of Happiness Studies*, 3, pp. 71–92.

Sieberhagen, C., Rothmann, S. and Pienaar, J., 2009. Employee health and wellness in South Africa: The role of legislation and management standards. *SA Journal of Human Resource Management*, 7(1), pp. 18–26.

Sikakane, L.E., 2003. *Subcontracting in Gold Mining: Western Deep Level Mine, Carleton-ville*. Unpublished Dissertation, MA in Industrial Psychology, Rand Afrikaans University (now the University of Johannesburg), Johannesburg. http://hdl.handle.net/10210/1334 (accessed 4 May 2016).

Siu, O.L., Phillips, D.R. and Leung, T.W., 2004. Safety climate and safety performance among construction workers in Hong Kong. The role of psychological strains as mediators. *Accident, Analysis and Prevention*, 36(3), pp. 359–366.

Takahashi, M., Nakata, A., Haratani, T., Otsuka, Y., Kaida, K. and Fukasawa, K., 2006. Psychosocial work characteristics predicting daytime sleepiness in day and shift workers. *Chronobiology International*, 23(6), pp. 1409–1422.

Von Holdt, K., 2003. *Transition from Below: Forging Trade Unionism and Workplace Change in South Africa*. Pietermaritzburg, South Africa: University of Natal Press.

Webster, E. and Omar, R., 2003. Work restructuring in post-apartheid South Africa. *Work and Occupations*, 30(2), pp. 94–213.

Webster, E. and Von Holdt, K., 2005. *Beyond the Apartheid Workplace: Studies in Transition*. Pietermaritzburg: University of KwaZulu-Natal Press.

13 Businesses in Postmasburg

Tshipe e lokile ('iron is good') –
but what about business?

Deidré van Rooyen and Johan van Zyl

Doing business in Postmasburg

Mining is very important to the national, regional and local economies of develop-ing countries. But local communities, and especially businesses, tend to become dependent on the mining sector and find themselves at the mercy of changes in international commodity prices because they rely too heavily on a single mining staple. Resource rich areas often fail to diversify their economy, forgetting that the resource on which they depend is not inexhaustible. It is often difficult for a specialised region to change its direction, but if a mining-dependent town does not develop non-mining businesses it will not survive.

The literature has much to say about the effects of mineral resource extraction on the surrounding regions. Most of this literature – geographical, economic, sociological and psychological – has concentrated on environmental awareness and practices and socio-economic well-being in mining towns and the perim-eters of resource rich areas. Some have focused on the effects of rapid growth of single-resource towns and some on the effects of mine downscaling and closure. Useful sources to consult on these topics both internationally and in South Africa, on which we have drawn to some extent in this chapter, are Neil et al. (1992); Leatherman and Marcouiller (1996); Randall and Ironside (1996); Rolfe et al. (2007); Vadgama et al. (2008); Winde and Stoch (2010); Lawrie et al. (2011); Putz et al. (2011); Rogerson (2011); McDonald et al. (2012); Phagan-Hansel (2013); Marais (2013); Chapman et al. (2014); Bec et al. (2015) and Marais and Nel (2016).

However, we found little that was specifically dedicated to the business sector in a growing small mining town. We therefore conducted a study of the sector in Postmasburg, based on a profile we compiled of the town's business sector from 2005 to 2013. Data were collected via a questionnaire administered to 55 business respondents and semi-structured interviews with key stakeholders from mining companies, the municipality, the business sector and civic organisa-tions. A snowballing approach with a purposive sampling method was used to make sure that all the stakeholders would be covered. This enabled us to explore opinions about and attitudes to the mining development in the small town and the surrounding region, to discover how the business sector in Postmasburg has been affected by the rapid growth of the town's mining sector, and to gain some general insights into how mining development can affect the business sector of a small mining town.

Staples theory, resource curse and Dutch disease

These theories have been discussed in in Chapter 1 of this volume. Here we consider what light they cast on economic diversification. The core of staples theory is the 'staples trap' (Gunton, 2003). A single-resource town is particularly at risk of being caught in this trap. Innis (1956, p. 382) describes towns like this as 'storm centres to the modern international economy', and Argent (2013, p. 327) elaborates the metaphor, saying they are 'subject to the cyclonic winds of rapid and intensive investment and disinvestment as demand, resource availability and corporate restructuring shift in direction and velocity'. The community is led into the staples trap through, for example, sponsorships for sports teams, and community events. The entire community may find itself in a local 'cognitive lock-in' (Tonts et al., 2013, p. 365). During prosperous times local communities, including the mine employees, enjoy affluence; but when the tide turns they often suffer 'truncated development' and despair (Barnes et al., 2001, p. 2139). The workforce is affected adversely during crisis times because they do not have alternative skills and opportunities other than those obtained from the natural resource base. Chapman et al. (2015, p. 361) associate this with 'weak backward and forward economic linkages and rather modest returns when compared to the value of the resources being extracted'. On a positive note, though, staples theory suggests the trap may be avoided if regional economic growth and development brings diverse investment opportunities (Measham et al., 2013).

The 'Dutch disease' (named after the negative effects of Holland's North Sea gas revenues on the Dutch manufacturing sector) is defined by Langton and Mazel (2008, p. 35) as the detrimental impact of 'economic distortion that export booms can induce in a mineral-dependent economy such that non-mining sectors suffer as a result, with exports becoming less competitive and wages more expensive'. Boom and bust cycles negatively affect economic development in the region. During booms, foreign currency influx causes the local currency to appreciate, in turn causing other industry to become more expensive and less competitive. Walker (2005) notes that the mining sector's volatility prevents the long-term growth that could have been achieved by investing in stable sectors like manufacturing and agriculture.

Another angle on the problems of mining regions is the 'resource curse' theory: the idea that nations with large natural resource endowments do not perform better economically than other nations (Auty, 1993). A boom will boost the economy in the short term but may damage it in the long term. The region may gain jobs during the initial phase of mining but eventually create a poor business climate as the economy becomes volatile and less diverse. Christopherson and Rightor (2012, p. 365) say this 'crowds out' low-cost labour supply sectors like agriculture and community programmes. The rich resource companies usually outbid other smaller businesses in terms of income, housing and opportunities and thus promote a mono-economy (Haslam McKenzie, 2013).

Understanding the macro-economic environment
for businesses

All businesses operate in a market which changes daily. The market has many subsectors that businesses must analyse to find gaps and opportunities. A useful mnemonic for the sectors is PESTLE: political, economic, social, technological, legal and environmental (Wiid, 2014). Often the government assessment ignores long-term capacity building and development and focuses only on short-term profits (Tonts et al., 2013). Gaps and opportunities in terms of PESTLE are not analysed meticulously. External pressures such as commodity prices plummeting, sometimes by well over 50%, can do severe damage to businesses (De Hoop, 2016). Therefore, as Sandbu (2006, p. 36) argues, non-renewable minerals should not be regarded as the 'backbone of the economy' but rather as a bonus to stimulate economic growth. Host communities should understand that the additional jobs, investment in infrastructure and infusion of cash that result from a boom will disappear in a recession. New small mining towns benefit substantially in terms of local economic growth as well as poverty alleviation (Owusu-Koranteng, 2008). But this does not happen automatically and the community should be aware of the need to reduce their dependence on the natural resource very early in the development of the mining sector in the region (World Bank and IFC, 2002).

Barkley (2001, p. 12) notes that economists differentiate between economic growth and economic development. The former is a measure of 'changes in the size of the local economy', whereas the latter is a measure of 'changes in population, employment, production of goods and services, housing stock, etc.' or 'a qualitative measure of variations in the local quality of life' as evidenced by 'poverty and infant mortality rates, level of education, mean family income, and quality of the housing stock'.[1] At a national level, economic growth is measured as gross domestic product (GDP). As applied to our topic, Barkley's distinction helps us see that although mining may cause the country's GDP to rise (economic growth) this does not necessarily improve the quality of life in a mining town (economic development). Smit et al. (1996) argue that improved economic development will result in better government services, more job opportunities and fairer distribution of income, individual freedom and stability. The converse also applies: more job opportunities and income lead to better economic development.

Rogerson (2012) notes that economic development is not only about growth in the economy but also about diversifying the local economic base to make the area economically sustainable once mining comes to an end. Keyes (1992) identifies two ways a mining town can diversify its economy: vertical diversification, where it adds businesses related to the mining sector, such as processing, transportation and mining other commodities, and horizontal diversification, where it adds businesses related to other economic sectors such as manufacturing or agriculture. Vertical diversification means the town still has a single economic base and thus remains vulnerable to the mineral economic cycle. It is important for a mining town to diversify at the start of the mining operations to prevent economic collapse and single sector dependence. A diversified economy is to the benefit of the mining investors, the local government and the business community in the surrounding region. As in other parts of the world, most South African mining towns are largely 'economically undiversified, single-resource small towns' (Pelser et al., 2012, p. 45).

Any fluctuations in the mining industry in South Africa can influence the market and its subsectors, especially in a mining town. In many of these towns the responsibility for economic development has been transferred to the mining company through the social and labour plans required in terms of the Mineral and Petroleum Resources Act No. 28 of 2002 (Cawood, 2004) and the corporate social responsibility of the large mining companies. This is often referred to as the 'company town syndrome' (Pelser et al., 2012, p. 45). Although Postmasburg is not a company town per se, much of the 'company town syndrome' also applies to the town.

The market economy of Postmasburg

The dominant industry in a town affects the local businesses. In the case of Postmasburg it is the mines that are largely responsible for local business conditions. Expansion in the industry increases local spending, because the mineworkers have more disposable income, and provides business opportunities for entrepreneurs with business opportunities. If the mines downscale the effect will be reversed.

According to Kumba (2014), the company that owns Kolomela mine, mining contributed 41% to the local economy in 2013. Besides their direct contribution, Postmasburg's mines also contribute indirectly to the secondary economy, particularly transport and communication (18.4%) and finance and business services (10.8%) (Kumba, 2014). Until about nine years ago, Postmasburg businesses did not benefit much from mine employees because the only major mine was Beeshoek, seven kilometres to the west of the town, which was fairly self-sufficient in terms of housing, education and recreational facilities. However, the development of Kolomela mine, which began in 2008, has considerably enhanced the procurement of local goods and services and indirectly through the buying power of employees of the mine, contractors and people in search of job opportunities.

Postmasburg's business profile

Using a technique similar to that described by Toerien and Seaman (2010), we classified Postmasburg's formal businesses into sectors to produce the business profile shown in Table 13.1. These were businesses listed in the Yellow and White pages of the Northern Cape telephone book for 2005, 2008, 2010 and 2013. We also approached some informal businesses in Postmasburg that were not listed in the telephone book, such as fruit sellers at the bus stop, as we needed their opinions too.

Table 13.1 Postmasburg's business profile, 2005–2013

Sector	2005		2008		2010		2013	
	%	N	%	N	%	N	%	N
Agriculture	4.9	11	5.1	10	4.9	11	4.2	10
Manufacturing	0.4	1	1.5	3	0.9	2	1.3	3
Engineering and technical services	6.3	14	6.6	13	8.0	18	5.5	13
Construction	1.3	3	3.6	7	4.0	9	4.2	10
Mining	1.8	4	2.5	5	3.6	8	3.8	9
Transport and earthworks	4.0	9	2.0	4	2.2	5	1.7	4
Retail (including vehicle sector)	33.0	74	32.5	64	28.4	64	28.0	66
Financial services	9.8	22	10.7	21	10.2	23	8.9	21
Telecommunications, legal and property services	3.6	8	5.1	10	4.4	10	5.1	12
Health and personal services	9.8	22	8.6	17	10.2	23	8.5	20
Tourism and hospitality services	5.8	13	4.6	9	4.4	10	7.6	18
Government services	9.4	21	8.6	17	9.8	22	10.2	24
Professional and general services	4.9	11	4.6	9	4.4	10	6.4	15
Non-profit sector	4.9	11	4.1	8	4.4	10	4.2	10
News and advertisements	0.0	0	0.0	0	0.0	0	0.4	1
Total	**100**	**224**	**100**	**197**	**100**	**225**	**100**	**236**

Source: Yellow and White Pages of telephone books 2005, 2008, 2010 and 2013 (authors' own interpretations)

Table 13.1 shows that the number of businesses listed in the telephone book increased in Postmasburg from 197 in 2008 to 236 in 2013. New mining developments in the Postmasburg region have contributed to the increases in several non-mining sectors. As expected, engineering and technical services (8% in 2010) increased during the construction period. The construction sector (4.2% in 2013) benefited not only directly from the mining development but also indirectly from the housing developments. The services provided by the government (social development, schools and clinics) increased slightly from 9.4% in 2005 to 10.2% in 2013. On the other hand, the retail sector decreased marginally, from 33% to 28% of the listed businesses. This may be because the national chains caused several smaller local retailers to close. Transport and earthworks companies decreased from 4% in 2005 to 1.7% in 2013. However, the telecommunications, legal and property services (5.1% in 2013) seem to have benefited from Kolomela mine opening in Postmasburg. This can be directly linked to the increase in property development and a booming housing market (see also Chapters 9 and 10 of this volume). Despite the new housing developments, however, there was still a high demand for mine employee accommodation, which increased the asking price for rents and housing sales. The businesses involved in tourism and hospitality services (guesthouses and overnight accommodation) therefore increased from 5.8% of the profile in 2005 to 7.6% in 2013. More professional and general services, such as labour brokers and security companies, were also established during 2010 (4.4%) and 2013 (6.4%). The profile shown in Table 13.1 and the explanations given above show that the diversification that has taken place in the Postmasburg business sector has been almost exclusively vertical. Most business developments in the past several years have been associated with the mining sector boom. Very little horizontal diversification (in other words, 'outside the box' entrepreneurial endeavour) has taken place.

Since 2015, the drop in iron prices has reduced the positive effect of the mines on Postmasburg businesses. Business owners told us that some new businesses had opened in town but soon closed as a result of the slowdown in mining activities. On the other hand, many more informal foreign-owned shops (known as 'spaza shops' in South Africa) have been established in all the neighbourhoods. Table 13.1 shows that manufacturing businesses stayed relatively low and constant at approximately 1% from 2005 to 2013. Furthermore, the absolute number increased from 1 to 3. This is rather remarkable for a small town. This has been bad for the economic development of the town because diversification has only really taken place vertically with a growth in economic sectors dependent on the mining cycle and not horizontally with new industries in the manufacturing sector (cf. Helmuth, 2009). We found only two examples of horizontal diversification: a business operating from a farm and the solar plant close to Postmasburg. Although retail and manufacturing sector had difficulty finding suitable employees (and being able to compete with the higher mine salaries), the mining developments did not affect their businesses because their market share was throughout South Africa and not only in surrounding areas.

Reflections from local businesses

Postmasburg businesses have felt the positive influence of mining since the construction of Kolomela mine began in mid-2008. The older mine, Beeshoek, established in 1968, had always had only a very slight influence because of its distance from the town and the fact that its employees live near the mine. But in 2013 this mine began offering its workers homeownership in the town, and therefore the purchasing power in Postmasburg has increased because employees from both mines now live in town.

According to Carrington and Pereira (2011), the mining industry as a whole does not support local businesses. Our findings show a more balanced result. A respondent from Assmang, the company that owns Beeshoek mine, says that 'in the old days the towns did not welcome the people that were working on the mines and now according to the Mine Charter the mine has to assist the town'. Many local businesses we interviewed, whether small or large, black-owned or white-owned, felt this was the case. The Mining Charter does not set specific targets for regional or local black economic empowerment (BEE) procurement, but Kolomela mine has committed itself to creating business opportunities for black-owned businesses in the Northern Cape generally and the Tsantsabane Municipality (of which Postmasburg is part) in particular. By 2014, 25% of the businesses procured by Kolomela Mine were locally based and black-owned. R860 million was injected into the local economy through this initiative. Black business owners have mobilised themselves into forums such as the Emerging Contractors' Forum, Tsantsabane Black Business Chamber and the Tsantsabane Local Business Forum, to put pressure on Kolomela Mine to fast-track localised BEE procurement (Kumba, 2014).

Most of the businesses (44 of 55) we surveyed were in formal structures, 10 were in informal structures and only one made use of business opportunities without shelter. We found many new businesses in Postmasburg. Of the 55 we interviewed, 31 were less than five years old. All the interviewed businesses were subdivided into sectors, 29 in retail and wholesale, 10 in personal services, nine in transport, four in catering and accommodation and two in financial services.

The success of a business depends largely on understanding the strengths and weaknesses of the local market and being able to adapt accordingly. One of our business respondents said he had bought his current business (a petrol station plus a food and general goods retail store) in 2003 before the opening of the Kolomela mine because of the opportunities presented by possible mining expansion. The paperwork took him many years, mainly because the petroleum company did not see a need for another petrol station in Postmasburg. As a result, he could not open for business until a few years after the opening of the mine. He was not the only entrepreneur who saw a business opportunity in Postmasburg after doing an environmental and market analysis, knowing a new mine was going to be established. His business is now thriving due to the planning he did ahead of the boom. As part of Kolomela's 2014 environmental impact assessment (EIA) and socio-economic assessment,[2] focus group discussions were conducted with various stakeholders in Postmasburg. During the discussion with educational stakeholders, it was noted that 'we suddenly had three tyre shops, which we never used to have' (Kolomela Mine, 2014). Entrepreneurs are always looking for gaps in the market and do not always do a risk analysis before they open their business. There may be potential for three tyre businesses while the mines are flourishing, but if the mines downscale one or more of these businesses may not be sustainable.

The large influx of job seekers attracted by the new Kolomela mine increased the opportunities and therefore also the buying power in Postmasburg. In our survey of 55 businesses, we asked which buyers make the greatest contribution to their turnover. We found that employees of the two main mines (Beeshoek and Kolomela) account for the highest percentage (45%) of the buying power. Both mines spend a substantial amount of money at businesses in Postmasburg. From our respondents' responses we calculated that on average 18% of their turnover comes directly from the mines. Examples of goods and services offered by businesses in Postmasburg that the mines and their employees make use of are steel parts, maintenance products, repair services and engineering services. Social grants accounted on average for 13% of the business owners' income.

Therefore, although Postmasburg's business owners have profited from spending by employees of the mining companies, we can see that many are still very dependent on grants. The target market of three-quarters of the new businesses (established one to five years ago) was individual buyers rather than companies. The prevalence of social grants suggests that their client base will remain largely intact even if the mines close.

Given the 2008 boom and the decline in iron ore prices that began in 2015, we asked businesses whether their turnover had declined, stayed the same or increased over the past two years. About two-thirds said they had recorded declines of 11 to 20%, only a quarter had recorded an increase (equal to the inflation rate, 6% to 8%), and only one said turnover had stayed the same. Reasons they suggested for the decrease in turnover included the South African economic downturn and the mining downturn, low or no salary increases for mineworkers (which meant less spending money), retrenchments of mineworkers and the drop in the price of iron. A local restaurant manager noted that 'there are not so many contractors any more, this is the reason for negative growth in income'. One business owner jokingly said: 'We are *Postmasplaas* [Postmasfarm] not Postmasburg, because we are not progressing but regressing'. The business owners put this down to a continuous increase in the number of residents, which is overloading the town's housing capacity, retrenched employees not leaving Postmasburg and very little diversification of the economy such as the solar farms in the area.

A lower turnover did not necessarily lead to lower profits. Twenty-nine of the business respondents said they had made a lower profit, compared to the 34 who reported a lower turnover. Reasons given by those who said they had a lower profit margin ranged from a decrease in turnover to fewer customers for the business or purchasing of less profitable products. The economic downturn and the higher import prices were also mentioned as further reasons for reduced profits.

Asked for their views about business opportunities and growth in Postmasburg in the next two years, 11 of the respondents predicted that the situation would stay the same, 22 that it would get worse and 22 that it would get better – an interestingly divided opinion. One of the respondents added an optimistic note, saying: 'People should just have the stamina to hold on – the iron ore price will rise again.'

A positive finding was that 35 of the respondents, about two-thirds, had undertaken new activities in the past two years. Six said they had hired more staff, seven had purchased new property and machinery, and nine had even opened new branches. Twenty-three expressed a positive outlook for the future of their business, 13 were planning a moderate expansion and four planned a large-scale expansion in the near future. Although this does seem positive, 10 respondents said they were considering closing down and one was already in the process of doing so. We could see that the thought of mining downturn was in the back of the minds of the entrepreneurs in this small town. Some said that more collaborative business planning should have been done during the boom part of the cycle and not left to the start of the bust.

Even though the new mining activities have enhanced the Postmasburg business sector in several ways, our respondents said they were still encountering barriers to the expansion of their operations, the main ones being competition ('more players in the market', mentioned by 11 respondents) and a shortage of customers (also mentioned by 11 respondents). Respondents mentioned in particular the recent increase in foreign-owned spaza shops.[3] Other competition they face comes from new larger retailers that have opened and a new shopping mall that has been built closer to the housing developments.

Twenty-two of our respondents complained about competition and lack of customers and nine complained about the economy and the commodity prices. This implies that just over half of our sample sees the reduction in mining activities as a threat to their business. Other hindrances to business expansion that our respondents mentioned were lack of access to finance (six respondents) and crime (five respondents). Although we heard about business expansions, and some positive outlooks on the business sector in Postmasburg were expressed, we also picked up a fair amount of negativity. The business sector is still reliant on the mining operations in the area and not enough entrepreneurial 'outside-the-box' ideas are being initiated. This means that horizontal diversification is minimal.

Conclusion

We can apply a Darwinian principle to the business situation in a town like Postmasburg: for a mining town, as for a species, it is not the strongest or the most intelligent which survive, but those most responsive to change. The literature on economic development supports this – it highlights the importance of economic diversification in a resource town. It makes sense to take full advantage of the opportunities provided by a mega project (like mining) in a small town so that the local community can survive even after the closure of a mine (World Bank and IFC, 2002). The local people say, in Setswana, *tshipe e lokile* ('iron is good'). But business needs to be good too. The promotion of small and medium enterprise development could stimulate the growth of the private sector and horizontally diversify the economic base of the town, in turn generating more employment opportunities to sustain the town. It is hence important for all stakeholders to contribute to the diversification process while the town is experiencing a boom. The sudden growth of the new Kolomela mine took many local entrepreneurs by surprise. Businesses were opened to take advantage of the growth in population and the mine employees' spending power. But the necessary (macro and market) environmental scan was often not completed to calculate the risks for businesses over time.

The new mining development in Postmasburg can be seen as having both a positive and a negative influence. The positive side is that the regional economy has been stimulated so investment opportunities have arisen. The negative is that Postmasburg suffers a cognitive lock-in due to generous sponsorships from Kolomela mine for sports teams and community events – an example of the 'staples trap' described earlier. The business sector has had short-term gains from the construction of the mine, with many contractors migrating into Postmasburg for job opportunities, but it faces the long-term consequences of a volatile economy with even less sectoral diversity than before.

Once again, we cannot stress enough that all stakeholders must prioritise long-term business planning while the mines are prospering rather than being caught unprepared when they decline. This planning must entail horizontal diversification into other sectors. Collaboration between the various stakeholders – local government, mining companies and local business chambers – could promote not just economic growth for Postmasburg but also sustainable economic development.

Notes

1 South Africa uses the Living Standard Measurement (LSM) to categorise sections of the population according to their quality of life. www.saarf.co.za/lsm/lsms.asp.
2 The EIA and socio-economic assessment were conducted by Synergistics Environmental Services and G3 Business Solutions, respectively.
3 These foreigners are mostly from Pakistan or Nigeria.

References

Argent, N., 2013. Reinterpreting core and periphery in Australia's mineral and energy resources boom: An Innisian perspective on the Pilbara. *Australian Geographer*, 44(3), pp. 323–340.
Auty, R., 1993. *Sustainable Development in Mineral Economies: The Resource Curse Thesis*. London: Routledge.
Barkley, D.L., 2001. *Employment Generation Strategies for Small Towns: An Overview of Alternatives*. Research Report 09–2001–02, Regional Economic Development Research Laboratory, Clemson University, Clemson, SC.
Barnes, T., Hayter, R. and Hay, E., 2001. Stormy weather: Cyclones, Harold Innis and Port Alberni BC. *Environment and Planning*, 33, pp. 2127–2147.
Bec, A., Moyle, B. and McLennan, C., 2015. Drilling into community perceptions of coal seam gas in Roma, Australia. *The Extraction Industries and Society*, 3(3), pp. 716–726.
Carrington, K. and Pereira, M., 2011. Assessing the social impacts of the resources boom on rural communities. *Rural Society*, 21(1), pp. 2–20.
Cawood, F., 2004. The mineral and petroleum resources development act of 2002: A paradigm shift in minerals policy in South Africa. *The Journal of the South African Institute of Mining and Metallurgy*, 104(1), pp. 53–64.
Chapman, R., Plummer, P. and Tonts, M., 2015. The resource boom and socio-economic well-being in Australian resource towns: A temporal and spatial analysis. *Urban Geography*, 36(5), pp. 629–653.
Chapman, R., Tonts, M. and Plummer, P., 2014. Resource development, local adjustment and regional policy: Resolving the problem of rapid growth in the Pilbara, Western Australia. *Journal of Rural and Community Development*, 9(1), pp. 72–86.
Christopherson, S. and Rightor, N., 2012. How shale gas extraction affects drilling localities: Lessons for regional and city policy makers. *Journal of Town and City Management*, 2(4), pp. 250–268.
De Hoop, H., 2016. South African mining sector faces a tough year. *Mail and Guardian*, 19 February. https://mg.co.za/article/2016-02-19-00-south-african-mining-sector-faces-a-tough-year/ (accessed 23 Novemeber 2016)
Gunton, T., 2003. Assessment of dependency and comparative advantage paradigms. *Economic Geography*, 79(1), pp. 67–94.
Haslam Mckenzie, F., 2013. Delivering enduring benefits from a gas development: Governance and planning challenges in remote Western Australia. *Australian Geographer*, 44(3), pp. 341–358.

Helmuth, A., 2009. *Economic Diversification of a Mining Town: A Case Study of Oranje-mund*. Master of Business Administration, Rhodes University, Grahamstown.

Innis, H., 1956. *Essays in Canadian Economic History*. Toronto: University of Toronto Press.

Keyes, R., 1992. Mine closure in Canada: Problems, prospects and policies. In: C. Neil, C. Tykklainen and J. Bradbury, eds. *Coping with Closure: An International Comparison of Mine Town Experiences*. London: Routledge, pp. 192–207.

Kolomela Mine, 2014. *Focus Group Discussion for Environmental Impact Assessment (EIA) for Educational Stakeholders*. Kolomela Training Centre, Postmasburg, 14 October 2014.

Kumba (Kumba Iron Ore), 2014. Kolomela Mine SEAT Report 2014. Anglo American PLC. www.angloamericankumba.com/~/media/Files/A/Anglo-American-Kumba/documents/kumba-socio-economic-assesment-tool-report.pdf.

Langton, M. and Mazel, O., 2008. Poverty in the midst of plenty: Aboriginal people, the resource curse and Australia's mining boom. *Journal of Energy and Natural Resources Law*, 26(1), pp. 31–65.

Lawrie, M., Tronts, M. and Plummer, P., 2011. Boomtowns, resource dependence and socio-economic well-being. *Australian Geographer*, 42(2), pp. 139–164.

Leatherman, J. and Marcouiller, D., 1996. Persistent poverty and natural resource dependence: Rural development policy analysis that incorporates income distribution. *Journal of Regional Analysis and Policy*, 26(2), pp. 73–93.

Measham, T., Haslam Mckenzie, F., Moffat, K. and Franks, D.M., 2013. An expanded role for the mining sector in Australian society? *Rural Society*, 22(2), pp. 184–194.

Marais, L., 2013. The impact of mine downscaling on the Free State Goldfields. *Urban Forum*, 24(4), pp. 503–521.

Marais, L. and Nel, E., 2016. The dangers of growing on gold: Lessons from the history of the Free State Goldfields, South Africa. *Local Economy*, 31(1–2), pp. 282–298.

McDonald, P., Mayes, R. and Pini, B., 2012. Mining work, family and community: A spatially oriented approach to the impact of the Ravensthorpe Nickel Mine Closure in remote Australia. *Journal of Industrial Relations*, 54(1), pp. 22–40.

Neil, C., Tykkylainen, M. and Brandbury, J., 1992. *Coping with Closure: An International Comparison of Mine Town Experiences*. London: Routledge.

Owusu-Koranteng, D., 2008. Mining and investment and community struggles. *Review of African Political Economy*, 35(117), pp. 467–473.

Pelser, A., Van der Merwe, A. and Kotze, P., 2012. Rethinking sustainability of small towns: Towards a socio-technical approach. In: R. Donaldson and L. Marais, eds. *Small Town Geographies in Africa*. New York: Nova, pp. 63–85.

Phagan-Hansel, K., 2013. Small towns become boomtowns. *Wyoming Business Report*, 14(9), pp. 3–25.

Putz, A., Finken, A. and Goreham, G.A., 2011. *Sustainability in Natural Resource-Dependent Regions That Experienced Boom-Bust Recovery Cycles: Lessons Learned from a Review of the Literature*. Center for Community Vitality, NDSU Extension Service, North Dakota State University, Fargo, ND.

Randall, J. and Ironside, R.G., 1996. Communities on the edge: An economic geography of resource-dependent communities. *Canadian Geographer*, 40(1), pp. 17–35.

Rogerson, C., 2011. Mining enterprise, regulatory frameworks and local economic development in South Africa. *African Journal of Business Management*, 5(35), pp. 13373–13382.

Rogerson, C., 2012. Mining-dependent localities in South Africa: The state of partnerships for small town local development. *Urban Forum*, 23(1), pp. 107–132.

Rolfe, J., Miles, B., Lockie, S. and Ivanova, G., 2007. Lessons from the social and economic impacts of the mining boom in the Bowen Basin 2004–2006. *Australasian Journal of Regional Studies*, 13(2), pp. 134–157.

Sandbu, M., 2006. Natural wealth accounts: A proposal for alleviating the natural resource curse. *World Development*, 34(7), pp. 1153–1156.

Smit, P.C., Dams, D.J., Mostert, J.W., Oosthuizen, A.G., Van der Vyver, T.C. and Van Gas, W., 1996. *Economics: A Southern African Perspective*. Cape Town: Juta.

Toerien, D. and Seaman, M., 2010. The enterprise ecology of towns in the Karoo, South Africa. *South African Journal of Science*, 106, pp. 24–33.

Tonts, M., Martinus, K. and Plummer, P., 2013. Regional development, redistribution and the extraction of mineral resources: The Western Australian Goldfields as a resource bank. *Applied Geography*, 45, pp. 365–374.

Vadgama, J., Cretney, A. and Doukas, A., 2008. Boom to bust: Social and cultural impacts of the mining cycle. *Energy, Mining and Sustainability in NW British Columbia*, 19 February, pp. 1–4.- https://www.pembina.org/reports/boombust-final.pdf (accessed 11 June 2016).

Walker, M., 2005. *Understanding the Dynamics and Competitiveness of the South African Mining and Minerals Processing Inputs Cluster*. Policy paper, Corporate Strategy and Industrial Development (CSID), University of the Witwatersrand, Johannesburg.

Wiid, J., 2014. *Strategic Marketing*. Cape Town: Juta.

Winde, F. and Stoch, E.J., 2010. Threats and opportunities for post-closure development in dolomite gold mining areas of the West Rand and Far West Rand (South Africa). Part 1: Mining legacy and future threats. *Water South Africa*, 36(1), pp. 69–74.

World Bank and IFC (International Finance Corporation), 2002. It's not over when it's over: Mine closure around the world. Mining and Development. Washington. www.worldbank.org/mining.

Section E

Conclusion

14 The way forward for Postmasburg

Lochner Marais, Fiona Haslam McKenzie,
Etienne Nel, Deidré van Rooyen and Philippe Burger

Will the mines continue to benefit the town?

For more than a century mining has dominated development in South Africa. The country's economic heartland, Johannesburg, grew out of the first gold mines. But in the 20th century and the early years of the 21st, mining development has been mostly in peripheral areas and, unlike Johannesburg, most have remained peripheral. Some of these areas have tried to diversify their economies but few have succeeded (Marais and Nel, 2016). In the last decades of the 20th century China's rise as a world economic power fuelled the demand for metals, and most of these metals are present in the sparsely populated desert areas of South Africa's Northern Cape. Our case study town, Postmasburg, has profited from the increased demand for its metals, but it continues to depend too heavily on them. Nationally, South Africa has undoubtedly benefited from the mines, but locally they have brought problems in the form of power struggles between multinational mining companies and small communities.

This book is a first attempt to document the interaction between mining companies and a local community. We have attempted to explain the complexities of community development in a mining town by studying it from a variety of perspectives. Marais et al (Chapter 1) reviewed the rise and demise of mining settlements. The existence of mining towns is sparked by the discovery of a resource, their prosperity is boosted by global market demand, a rush follows to extract the resource, momentum builds around the possibilities of employment, livelihoods, business development and capacity building – and little heed is taken of what will happen when the resource runs short.

As we noted in Chapter 1 (Marais et al.), a substantial body of work is available on resource towns. Early research on the social aspects of mining in South Africa looked mostly at the gold and diamond mines (Crush, 1994); more recently, it has turned to the platinum mines (Capps, 2012; Manson, 2013; Mnwana, 2014). The iron ore mines have not yet received as much attention. What makes this book different is its comprehensive, multi-method, cross-disciplinary examination of the rapid growth of one small mining town and how it has been affected by the life cycle of its mines. Its findings provide a benchmark for researchers from a variety of disciplines who want to measure change over time in a particular place. It fills a gap in the literature on mining communities and its treatment of the consequences of mining creates a research niche. Many of the conclusions from our research in Postmasburg are generalisable to other communities in other locations where different resources are mined.

The book highlights the way mining communities depend on the mines for their social and economic sustainability. It describes the ways the mining companies and the community function and interact at important stages of the life cycle of a mine. The concept of community sustainability, as applied to mining towns, is highly contentious. The cyclical nature of mining has economic, environmental and social implications that threaten the sustainable development of communities and regions. The immediate, most noticeable social effects are the difficulties that low and moderate income households face in accessing affordable housing. The cycle of poverty continues for some despite the affluence of many others in mining communities. (On these topics, see Brereton and Pattenden, 2007; Rubin and Harrison, 2016; and Ntema et al., 2017). While it is reasonable to expect that mining will contribute to the development of communities, this line of argument tends to overstate the causal link between housing shortages and mining company employment practices, particularly those dependent on migrant labour.

Theoretical implications

Much of the research on the effects of mining has been done from a national perspective, but an increasing body of work focuses on the local effects, drawing on various theories to explain the negative implications (see Chapters 1 and 2). Staples theory says mining companies in remote areas often bypass the regional economies in which they are located, seldom procuring locally but importing not only goods and services but also labour from elsewhere. The resource curse and Dutch disease theories say the mining industry discourages local economies from diversifying. Social disruption theory points to negative social effects, such as massive in-migration damaging the social fabric of existing communities. Negative effects on the local community are also explained as the result of neoliberalism in the mining industry bringing about a change in production methods. The move towards shift work and block-roster shifts has led to higher salaries and changed the relationships between mining companies and local communities and between mineworkers and local communities. The research that produced the chapters in this book was done against the background of these theoretical frameworks.

The authors of some chapters mention the lack of local procurement in Postmasburg. They say the mining companies' supply chains often bypass local businesses – this despite claims by the companies that they have increased local procurement (see Chapter 13 by van Rooyen and van Zyl and Chapter 6 by Du Plessis and Abrahams). This shows that staples theory is to some extent relevant to Postmasburg. Mostly, though not exclusively, it is black business people who feel excluded from the supply chains to the mines.

This issue is also raised by Drewes and Stewart in Chapter 10 in connection with housing construction in Postmasburg, where one of the mining companies' use of contractors and developers from Gauteng aroused the resentment of local entrepreneurs. We found little evidence of development in other economic sectors, apart from the hospitality industry (see Chapter 13). This indicates that the development of Postmasburg's economy is only vertical (and that minimally) and not horizontal (see Keyes, 1992). This is the situation predicted by Dutch disease theory. It would, however, be unreasonable to expect an extensive manufacturing sector to be established in and around Postmasburg, given the town's remote location, and South Africa's current patterns of production and lack of economies of scale also hamper such an approach.

Despite exhibiting some of the symptoms described by the Dutch disease, resource curse and staples theories, Postmasburg is also distinctly different in a number of ways. To a large extent, the secondary (but not the primary) spin-offs of mining are benefiting the town's local entrepreneurs. People employed by the mining companies buy in Postmasburg. This has generated new retail developments (though the downscaling in 2015 caused some shops to close). In contrast to the company-town models of the 1950s, the increase in the mining workforce has provided local entrepreneurs with opportunities and created local jobs (outside mining). But the entrepreneurs struggle to access mining supply chains, mainly because of skills barriers and lack of economies of scale. We might wonder, though, whether this access would necessarily be beneficial, since it could increase the town's dependence on mining. Again in contrast to the company-town model, mining around Postmasburg is providing the local government with increased revenue (see Chapter 7 by Hendriks and Marais). However, the municipality lacks the capacity to cope with the increased demand for basic services (also see Chapter 6 by Du Plessis and Abrahams).

Researchers have noted that fly-in-fly-out labour can increase the staples theory effect: the bypassing of local providers. In Australia the benefits of mining are channelled to the country's larger urban areas and the local communities lose out. When the mines near Postmasburg were developed, the mining companies made a special effort to ensure that a stable and local labour force would be created. This led to an increase in the number of new settlements and an expansion of the Postmasburg business profile (particularly in retail and the hospitality services) (see Chapter 13 by van Rooyen and van Zyl). Nevertheless, the lack of local procurement and investment is an ever-present concern for entrepreneurs and business people in Postmasburg.

Among the negative economic effects of mining development in Postmasburg, we noted that local house prices and housing rentals have increased more than the inflation rate, resulting in increases in rates and taxes (see Chapter 5 by Denoon-Stevens et al.). Non-mineworker households pay larger percentages of their incomes to local services and taxes than mineworker households do (see Chapter 11 by Burger and Geldenhuys). Another indicator of new inequalities is that both mine-employed mineworkers and contractor mineworkers earn higher incomes than do local residents (see Chapter 11 by Burger and Geldenhuys). To remain internationally competitive, mining companies, where possible, have mechanised their production processes. The open-cast mines near Postmasburg are the result of such mechanisation, and since mechanisation requires better trained mineworkers they are paid higher salaries. The resulting income disparity could lead to social conflict between mineworker and non-mineworker families. However, non-mine-worker households in Postmasburg have a higher degree of labour force partici-pation, which indicates a positive local spin-off from mining and should redress the balance somewhat (see Chapter 11 by Burger and Geldenhuys). Economic effects have social implications too. Bearing out the predictions of social disrup-tion theory, concerns were expressed about social ills such as increased crime and drug and alcohol abuse, and about the inability of the police and the social support systems to deal with these problems (see Chapter 6 by Du Plessis and Abrahams).

The effects of neoliberalism in a mining town were discussed in Chapter 1 (see Table 14.1). Though block-roster shifts have not as yet been institutionalised in South Africa, longer shifts have become more common in recent years. The absence of block-roster shifts means that migration trends in mining in South Africa are less pronounced than those occasioned by the fly-in-fly-out arrange-ments in Australia and Canada. The creation of settlements and housing for Post-masburg mineworkers by their employers has brought a greater degree of stability to this town, and highlights the power of mining companies and the limited capac-ity of the local government.

Although the mines and the municipalities in South Africa have entered into partnerships, the mines dominate by virtue of their economic superiority and their power to create and withdraw jobs and local investment. The Tsantsabane Local Municipality is largely unable to question or direct such processes, so it has to comply with them and deal with the long-term risks of settlement maintenance. However, the effects of the mining companies' dominance are not always negative; for example, it has resulted in well-planned stands and good housing in Postmas-burg. What is more problematic is that national, provincial and local governments do not have the power to question the activities of the mining companies or in some case their might be a lack of political will. One outcome has been the creation of big mining settlements in Postmasburg (largely due to government requirements not to create a company town). Both the government and the mining companies accepted these developments and the approach was not questioned.

Three issues are pertinent here. Firstly, the long-term maintenance of the new town development requires local government capacity to maintain these settle-ments, but the Tsantsabane Local Municipality lacks this capacity. Secondly, there is the question of long-term settlement and the municipal management of risks associated with these settlements in the event of the inevitable mining decline. Denoon-Stevens et al. (Chapter 5) have noted that long-term planning is largely absent in Postmasburg, mainly because of the mining companies' immediate need to house their workforce and the perceived short-term community development benefits derived from town expansion. What happens in the long run is either considered not important or not considered at all. Thirdly, nobody has questioned the fact that Assmang provides homeownership and that Kumba wants to fol-low the same route by transferring its rental houses to owners. Questions about who carries the long-term risks have not yet been raised. In the end, all levels of

Table 14.1 Characteristics of the mining sector internationally and in South Africa, with particular reference to Postmasburg

	Criteria	Modern/industrial period, 1950 to mid-1980s	Post-industrial/neoliberal period, since mid-1980s	South Africa/Postmasburg
Nature of mining companies and global mining trends	How far multinational corporations dominate mining	Largely dominated by local mining companies	Largely dominated by multinational corporations	Largely dominated by multinational corporations
	Major trend in the mining economy	Boom ended in the mid-1980s	Boom since early 2000s ended in 2014/15	Boom since early 2000s, ended in 2014/15 Global financial crisis caused drop in commodity prices, but prices recovered quickly after 2008
Changes in the labour regime	Working hours	40-hour working week Daytime work only Full-time mine employment	Block-roster shifts (e.g. 4 days on, 4 days off, or 2 weeks on, 2 weeks off) Shifts (usually 12 hours, day or night) 24-hour production cycles Contract work Production 7 days a week Extended periods off	No block-roster shifts Mainly 12-hour shifts 24-hour production cycles Contract work present but not dominant Production: 7 days a week No extended periods off
	Nature of employment	Employed full-time by the mining company	Increasingly employed as contract workers	Contract work mainly related to construction and peripheral activities, but percentage of contract workers growing
	Duration of work	Lifelong or for as long as the mine is in operation	Short-term contracts	Mainly longer-term contracts
	Salary package	Large-scale non-salary benefits Moderate salaries	Only salary benefits Large salaries	Mineworkers still have work benefits (pension, medical aid) Substantial salary increases for open-cast and mechanised mining – still much lower than international standards

(Continued)

Table 14.1 (Continued)

Criteria		Modern/industrial period, 1950 to mid-1980s	Post-industrial/neoliberal period, since mid-1980s	South Africa/Postmasburg
Changes in mining towns	Mining production methods	Labour intensive	Capital intensive Mechanisation Outsourcing – for both non-direct and direct services	Capital intensive Increasingly mechanised (except for platinum and gold mining, where rock-drillers still dominate production) Mainly in peripheral activities
	Labour legislation	Strict labour legislation Labour is unionised	Smaller role for unions	Unions still dominant, but less so for contract workers
	Settlement permanence	Mostly permanent (as long as mine production continues) Company towns	Mostly non-permanent workforces Worker camps/'fly-in-fly-out' workers	Mostly a permanent workforce Migrant labour still used in some mining, but minimal in Postmasburg
	Housing types	Houses provided by the mining company	Privatisation Worker camps 'Hotbedding'* Informal settlement development Re-emergence of compounds	Privatisation Good mining settlements and housing but also some informal settlement development
	Town management	Many towns initially managed by mines	Transferred to local government	Town management transferred to local councils
	Community cohesion	Seen as permanent	Increasingly seen as temporary	Government policy emphasises stability and permanence of mining settlements and communities

Implications for host communities	Positive local implications but long-term negative consequences depending on mine's lifespan	Economic exclusion / Less local spending	Local entrepreneurs feel economically excluded / Substantial secondary benefits from local spending by mineworkers
Financial risks / Social infrastructure	National government / Some underinvestment	Local communities / Continued underinvestment	Local communities / Government commitment to spend in mining areas
Governance models	Mining towns managed by mines or by local municipalities (where these existed) that depended heavily on mine housing	Mining companies had withdrawn by late 1980s / Recently, corporate social responsibility (CSR) to provide social infrastructure / Increasing emphasis on partnerships for development / Hybrid governance models	Social and labour plans to be dovetailed with integrated development planning (local strategic planning) / Outcomes disappointing: little evidence of partnerships, collaborative planning or hybrid governance models
Impacts of mine closure — Local impacts	Extreme	Local consequences of mine closure reduced by 'fly-in-fly-out' system	Mining settlements remain vulnerable to mine decline and closure

* 'Hotbedding' is shift work in which two employees use the same bed one after the other in a 24-hour cycle.

government accept the mines' housing arrangements without questioning them. In some instances, their plans are supported by the government's policy directives. The dominant economic role of the mines in power relations means that the mines get what they want. A poorly resourced local municipality consequently has very little ability to question local policy directives or to influence the mining companies' decisions. The outcome is merely the result of mining needs and of the power inherent in large companies.

Although these are not necessarily negative outcomes, there is much scope to rethink mainstream strategic planning at the local level for the complex reality of large-scale industry and community development. Mining companies have gone a long way towards subscribing to notions such as 'sustainable mining'. The same is true of non-mining activities like corporate social responsibility (CSR), settlement creation and housing provision. There are some indications of continued problems, as predicted by staples theory and by the Dutch disease, resource curse and social disruption theories, as discussed in Chapter 1 (by Marais et al.). There are also signs that mining companies continue to dominate in a neoliberal economic climate, but their dominance is not as absolute as it was in the days of company towns. Although few primary linkages exist between Postmasburg and the mining companies, the creation of settlements and housing for mineworkers at least allows the town to benefit from secondary linkages. Yet to some extent these settlement and housing developments also attest to the power of mining companies, since they transfer some of the long-term risks to individual households. At the same time one cannot ignore the counter-argument that they also transfer long-term benefits to individual households, who will enjoy capital gains – if and when the local housing market booms. Assmang, by privatising homeownership, has transferred responsibility for maintenance and long-term liability to its employees, and Kumba intends to do the same.

Planning and policy implications

Several clear messages for mining towns emerge from the studies conducted for inclusion in this book. The first is the importance of planning for the mine's life cycle – from exploration, through extraction to closure. As Laurence (2005, p. 285) notes, 'the excitement and fanfare that surround the opening of a new mine is never present when it finally closes'. Failing to plan for closure, or at least for downscaling, of the mine can prove to be an expensive economic, social and environmental oversight. Denoon-Stevens et al. (Chapter 5) offer many reasons for this, not least that predicting or, to be more precise, *managing* the future takes considerable effort, data, trust, communication and cross-disciplinary insights into complex situations. Managing the day-to-day minutiae and responsibilities is a convenient distraction, and political concerns and short-term electoral priorities often get in the way of prescient and strategic planning. Some of the challenges are discussed in the chapters by Drewes and Campbell (Chapter 4) and Du Plessis and Abrahams (Chapter 6).

The second is the need to improve coordination within and between the different levels of government, between mining companies and government and between mining companies and communities. This is a recurring theme in this book, underscoring the importance of having transparent governance frameworks and adhering to them. Clearly there are considerable economic benefits – for South Africa, the mining companies and the ancillary services – to be derived from mining investment and resource extraction. But without a clearly defined, inter-related governance framework with checks and balances to ensure seamless integration of national, provincial and local governments, the potential benefits and opportunities at the local level are likely to dissipate. Addressing these issues requires the establishment of new governance mechanisms at the national, provincial and local levels to enable companies and these different levels of government to share information and collaborate on matters of common concern (Haslam McKenzie et al., 2009).

The book's third message is about power relations. The notion of power is both an overt theme and a subtext throughout this book. It is on the authorities who provide employment and accommodation, grant contracts, develop land and start businesses that many of the benefits to be derived from mining depend. However, the way they wield their power is often neither clear nor transparent (see Chapter 2 by Marais and Ntema). In many mining towns, excessive power of the mines is accompanied by lack of capacity of the local authority. South Africa's Mining Charter seeks to redress the economic inequalities associated with colonialism and apartheid (see Chapter 1 by Marais et al.) through the municipalities' integrated development plans (IDPs) and the social and labour plans (SLPs) developed by mining companies and mandated by the Minerals and Petroleum Resource Development Act 28 of 2002, but these plans do not always align. Furthermore, as there is no formalised requirement for broad stakeholder engagement or regular monitoring or assessment in the SLP, these are largely absent from local practice. Interpretation and implementation of local plans or the social licence have considerable latitude and therefore, as highlighted by Marais and Ntema in Chapter 2, create opportunities for tokenism, nepotism and inefficiency.

To achieve good governance and development goals requires transparent leadership (see Chapter 12 by Kotzé and Nel). In addition to the general problems, every industry, resource sector and community faces specific challenges that require careful planning, tactical investment and strategic management (Hilson and Murck, 2000) to maximise the prospective benefits. Transparent leadership of the power dynamic is important if the weaknesses of the current arrangements of Postmasburg and other mining towns are to be addressed. Leadership in a mining town, ideally, is not limited to the mine management, the municipality or the community authorities. It requires mutual respect, open communication and trust between all stakeholders. However, if relationships between the authorities and the workers, and between different categories of workers, are something to go by (see Chapter 2 by Marais and Ntema and Chapter 11 by Burger and Geldenhuys), these prerequisites are likely to remain aspirational. Without senior government leadership and commitment it is unlikely that a coordinated strategy will be developed. Industry groups have commercial priorities that take precedence unless mandated otherwise, and community-based groups such as non-governmental organisations are under-resourced and often overcommitted.

The fourth important message of this book is that public policy must be appropriate to meet the growth challenges inherent in the complexity, scale and speed of a resources boom, and sufficiently robust to deal with the implications of mine downscaling and closure. Chapter 2 (Marais and Ntema) highlighted some indicators of shortcomings in policy and governance, such as a lack of accurate information to inform planning, fragmentation of responsibility, confusion of roles and lack of forums capable either of dealing with bad practices and conflicting interests or mediating between various stakeholders. The national and provincial government departments responsible for assisting the local government could play a much more direct role in supporting local municipalities in a mining town like Postmasburg.

The fifth message is that the mining companies must take their corporate citizenship seriously. The expectation is that the companies will operate in accordance with the interest and welfare of those community groups that are affected by their operations (Hilson and Murck, 2000; Brereton and Pattenden, 2007; Haslam McKenzie et al., 2009; Harvey and Bice, 2014). But mandatory CSR programmes and imposed regulations have been found to be less than effective (Hamann, 2004; Székely, 2006; Harvey and Bice, 2014) without commitment and investment in developing long-term trust and a thorough understanding of what the community needs. Communities are often given money for infrastructure or projects they neither need nor want, which in turn could lead to over-reliance on mining. This raises the question as to whether programmes to promote 'sustainability' are themselves sustainable. The provision of large-scale ownership housing in Postmasburg comes to mind.

As highlighted in Chapter 1 (Marais et al.) and in Chapter 6 (Du Plessis and Abrahams), respect, openness and information sharing continue to be generally absent in relationships between the mining companies and the Postmasburg community. Company initiatives such as the living-out allowances – purportedly a revitalisation strategy following the Marikana tragedy in 2012, intended to improve mineworkers' socio-economic and living conditions – have not achieved their objectives but instead exacerbated informal settlement development and shifted the burden of infrastructure provision to the local government. Similarly, bonuses paid in 2011 – in some cases, equivalent to two years' salary – have caused local inflation and increased the cost of living and thus had broader implications for those beyond the mine workforce.

Following on that, the sixth message is that new ways need to be found to provide housing for mineworkers. As Chapter 9 (Cloete and Denoon-Stevens) shows, similar unintended consequences have resulted from the government-mandated policy of helping mineworkers to own their homes. On the surface, this initiative purports to address homeownership. At a deeper level though, it absolves mining companies from long-term housing commitment and renders homeowners vulnerable to the vagaries of the housing market, which are amplified in a mono-economy exposed to international market forces. Chapter 10 (Drewes and Stewart) describes a company housing initiative in which the purchasing arrangements for the homes are linked to employment. This is very similar to many other mining company homeownership schemes in South Africa. Underwritten by company subsidies, the initiative addresses some of the discriminatory housing stratification practices and serves to integrate mineworkers into existing communities. It also addresses some – though not all – of the concerns associated with mine downscaling.

The seventh message is that towns like Postmasburg urgently need to plan for a future without the mines. Throughout the book, the authors note implicit expectations among the interviewees that the mine will not last for ever. Bice (2013, p. 139) notes that 'companies and communities are in complex relationships' and that many companies 'try to do the right thing without realizing that well-meaning CSR programs can create a troubling dependency over the long term'. It is evident that businesses in Postmasburg depend on the ongoing existence of mining. In Chapter 13 van Rooyen and van Zyl highlight the importance of horizontally diversifying the local economy while the mines are fully operational and maximising any opportunities to enhance local training, develop skills and build capacity. The limited life of a mine also has implications for planning. Infrastructure must be planned so that it can easily be closed down and the land likewise easily rehabilitated. Postmasburg could investigate the civil engineering principle of 'modular infrastructure' and consider how the functions of the infrastructure provided during the mining boom can be changed. The town planners should give more thought to land use, including how quickly the planned use can be changed when the mines decline. For example, during a boom schools could be planned in such a way that they could become retirement homes when mining operations have ground to a halt.

The need to define the local responsibilities of mining companies is the eighth message. The local responsibility of mining companies, a theme running through the book, is an international concern. Different ways have been found of ensuring that mining companies become involved in local development. In many cases this is achieved via CSR programmes. In Western Australia, the Royalties for Regions Programme redistributes a percentage of mining royalties back to mining regions. South African legislation has paved the way for collaborative planning between the mining companies and local government. Mining legislation requires the development of SLPs and local governments are required to develop IDPs. The former have been hailed as international good practice (Rogerson, 2011). South Africa has seen some examples of collaborative planning and implementation (see Chapter 4 by Drewes and Campbell). However, collaboration of this kind has focused mainly on the initial settlement planning and housing provision rather than taking a long-term view of the mine's life cycle. Collaborative planning beyond these initial partnerships is rare, which does not mean that mines are not investing in the local area in various ways. There are numerous examples of local spending by mines – most of this in the form of CSR that, conveniently for mining companies, happens not to require collaborative planning. CSR planning is inevitably short-term. Denoon-Stevens et al. (Chapter 5) have aptly noted that planning by the Tsantsabane Local Municipality has a narrow focus and does not consider long-term implications. Furthermore, IDPs are driven by provincial and municipal governments, and mining is a national competency. The national department has limited interest, knowledge or concern with municipal government.

The ninth message concerns the need to question the advisability of creating a permanent town around a mine. Drewes and Campbell (Chapter 4) and Drewes and Stewart (Chapter 10) make a compelling case for permanent settlement and housing development in Postmasburg. They make two main points: that future investment in Postmasburg will support the ongoing development of an existing regional centre, so the town has, in theory, an economic function beyond mining, and that Postmasburg has been lauded for promoting integrated communities rather than just mining communities. These principles have also been supported by government policy that aims to prevent isolated mining settlements. Yet we should also question these principles and their application in Postmasburg. Despite the existence of the Tsassamba Committee, a partnership committee between the mines and the municipality (see Chapter 4 by Drewes and Campbell), mandated to develop the land and provide bulk infrastructure, some questions can still be asked about the process of developing Postmasburg and whether, in some cases, company towns might be the right way to go. Such towns do have their advantages, though the concept should not be blindly promoted. They do not shift the burden of maintenance onto poor and incapacitated local authorities; maintenance remains the mining company's responsibility. The prospect of mine closure (a particular risk for remote communities) does not add to the financial or social risk of households in a company town because they do not own their houses. Finally, the rehabilitation of a company town after mine closure is, in principle, easier than it would be in an integrated settlement.

A further consideration is that the government's guidelines for creating integrated settlements rather than mining towns could themselves spawn new inequalities. The international literature points to inequalities between mineworkers and the original inhabitants of what have become mining towns. This is especially the case in Australia. Burger and Geldenhuys (Chapter 11) touch on this issue, showing that mine-employed mineworkers receive higher incomes, have more assets and perceive their economic well-being to be better than that of contractor mineworkers. The latter are in turn likely to be better off than local residents who do not have the advantage of inflated mining industry wages and other benefits. Burger and Geldenhuys's comparison of the two types of mineworkers reveals that the alleged inequalities are less pronounced in Postmasburg than commonly assumed by analysts. Although this book does not touch on issues of social cohesion between mineworkers and non-mineworkers, it was clear from our study that inequalities between them could be problematic for long-term social cohesion in mining towns like Postmasburg. Although class differentiation is normal, the question is, what kind of class differentiation is taking place?

A final message concerns mineworkers' psychological well-being. The international literature has alerted us to mental health problems in remote mining towns, where women in particular struggle to cope (see Chapters 2 by Marais and Ntema and Chapter 12 by Kotzé and Nel). Block-roster shifts and fly-in-fly-out arrangements have added other pressures that affect mental health. In Chapter 12 Kotzé and Nel report that mineworkers in Postmasburg have relatively high levels of work engagement, and although their work occasionally intrudes into their private lives this does not badly affect their psychological well-being. Payment of bonuses was found to be one of the main reasons for this, along with substantial improvements in labour practice on South African mines in the past two decades.

Further research

This book would not be complete if the authors were to neglect to suggest topics for future research. Although this is a comprehensive case study of Postmasburg, a number of research gaps have yet to be filled.

Postmasburg mines are open-cast iron-ore mines, which means they are largely mechanised and thus require skilled and well-trained employees. We found that Postmasburg's mineworkers were relatively well paid, their living conditions were adequate and their work engagement levels were generally acceptable. Would the same trends be apparent in underground mining? Rock-drillers still dominate mining employment in the gold and platinum mines, where salaries are substantially lower than in the more mechanised mines. Replicating this study in areas where underground mining is common should fill a knowledge gap by extending the research to include industries that still require substantial manual labour.

Further research is needed on inequalities between contract mineworkers and permanent mineworkers. Our study found that some inequalities do exist. Yet once these inequalities are considered at the household level they are found to be less pronounced. In our opinion, other case studies in different mine settings could help researchers and policy makers to understand the precise nature of these inequalities.

Research is needed on social cohesion between mineworkers and non-mineworkers in mining towns like Postmasburg. How do the original residents experience mineworkers? Has mining negatively affected the economic well-being of the original residents? Our study of Postmasburg shows that higher house prices, higher rentals and substantial increases in rates and taxes could leave these households at a disadvantage. However, on the positive side we also found an increase in the labour force participation rate of households not employed by mining companies. Are these differences and inequalities more pronounced in towns dependent on other kinds of mining?

Changing migration patterns have not received much attention in this book. The history of mining in South Africa is strongly linked to migrant labour and migration patterns. Formal work and higher salaries have changed migration trends. Ample opportunities thus remain to study these trends in Postmasburg and elsewhere. What drives migration patterns and to what extent are they a continuation or a discontinuation of patterns enforced under apartheid rule? How do the migration patterns of permanent mineworkers and contract mineworkers differ? The considerable growth of informal settlements in and around Postmasburg also warrants further research. What drives the creation of these informal settlements? Who are the people living here and how does one plan for such settlements in mining towns?

Our study was based largely on a study of policy and planning documents, followed by structured household or individual interviews and complemented by a range of qualitative interviews with key informants. We believe our methods have contributed to a better understanding of mining-community relationships in Postmasburg. They do not, however, say much about the lives of mineworkers in a peripheral location like Postmasburg. There is thus a need for ethnographic research in South Africa's remote mining towns.

This book has also laid the foundation for considering the future of Postmasburg. Much more research can be done to explore different scenarios, the potential of changing land use and planning for the boom-bust cycles of mining.

References

Bice, S., 2013. No more sun shades, please: Experiences of corporate social responsibility in remote Australian mining communities. *Rural Society Journal*, 22(2), pp. 138–152.

Brereton, D. and Pattenden, C., 2007. *Measuring What Matters: Monitoring the Contribution of New Mining Project to Community Sustainability*. Paper presented at the 3rd International Conference on Sustainable Development Indicators in the Minerals Industry, 17–20 June, 2007, Milos Island, Greece.

Capps, G., 2012. A bourgeois reform with social justice? The contradictions of the minerals development bill and black economic empowerment in the South African platinum mining industry. *Review of African Political Economy*, 39(132), pp. 315–333.

Crush, J., 1994. Scripting the compound: Power and space in the South African mining industry. *Environment and Planning D: Society and Space*, 12(3), pp. 301–324.

Hamann, R., 2004. Corporate social responsibility, partnerships, and institutional change: The case for mining companies in South Africa. *Natural Resources Forum*, 28, pp. 278–290.

Harvey, B. and Bice, S., 2014. Social impact assessment, social development programmes and social licence to operate: Tensions and contradictions in intent and practice in the extractive sector. *Impact Assessment and Project Appraisal*, 32(4), pp. 327–335.

Haslam McKenzie, F., Phillips, R., Rowley, S., Brereton, D. and Birdsall-Jones, C., 2009. *Housing Market Dynamics in Resource Boom Towns, Perth*. Australian Housing and Urban Research Institute. www.ahuri.edu.au/publications/p80370/.

Hilson, G. and Murck, B., 2000. Sustainable development in the mining industry: Clarifying the corporate perspective. *Resources Policy*, 26, pp. 227–238.

Keyes, R., 1992. Mine closure in Canada: Problems, prospects and policies. In: C. Neil, C. Tykklainen and J. Bradbury, eds. *Coping with Closure: An International Comparison of Mine Town Experiences*. London: Routledge, pp. 192–207.

Laurence, D.C., 2005. Optimisation of the mine closure process. *Journal of Cleaner Production*, 14, pp. 285–298.

Manson, A., 2013. Mining and 'traditional communities' in South Africa's 'platinum belt': Contestations over land, leadership and assets in North-West Province, 1996–2012. *Journal of Southern African Studies*, 39(2), pp. 409–423.

Marais, L. and Nel, E., 2016. The dangers of growing on gold: Lessons from the history of the Free State Goldfields, South Africa. *Local Economy*, 31(1–2), pp. 282–298.

Mnwana, S., 2014. Mineral wealth–'in the name of morafe'? Community control in South Africa's 'platinum valley'. *Development Southern Africa*, 31(6), pp. 826–842.

Ntema, J., Marais, L., Cloete, J. and Lenka, M., 2017. Social disruption, mine closure and housing policy: Evidence from the Free State Goldfields, South Africa. *Natural Resources Forum*, 41(1), pp. 31–40.

Rogerson, C., 2011. Mining enterprise and partnerships for socio-economic development. *African Journal of Business Management*, 5(14), pp. 5405–5417.

Rubin, M. and Harrison, P., 2016. An uneasy symbiosis: Mining and informal settlement in South Africa with reference to the platinum belt in North West province. In: L. Cirolia, T. Görgens, M. Van Donk, W. Smit and S. Drimie, eds. *Upgrading Informal Settlements in South Africa*. Cape Town: Juta, pp. 145–173.

Székely, F., 2006. Responsible leadership and corporate social responsibility: Metrics for sustainable performance. *European Management Journal*, 23(6), pp. 628–647.

Index

Note: Page numbers in *italics* indicate figures; page numbers in **bold** indicate tables.